WILLS AND ADMINISTRATIONS

OF

NORTHUMBERLAND COUNTY, PENNSYLVANIA

Including
Wills and Administrations
of

Union, Mifflin and Indiana Counties

All formerly a part of Northumberland

County, Pennsylvania

Compiled by

CHARLES A. FISHER

Southern Historical Press, Inc.
Greenville, South Carolina

Originally Published 1950:
Selinsgrove, PA.

SOUTHERN HISTORICAL PRESS, INC.
PO BOX 1267
Greenville, SC   29601

ISBN #978-1-63914-106-7

Printed in the United States of America

WILLS AND ADMINISTRATIONS
OF
NORTHUMBERLAND COUNTY, PENNSYLVANIA

INCLUDING

WILLS AND ADMINISTRATIONS
OF
UNION, MIFFLIN AND INDIANA COUNTIES

ALL FORMERLY A PART OF NORTHUMBERLAND
COUNTY, PENNSYLVANIA

COMPILED BY
DR. CHARLES A. FISHER, F.I.A.G.
SELINSGROVE, PENNA.

INTRODUCTION

WHEN NORTHUMBERLAND COUNTY WAS FORMED IN 1772, IT WAS THE LARGEST COUNTY IN THE STATE OF
PENNSYLVANIA. TWENTY-SEVEN COUNTIES HAVE BEEN FORMED, WHOLLY, OR IN PART, FROM THE ORIGINAL AREA.
THE WILLS AND ADMINISTRATIONS GIVEN IN THIS COMPILATION ARE ABSTRACTS OF THE RECORDS OF THE FOUR
COUNTIES MENTIONED ABOVE. UNION, MIFFLIN, AND INDIANA COUNTIES WERE TAKEN FROM THE ORIGINAL NORTH-
UMBERLAND COUNTY. THE OTHER COUNTIES ARE ARMSTRONG, BARDFORD, CAMERON, CENTER, CLARION, CLEARFIELD,
CLINTON, COLUMBIA, ELK, FOREST, JEFFERSON, LACKAWANNA, LUZERNE, LYCOMING, MCKEAN, MONTOUR, POTTER,
SULLIVAN, SUSQUEHANNA, TIOGA, VENANGO, WARREN, AND WYOMING. THIS WORK CONTAINS WILLS AND ADMINIS-
TRATIONS OF

NORTHUMBERLAND COUNTY (1772-1813)
MIFFLIN COUNTY (1789-1793)
UNION COUNTY (1813-1818)
INDIANA COUNTY (1818-1849)

FEBRUARY, 1950.

OTHER WORKS BY THE SAME COMPILER

GENEALOGY OF THE WOODLING FAMILY, 1936
GENEALOGY OF THE MICHAEL FISHER FAMILY, 1937
THE SNYDER COUNTY PIONEERS, 1938
ABSTRACTS OF THE SNYDER COUNTY PROBATE RECORDS, 1940
CENTRAL PENNSYLVANIA MARRIAGES (1700-1896), 1946
EARLY PENNSYLVANIA BIRTHS (1675-1875), 1947
EARLY CENTRAL PENNSYLVANIA LINEAGES, 1948

DATE ISSUED	DECEASED PERSON	LETTERS GRANTED TO	SURETIES FOR THE ADMINISTRATOR.
1772			
12/18	WELANT, MICHAEL	MAGDALENE WEILAND (WIDOW)	NOT MENTIONED
1773			
1/21	JOHNSON, RICHARD	JOHN BUCHANAN	" "
5/26	ESPER, SIMON	BARBARA ESPER (WIDOW)	" "
11/23	WILSON, JOHN	JANET WILSON "	" "
1774			
3/29	ROBESON, THOMAS	RICHARD ROBESON (BRO.)	" "
4/5	DEWITT, PAUL	CATHERINE DEWITT (WIDOW)	" "
9/21	EVANS, ROGER	JAS. CHISNELL (PARTNER)	" "
8/3	PARKS, DAVID	JAMES GILER	" "
1775			
4/24	GRANT, ALEXANDER	ANN GRANT (WIDOW)	" "
4/26	STONE, ABRAHAM	BARBARA STONE (WIDOW)	" "
5/10	FINLEY, JOHN	JACOB GROSJEAN	" "
8/12	SHIELDS, EDWARD	GEORGE MCCULLOUGH	" "
1776			
1/3	MCWILLIAMS, HUGH	REBECCA MCWILLIAMS (WIDOW)	" "
2/6	DRAKE, JOHN	ELIZABETH DRAKE (WIDOW)	" "
1777			
4/29	IRWIN, RICHARD	JEAN IRWIN (WIDOW)	THOMAS HEWITT, JAMES MCMAHON
5/3	TURNER, WILLIAM	JOSEPH GRAY	JAS. POLLOCK, JNO. HARRISON
5/30	KELLEY, SARAH	JAMES WHITE	JAS. GILES, JAS. HAMPTON
5/19	NEIGH, J. NICHOLAS	MARGARET NEIGH	MARTIN KERSTETTER, S. BROSIUS
6/3	" "	" "	JAC. HAVERLING, JOHN SHEAVER
12/15	DAUGHERTY, WILLIAM	PHILIP FRICK	JOHN PAINTER, SAM ALLEN
1778			
4/2	CAMPBELL, JOHN	JOHN CAMPBELL, JR.	ADAM CAMBLE, GOTLIEB LEFFLER
4/8	BREEZE, NEHEMIAH	RUTH BREEZE	WM. SIMS, ELIAS YOUNGMAN
4/27	GREGG, ROBERT	WILTON ATKINSON	EDWARD MCCABE
5/22	TURNER, ANDREW	DAVID TURNER	JAS. HARRISON, JAMES ESPY
6/11	BROWN, DANIEL	RALPH SLACK	JOHN CARPENTER, L. MCCARTNEY
8/20	MURRAY, WILLIAM	JAMES MCCORMACK	NEAL MCCOY, LAUGHLIN MCCARTNEY
9/7	SALTSMAN, ARTHUR	ROBERT RICHEY	COOKSON LONG, J. ASHBRIDGE
9/26	CRAWFORD, HENRY	JOHN BUYERS	JOHN REIM, ELIAS YOUNGMAN
11/5	ARMSTRONG, SAMUEL	FLEMING WILSON	SAM HUNTER, WM. SAWYERS
11/5	KNEPP, CALEB	JOHN BRADY	" " " "
11/25	KERR, ROBERT	REBECCA FELCH	CHAS. BAGNELL, W. ATKINSON
1779			
1/10	MCWILLIAMS, ROBERT	ELIZABETH & JOHN MCWILLIAMS	WILLIAM COOK, THOS. HAMILTON
2/23	JONES, LEVI	EDWARD HUFF	JOHN MORRISON, DAVID BEAN
3/27	COVENHOVEN, ALBRIGHT	SARAH COVENHOVEN	WM. COOK, DAVID MCKENNY
4/12	WHITMORE, GEORGE	JACOB FULMER	JOHN BLAIR, ROB. REYNOLDS
4/12	BAIRD, JOHN	WILLIAM BAIRD	TOM ROBINSON, JOHN CARUTHERS
5/7	LEPLEY, MICHAEL	JACOB LEPLEY	JOHN REED, ISRAEL PASCHALL
5/24	PARKER, JAMES	ALEXANDER EWING	JOHN BUYERS, JAMES MCLEES
5/25	EWIG, PHILIP	ADAM EWIG	MICH. HESSLER, MAT. STRINGLE
6/5	CROWNOVER, JAMES	ESTHER CROWNOVER	JOHN LEE, JOSEPH NEWMAN
6/12	BRIDGENS, THOMAS	JOHN MORRISON	TOM ROBINSON, JAS. CRAWFORD
6/12	LEPLEY, MICHAEL	JOHN NYE	ADAM GIFT, JAC. HASSINGER

1779			
7/24	CRAWFORD, WILLIAM	JAMES CRAWFORD	L. MCCARTNEY, JOHN MCHENRY
7/24	LAUGHLIN, WILLIAM	WILLIAM GRAY	WM. COOK, WM. SHAW
8/16	BOONE, CAPT. HAWKINS	JEAN BOONE	JAMES MURRAY, JAMES HAYES
"	" " "	ROBERT MARTIN	CHAS. GILLESPIE, JONATHAN LODGE
8/25	BIGNAL, CHARLES	MARTHA BIGNAL	WILLIAM SIMS, ANDREW PIATT
"	SALTSMAN, GEORGE	ROSANNA RICHEY	JOHN WALKER, DANIEL CRUGER
8/26	LIEFF, FRED	SARAH LIEFF	STEPHEN CHAMBERS, BEN ALLISON
10/12	COX, SAMUEL	HANNAH COX	DAVID MCKENNY, JOSEPH NEWMAN
11/25	TREASTER, GEORGE	MARTIN TREASTER	GEO. TROUTNER, MELCHOIR STOCK
12/7	BRADY, CAPT. JOHN	MARY & SAMUEL BRADY	ROB. LYON, JONATHON DODGE
11/1	PLUNKETT, ROBERT	WILLIAM PLUNKETT	JOHN HARRIS, JR., WM. MACLAY
"	DEEM, ADAM	THOMAS DEEM	ROB. LYON, WILLIAM HOFFMAN
11/26	MCKNIGHT, JAMES	MARTHA & JOHN MCKNIGHT	WM. MACKEY, ARCHIBALD QUAY
1780			
4/4	HAINES, JAMES	JOHN SUTTON	SIMON COOL, CLARY CAMPBELL
4/18	SOLOMON, JOHN	ANN & JOS. SOLOMON	DAN GOODSEN, MOSES VANCAMPEN
4/19	DASSON, DANIEL	JOHN EWART	ANDREW CLARK, GEORGE CALDWELL
6/16	WATT, SAMUEL	JAMES GIBSON	JAMES HAMON, NEAL MCCOY
7/8	CURRY, ROBERT	JEAN CURRY & J. MCHARG	JOHN CLARK, JOHN BLACK
7/23	WATSON, CAPT. PATRICK	DAVID WATSON	" " AND. CULBERTSON
8/22	MINIAN (MINIUM?), JACOB	MARY MINIAM	PETER ALLEMAN, SEB. BROGIUS
"	LASH, STEPHEN	JOHN ADAM LASH	" " " "
8/24	ROW, GEORGE, SR.	GEORGE ROW, JR.	ANDREW MORR, GEORGE CONRAD
9/15	MEADS, ASHEL	DARIUS MEADS	ABE DEWITT, BERNARD EARGOOD
9/19	SHEFFER, CONRAD	CATHERINE SHEFFER	STOPHEL GETTIG, WILLIAM BAKER
10/10	CLARK, JAMES	JEAN CLARK	DAVID DEAN, JAMES PATTON
10/14	MCCRACKEN, HENRY	MARY MCCRACKEN	ROBERT FRUIT, GEORGE MOORE
10/28	THOM, JAMES, JR.	JAMES THOM, SR.	WALTER CLARK, JOHN FORSTER
11/30	BAKER, WILLIAM, SR.	ADAM BALT	JOHN REAGER, JOHN STROUP
1781			
2/20	LIVINGOOD, GEORGE	JOHN & JAC. LIVINGOOD	PETER WITMER, ZACH. SPANGLE
2/27	ETZWEILER, GEORGE	MARY ETZWEILER	W. ATKINSON, PETER ALLEMAN
4/6	JOHNSTON, WILLIAM	ISABEL JOHNSTON	WM. MCKNIGHT, CHAS. GILLESPIE
8/14	CAMPBELL, WILLIAM	JAMES ALEXANDER	MARTIN TREASTER, GEO. CLEVER
10/19	TREASTER, MARTIN	ELIZABETH TREASTER	" " " "
11/29	DOUGAN (DUGAN?), WM.	JOHN CLARK	JOHN EWART, DAVID MEAD
1782			
1/29	HAMILTON, ALEXANDER	ANN & JOHN HAMILTON	JOHN CHATAM, JAMES ESPY
4/16	WEITZEL, CAPT. CASPER	JOHN WEITZEL	SAMUEL HUNTER, WILLIAM GRAY
4/29	SMITH, JOHN	CATH. SMITH NORCON & DANIEL NORCON	
5/18	YOST, JOHN	MARGARET YOST	JOHN WEITZEL, MATTHEW SMITH
5/28	GEORGE, WILLIAM	THOMAS FERGUSON	EDWARD HUFF, WILLIAM REED
5/30	MILLER, JACOB	MARGARET MILLER	JACOB FULLMER, GEORGE WOLF
6/22	MCKENNY, MORDECAI	JACOB MCKENNY	DAVID MCKENNY, CORNELIUS LOW
7/18	ARNOLD, LORENTZ	MARY ARNOLD	ADAM BOLENDER, JAC. HASSINGER
8/12	LINDSEY, JOHN	JAMES LOGAN	JOHN CLARK, JAS. COUGHRAN
8/20	ASHBRIDGE, JONATHON	SARAH ASHBRIDGE	WILTON ATKINSON, DAVE MCKENNY
8/30	OPP (APP?), JOHN	PHILIP OPP	STOPHEL GETTIG, JOHN CLINGMAN
8/31	LEE, MAJ. JOHN	JOHN LOWDEN	SAMUEL HUNTER, DAVID MEAD
9/9	FURROW, STOPHEL	MICHAEL ROPE	JOHN EWART, BANJAMIN ALLISON
9/13	WALKER, JOHN	JEAN & BEN. WALKER	HENRY STERRETT, JOHN CHATHAM
9/18	KEMPLIN, CAPT. THOMAS	MARY KEMPLIN	RICH. MANNING, THOMAS FORSTER
10/11	WATT, JAMES	FREDERICK WATT, JR.	AND. CULBERTSON, GEORGE WOLF
10/14	DEAN, DAVID	JOHN SCOTT	JAMES HAMON, DAVID MEAD
10/21	MARTIN, JOHN, SR.	JOHN MARTIN, JR.	JAMES MURRAY, WILLIAM REED
10/22	TREASTER, MARTIN	JACOB TREASTER	JAS. CRAWFORD, JOS. LORENTZ
11/8	WILSON, JAMES	GEORGE MOORE	RICH. SHEARER, JAMES VANDIKE
11/10	LEE, EDWARD	JAMES ESPY	JOSEPH EAKER, JOHN PAINTER
11/29	BARTGES, CHRISTOPHER	WILLIAM GILL	GEO. OVERMIRE, MICHAEL FOCHT

2

1782			
12/10	THOMSON, MATTHEW	REBECCA THOMSON	ARCHIBALD QUAY, DAVE MCKENNY
12/19	SMITH, ADAM	CATHERINE SMITH	HENRY AURAND, JACOB METZGER

1783			
1/10	CROCKETT, THOMAS	ROBERT CROCKETT	PHILIP OPP, NATHANIEL BARBER
1/25	NICKLE, HUGH	MARY NICKLE	THOMAS FORSTER, ROBERT TAGGART
3/3	MILLER, ZEPHNIAH	EZEKIEL MILLER	JOHN FAULKNER, CHRISTIAN GORMAN
3/7	MCGENNETT, CHARLES	ELIZABETH MCGENNETT	WILLIAM GRAY, MATTHEW SMITH
4/4	MCCANDLISH, WILLIAM JR	WM. MCCANDLISH, SR.	" " JOHN CHATHAM
5/5	DIEM, THOMAS	PHILIP FRICK	JAS. CRAWFORD, DAN. MONTGOMERY
5/29	COOL, CAPT. SIMON	MARY COOL	WILLIAM REED, WILLIAM LAYTON
6/14	WATSON, WILLIAM	SUSAN WATSON	HENRY STERRET, JOHN MCPHERSON
7/4	MOODY, ROBERT	ABIGAIL MOODY	JOHN CLINGMAN, DANIEL CRUGER
8/14	POAK (POLLOCK?), JAMES	MARY & JOS. POAK	WM. WILSON, JAMES MCCLANAHAN
10/10	ESBENSHIP, JACOB	SYBILLA ESBENSHIP	THOMAS PRICE, GEORGE ULRICH
10/27	BOLBEE, MARTHA	JACOB LINKS	JAMES STEADMAN, JAMES MOORE
10/31	ROUSHER, JOHN NICHOLAS	GERTRUDE ROUSHER	MARCUS PONTIUS, PETER MELICK, JR.
11/5	JOHNSTON, JOHN	JAMES STEADMAN	JACOB LINKS, WILLIAM MARSHALL
11/25	PUMROY, JOSEPH	ISAAC PUMROY	PETER FOLK, ABRAHAM MCKINNEY
11/27	TRINKLE, MATHIAS	CHARLES TRINKLE	GEORGE OVERMIRE, JACOB HARPSTER
11/27	LODGE, JONATHAN(SHERIFF)	MARY LOTGE, J. SCOTT	THOMAS ROBINSON, JAMES ESPY
11/28	LAMB, MICHAEL	CHRISTIAN STORM	BENJAMIN MILLER, WM. CHARTERS
11/29	LYCANS, JOSEPH	THOS. LYCANS (LYKENS?)	WILLIAM GRAY, WALTER CLARK

1784			
2/27	HEMROD (HIMROD?), SIMON	AARON HEMROD	ROBERT FRUIT, JOHN SCOTT
3/27	HOUCK, JACOB	MARG. HOUCK, JAS. TAYLOR	JOHN HALL, ADAM RENN
6/9	GORMAN, CHARLES	REBECCA GROMAN	JOHN LYONS, BARNHARD RENN
6/9	OGDEN, NATHAN	JOSEPH OGDEN	WM. HOFFMAN, JOHN FAULKNER
6/15	BLACKLEY, MATTHEW	SARAH BLACKLEY	WILLIAM WILSON, THOMAS GRANT
7/8	BODINE, ISAAC	RICHARD MANNING	LUDWIG GOSS, JOHN MEAD
8/13	DUNKELBERGER, PHILIP	DANIEL WELKNER	ADAM RENN, WILLIAM APLEY
9/15	STEPHENS, JOHN	CATHERINE STEPHENS	LUDWIG GOSS, BERNHARD EREGOOD
9/25	HOPKINS, ROBERT	NATHAN CEARY	HENRY ANTES
10/8	SWISHER, PHILIP	CATHERINE, SWISHER	JOHN SCOTT, WILLIAM HUTCHINS
11/8	MEISER, MICHAEL	JOHN MEISER	JACOB ECKHART, HENRY RINE
11/9	GILLESPIE, WILLIAM	REBECCA & JOHN GILLESPIE	ADAM CLARK, JAMES MCMAHAN
11/13	YEAKLEY, GEORGE	HANNAH & GEORGE YEAKLEY	NICHOLAS BUBB, SEBASTIAN BROSIUS
11/24	WILLETTS, ISAAC	THOMAS WILLETTS	ISAAC COLDEN, WILLIAM DAVIS
11/25	GARRETT, ELISHA	ABE CARTWRIGHT	WILLIAM WILSON, JAS. CRAWFORD
11/26	JOB, JOHN	MAGD. & JOHN JOB, JR.	ABRAHAM SNYDER, PETER ALWOOD
11/29	LAVISTON, JOHN	DANIEL LAVISTON	JOHN WATT, DAVID LAVISTON
12/30	BLACK, WILLIAM	JEAN BLACK	JAMES MCMAHAN, ALEX. MCMULLEN

1785			
1/8	DEWITT, ABRAHAM	ELINOR DEWITT	PETER VINCENT, PETER KERLIN
1/15	ADAMS, GEORGE	GEORGE TROUTNER	CHAS. MEYER, NICHOLAS MOCKELL
1/16	BORRAH, PETER	JACOB BORRAH	FRED MILLER, VAL. LAUDENSLAGER
2/12	HENDERSON, JAMES	JOHN WILSON	ADAM WOLF, ISAAC WILSON
2/14	MCKENNY, DAVID	REBECCA & ABRAHAM MCKENNY	LUDWIG GOSS, THOMAS HEWITT
2/16	MCCORMICK, ALEXANDER	JOHN MCCORMICK	WILLIAM WILSON, ALEX. HUNTER
4/16	CAMPBELL, JOHN	JEAN & TOM CAMPBELL	" " PAUL GEDDIS
5/26	ROSS, GUSTAVUS	MARTHA ROSS	RICHARD ALLISON, SAMUEL HARRIS
5/26	HORSEFALL, WILLIAM	SAMUEL BOONE	JOHN REIM, ELIAS YOUNGMAN
6/3	CROOKS, SAMUEL	HANNAH & HENRY CROOKS	WILLIAM LEACOCK, PETER KERLIN
6/21	MORRISON, GEORGE	JEREMIAH MORRISON	EPH. MORRISON, JOSEPH BARNETT
8/25	HUGHES, JAMES, JR.	JAMES HUGHES, SR.	WILLIAM HEPBURN
9/19	READER, JOSEPH	JOHN & DOROTHY SUTTON	" WYCOFF
9/28	GIBSON, THOMAS	JOSEPH BARNETT	THOS. ROBINSON, HUGH WHITE

1785			
9/28	MCFADDEN, HUGH	MARY MCFADDEN	THOMAS ROBINSON, JOSEPH BARNETT
9/30	IRWIN, ALEXANDER	WILLIAM IRWIN, SR.	WILLIAM MCADAM
11/22	HUGHES, JAMES, SR.	JOHN HUGHES	WILLIAM LEACOCK, CLARY CAMPBELL
11/23	COTNER, TOBIAS	CHRISTINA COTNER	HENRY BILLIG, MICHAEL GOWEN
11/24	DONALDSON, ALEXANDER	JANET DONALDSON	ROBERT FLEMING, JAMES WITMAN
11/24	EMERY, DAVID	JOHN EMERY	GODFREY GRAY, GEORGE BENFER
12/9	DERR, LUDWIG	GEO. DERR, WALT. CLARK	CHRISTOPHER GETTIG, JOHN TOMB
1786			
2/28	FREELAND, GARRET	MICHAEL FREELAND	FLEMING WILSON, ----- VINCENT
5/1	HALL, PETER	PETER & BARBARA HALL	ADAM GILGER, JACOB GOSS
5/18	TRINKLE, CHARLES	ELIZABETH TRINKLE	PETER KEISTER, F. DRUCKENMILLER
5/18	GROVE, GEO. MICHAEL	ADAM & MARY MARGARET GROVE	JOS. LORENTZ, CHRISTOPHER GEYTIG
5/24	FOX, JOHN	MARGARET & CHRISTIAN FOX	ADAM GILGER, CHRIST CHISSLER
5/25	PAUL, WILLIAM, SR.	WM. PAUL, JR.	ABRAHAM LATCHA, JOHN DUNLAP
8/7	JENKINS, JAMES, SR.	PHEBE, WM., & JAMES JENKINS, JR.	DANIEL MONTGOMERY, L. KEENE
8/12	HIORN, WILLIAM	JAMES WILLING	RICHARD WILLING, THOS. PALMER
8/23	MILLER, DAVID	VAL. LAUDENSLAGER & GEORGE ULRICH	GODFREY GRAY, PETER MAURER
8/24	ALLISON, MARY	HUGH MCCLEAN	WILLIAM MCGRADY, JOHN MCALWAIN
8/30	LEE, STEPHEN	ANN & ZEBULON LEE	JOHN MCNEAL, GILES PALMER
10/20	CAMPBELL, ANDREW	JOHN EWART	JAMES MCLEES, PHILIP OPP
11/8	DIMSY, CORNELIUS	ANN DIMSY	PETER WILSON, SAMUEL EDDINGS
11/25	HUFFMAN, PHILIP	PETER BUCK	JOHN WEITZEL, CHRISTOPHER GETTIG
11/28	MCCANDLISH, WILLIAM	DANIEL DAUGHERTY	ALEXANDER JOHNSTON, JAMES IRWIN
1787			
1/1	BROWN, ELIAS	JOHN MONTGOMERY	DAN MONTGOMERY, ROBERT GIFFIN
1/17	BRENNER, LUDWIG	ELIZABETH BRENNER & FREDERICK ALBRIGHT	JAC. ECKHART, JOHN REICHENBACH
1/30	GRAY, NEAL	MARY & JOHN GRAY	JOSEPH POAK, ROBERT MARTIN
2/4	ROBISON, PETER	SUSAN ROBISON	WILLIAM LEWIS, MARY ROBISON
2/12	SCUDDER, JOHN	JOHN ROBB	JOHN LYTLE, WALTER CLARK
2/17	PATTON, JOHN	JOHN SCOTT	" GAMBLE, JOHN MCPHERSON
4/28	MORDACH, JAMES	ROBERT MORDACH	WILLIAM GRAY, THOMAS JORDAN
5/2	AUMILLER, PHIL. CONRAD	CONRAD AUMILLER JACOB BORRAH	JOHN AUMILLER, SIMON BICKLE
5/19	SNYDER, JOHN (BRO. OF THE GOV.)	MARY & SIMON SNYDER	ALBRIGHT SWINEFORD, GEO. ULRICH
5/24	KEALY, ABEL	JEREMIAH MORRISON	ANDREW BARNELL, JOHN ROBISON
5/28	LOY, ADAM	CHRISTINA LOY	ADAM GILGER, CHRISTIAN SCHISTER
6/9	LEWIS, LEMEUL	CHARLES GOSIN	DAVID MEAD, CHRISTOPHER GETTIG
6/29	SHIPMAN, JOHN	ANN SHIPMAN	ROBERT FRUIT, GEORGE STEEPLES
8/6	KENNEDY, JAMES	ROBERT REYNOLDS	DAVID MEAD
8/30	HALL, JOHN	JAMES MCKELVEY	JOHN ROBB, JOHN LYTLE
10/10	MCGINLEY, HUGH	PETER JOS. MCGINLEY	THOMAS GRANT, THOMAS HAMILTON
1788			
3/6	GREEN, MARGARET	JOSEPH GREEN	DANIEL REESE, ROBERT LYON
4/1	AURAND, JACOB	JOHN AURAND	FREDERICK GETTIG, MICHAEL FOCHT
4/3	KETTERLY, PETER	MICHAEL ROAD	PETER FERST, FREDERICK ANTES
4/7	HAIN, GEORGE, SR.	JOHN HAIN	AARON LEROY, JACOB DREISBACH
5/6	HOGG, JAMES	JAMES HALL	WILLIAM COOK, ROBERT LYON
5/7	LEACOCK, WILLIAM	MARY LEACOCK	JOHN MACKEY, LAUGHLIN MCCARTNEY
5/9	TAGGART, THOMAS	MARY TAGGART	" " DAN MONTGOMERY
5/27	WALKER, JEAN	JOSEPH WALKER	ROBERT LYON, JOHN SCOTT
8/21	MARSHALL, JOSEPH	JAMES DAVIDSON	BEN LYON, EZRA PATTERSON※
8/27	WATSON, JAMES	ROBERT ALLISON	WILLIAM SHAW, JAMES BUCHANAN
8/29	NEELEY, JOHN	MARY NEELEY	JAMES & JOHN MITCHELTREE
8/30	BALL, THEOMOND	BLACK HALL BALL	JOHN BOYD, STEPHEN CHAMBERS

4

Date	Name		
9/11	CLELAND, WILLIAM	ELIZABETH CLELAND	JOHN MACKEY, WILLIAM BONHAM

1789

Date	Name		
1/17	GREENLEE, WILLIAM	JAMES GREENLEE	GEORGE MCKEAN, SAMUEL BEATTY
2/4	DAVIS, MARGARET	SAMUEL JACKSON	DANIEL REESE, JAMES WAGSTAFF
2/14	MARKLEY, SIMON	GEORGE MARKLEY	JACOB ECKHART, PETER MARKLEY
2/23	REARICK, JOHN, SR.	MARY, WILLIAM & JOHN REARICK, JR.	JACOB WISE, GEORGE OVERMIRE, JR.
4/6	MELICH, PETER, SR.	MARY & PETER MELICK, JR.	DANIEL GOODEN, SAMUEL BOONE
5/7	DAVIS, STEPHEN	ELINOR DAVIS	THOMAS ELDER, EDWARD GRIMES
8/29	MCCLANAHAN, JAMES	WILLIAM CLARK	WALTER CLARK, FLAVEL ROAN
8/29	" , DAVID	ANDREW MCCLANAHAN	MATTHEW LAIRD, JAMES LOWREY
10/1	WALKER, WILLIAM	REBECCA WALKER	CHARLES STEWART, THOMAS FORSTER
10/6	KEIGER, GEORGE	MARGARET KEIGER	HENRY DOUTY, HENRY BUCHER
12/16	IETSEL, MARGARET	GEORGE SHEAVER	HENRY AURAND, JOHN HAINES

1790

Date	Name		
1/3	LEVINSTON, DAVID	AGNES LEVINSTON	DAN MCDONALD, SR., DAN MCDONALD, JR.
2/9	TEEPLE, GEORGE	MARY TEEPLE	JOHN BLAIR, JACOB SHIPMAN
2/23	SHOEMAKER, PETER, SR. (WIFE, CATHERINE)	PETER & JOHN SHOEMAKER	MELCHOIR STOCK, DANIEL WITMER
3/29	HAWK, GEORGE	THOMAS HAWK	JAMES SILVERWOOD, CASPER SNYDER
6/22	TROXEL, GEORGE	CATHERINE & JOHN TROXEL	HENRY AURAND, NICHOLAS STROH
6/24	LEARY, DENNIS	JOHN MEARS	JOSEPH LORENTS, CHARLES GOBIN
8/6	KERSTETTER, LEONARD	LEONARD KERSTETTER, JR.	JOHN BINGAMAN, JACOB BROSIUS
10/1	HAMILTON, JAMES	THOMAS HAMILTON	THOMAS GRANT, WILLIAM COOK
10/7	SWISHER, LOW	MARY SWISHER	MART SHELLENBERGER, ROB. EASON
10/--	BERRY, GARRET	MARK WILLCOCK	GEN. DANIEL MONTGOMERY
10/26	WIERBACH, JOHN	CATHERINE WIERBACH	ABRAHAM PIATT, CHRISTOPHER HANEY
11/12	WILSON, ISAAC	MARTIN REESE	WM. FISHER, JAMES LATTIMORE

1791

Date	Name		
3/22	MOOR, JOHN	JAMES MOORE	ROBERT MARTIN, JOHN GRAY
4/13	JOHNSTON, JOHN	JEAN & WM. JOHNSTON	" " JAMES FORSTER
5/10	HEFFER (HAFER?), AND.	ELIZ. & FRED HEFFER	CHARLES MEYER, THOMAS PRICE
5/13	ZELLER, HENRY	JOHN ZELLER	CHRISTOPHER ZIMMERMAN
7/25	GRANT, GEORGE	THOMAS GRANT	WILLIAM GRAY, WILLIAM MCCURDY
8/6	GABLE, DANIEL	BARBARA & ADAM GABLE	WILLIAM DOBSON, CASPER GABLE
8/13	ZIMMERMAN, JACOB	FRANCIS RHOADS	FRANCIS RHOADS, JR., JOS. LORENTZ
8/15	LATSHA, ABRAHAM	JACOB LATCHA	CHAS. STEWART, BRITTAIN CALDWELL
8/23	BROWN, WILLIAM	JEAN, JOSEPH & SAMUEL BROWN	JOHN LYTLE, JAMES HAYS
8/31	TOMB, JOHN	MARGARET TOMB	JACOB TOMB
10/3	MARKLEY, PETER	ELIZABETH MARKLEY	JOHN GRAYBILL, FRED. STEESE
10/5	COOLY, JONATHAN	WILLIAM HEPBURN	WILLIAM COOK, JAMES HEPBURN
11/2	PFILE, GEORGE (WIFE, FRENNIE)	HENRY PFILE	JACOB ECKHART, GEORGE MARKLE
11/4	GREGG, WILLIAM	RACHEL GREGG	CHARLES GOBIN, JOHN CHILDS
11/9	MCKINLEY, JAMES	JOHN MCKINLEY	PETER KERLIN, ROBERT COLDREN
11/9	PEARSON, JOHN	GEORGE PEARSON	PAUL BALDY, JOSEPH LORENTZ
12/2	TORBET, JOHN	DAVID TORBET, JOHN ALLEN	WILLIAM COOK, JOHN MOFFATT

1792

Date	Name		
1/4	PIATT, ABRAHAM	ANN PIATT	JOHN KELLY, WILLIAM GRAY
2/23	SELIN, MAJ. ANTHONY (FOUNDER, SELINSGROVE, PA.)	SIMON SNYDER	CHAS. MEYER, ALBRIGHT SWINEFORD
3/2	PERINE, ELIZABETH	RICHARD PERINE	WILLIAM HASLET, PERKINS LOVELL
3/20	THROPTOE, ANDREW	PAUL LEBO	JOHN NOTESTINE, GEORGE THOMAS
3/20	RHOADS, JOHN	JOHN NOTESTINE	FRED BENT, JACOB SERVER (ZERBE?)
3/20	KAIN, JOHN	" "	" " " " "
5/25	HAIN, WILLIAM	CONRAD HAIN	JOSEPH LORENTZ, GEORGE WOLF
5/29	ARMOR, THOMAS	ROBERT BIGHAM	JOHN MCPHERSON
6/5	SEELY, ISAAC	ELIZABETH SEELY	TOM FOSTER, DANIEL MONTGOMERY

1792

Date	Name		
6/8	HODGENS, SAMUEL	ELIAS REGAR	JOHN HASSINGER, JOHN THOMAS
"	WELCH, JOHN	" "	" " " "
"	BOARDMAN, MOSES	JOHN HASSINGER	ELIAS REGAR " "
"	EASTWOOD, CHARLES	ELIAS REGAR	JOHN HASSINGER " "
"	CARIFF, MILES	GEORGE HAACK	" " ELIAS REGAR
6/25	LATELY, JOHN	JEAN CURRY	JERE SIMPSON, JOHN MCHARD
6/25	BUTLER, RICHARD	JOHN BUTLER	JOS. LORENTZ, MITCHELL BENNETT
7/9	O'DANIEL, DANIEL	JOSEPH LORENTZ	JOHN MCHARD, CHRISTOPHER WITMER
"	JOHNSTON, JOHN	CHARLES GOBIN	MICHAEL MILLER, WILLIAM MCADAM
"	ROSMAN, JOHN	ELIAS REGAR	JOHN HASSINGER, GEORGE THOMAS
"	KALABASH, ANTHONY	JOHN MITCHELL	ELIAS REGAR " "
"	BARNITZ, JACOB	" "	" " " "
7/13	GOBIN, HUGH	CHARLES GOBIN	MICHAEL MILLER, WILLIAM MCADAM
8/1	MILLER, ALEXANDER	ELIZABETH MILLER	JAMES MCMAHON, WILLIAM FISHER
8/11	SHEFFER, FRANCES	" SHEFFER	CONRAD WEISER, STEPHEN LENKER
8/26	MCGIBBEN, JOHN	THOMAS MCGIBBEN	PETER ZERBE, CHRISTIAN WERTZ
8/29	BARGER, CHRISTIAN	CARTOUT BAGER	SOLOMON REED, DANEIL BOGAR
9/20	BARBER, SAMUEL	MARTHA BARBER	WM. MCCURDY, JOHN JOSEPH HENRY
"	KNEELAND, THOMAS	FRED BENT	JOHN NOTESTEIN, JOHN KERNER
"	RHOADS, JOHN	JOHN NOTESTEIN	FRED BENT, JACOB ZERBE
"	KAIN, JOHN	" "	" " "
9/22	SULLIVAN, THOMAS	JOHN SHUTTS	GEO. THOMAS, JOHN GARNER (KERNER)
"	DUNSCOMD, JAMES	JACOB SERVER (ZERBE?)	" " " "
"	INGLEDOE, THOMAS	PAUL LEBO	" " " "
"	MCFARLANE, JAMES	JOHN KERNER	" " JACOB SERVER
"	BRENNER, JOHN	FRANCIS BRENNER	JOHN KERNER, JOHN BERRY
"	WILLIAMS, THOMAS	JOHN SHUTTS	" " GEORGE THOMAS
"	ROUSH, JOHN	GEORGE ROUSH	TOBIAS BICKEL, NICHOLAS MERTZ
11/6	CURRY, JOHN	JOHN ALEXANDER	JOHN MACKEY, JOHN MONTGOMERY
"	HAUN, SAMUEL	FLAVEL ROAN	CHARLES GOBIN, JOHN THOMPSON
11/21	GOODMAN, HENRY	GEORGE GOODMAN	GEORGE AURAND, JOHN HASSINGER
"	BRAIZLER, ROBERT	" "	" " " "
11/22	BEAVER, CHRISTOPHER	ADAM BEAVER	" " GEORGE GOODMAN
"	" WILLIAM	" "	" " " "
11/26	ARMER, PETER	JOHN BEAVER	GEORGE HAACK, JOHN HASSINGER
"	BROMLEY, JOHN	" "	" " " "
11/27	DELL, LEONARD	ADAM BOLLENDER	JOHN BEAVER " "
"	FISHER, JOHN	" "	" " " "
12/14	CORTING, GEORGE	PATRICK CORTING	JOHN DOWNEY, SAMUEL NEIL
12/12	ALCOM, JAMES	JOHN ALCOM	JAMES ANDREWS, JOHN ROBERTS
12/21	GIBBONS, EDWARD	ELIZABETH GIBBONS	JOS. LORENTZ, ELIAS YOUNGMAN
12/24	FOLLMER, MICHAEL	ELIZABETH & HENRY FOLLMER	JOHN FOLLMER, FRED FOLLMER

1793

Date	Name		
1/9	STEPHENS, JOHN	JOHN KARNER	PETER SERVER, PETER CLEMENS
"	MULLEN, JOHN	CHRISTIAN WERTZ	JOHN KARNER " "
"	SILVER, AMOS	PETER CLEMENS	" " JOHN NOTESTEIN
"	MURRAY, FRANCIS	PETER SERVER	" " JACOB SERVER
"	MCKUSH, JOHN	CHRISTIAN WERTZ	" " PETER CLEMENS
"	SOCKMAN, ANDREW	PETER CLEMENS	" " JOHN NOTESTEIN
"	WHITE, JOHN	JOHN NOTESTINE	PETER SERVER, CHRISTIAN WERTZ
"	WINTER, JAMES	" "	" " " "
"	BEAR, JOHN	ELIZ. & SAMUEL BEAR	ISAAC BEAR, JOHN KELLY
"	DAVIDSON, JAMES	JOHN KARNER	PETER SERVER, PETER CLEMENS
"	DEVORE, DAVID	PETER SERVER	JACOB " CHRISTIAN WERTZ
"	TORNEY, JOHN	JACOB "	PETER " " "
"	WILSON, JOHN	" "	" " " "
1/14	BORCHERT, MICHAEL	CHRISTOPHER BICKEL	JOHN HOWELL, STEPH. TOUCHMAN
"	MOYER, NICHOLAS	STEPHEN TOUCHMAN	" " CHRISTOP. BICKEL
"	SHAFFETT, FRANCIS	" "	" " " "

6

1793

Date	Name	Column 3	Column 4
1/14	SERVER, PETER	JOHN HOWELL	STEPHEN TOUCHMAN, STOPHEL BICKEL
"	KERSHNER, JACOB	CHRISTOPHER BICKEL	" " JOHN HOWELL
"	OGLEBEE, JOHN	JOHN HOWELL	" " CHRIST, BICKEL
1/30	LEECH, DANIEL	JACOB METZGER	" " " "
1/30	BEGDEL, NICHOLAS	" "	" " " "
3/25	WEISNER, JACOB	ISAAC WIGGINS	NATHANIEL LEE, JOHN HUGHES
4/3	SMITH, NICHOLAS	CATHERINE SMITH	NICHOLAS WELCH, JAC. HAVERLING
4/16	WHITE, JOSHUA	ANN WHITE	GEN. DANIEL MONTGOMERY
4/23	DEELMAN, PETER	ANNA MARIA DEELMAN	BEN & HENRY SHOEMAKER
4/24	SMITH, EZEKIEL	GEORGE NELSON	JAS. STEVENSON, PETER WEIRICK
4/29	ENOCH, ABRAHAM	ADAM BOLLENDER	ADAM HOLE, CHRISTIAN WERTZ
"	YOUNG, CHRISTIAN	" HOLE	" BOLENDER " "
"	ACKINS, ROBERT	" " "	" " " "
"	GRONER, HENRY	CHRISTIAN WERTZ	" " ADAM HOLE
5/20	TURNER, MORRIS	PHILIP MAUS, JR.	PHILIP MAUS, SR., NICH. ROUSHER
6/1	ERTLE, VALENTINE, SR.	SOPHIA & VAL. ERTLE, JR.	ADAM APPLE, JACOB MEYER (MOYER)
7/2	CARLING, GEORGE	JOHN NOTESTINE	ADAM HOLE, JOHN WINTER
8/13	MCENTIRE, DONALD	JAMES TONAR	CHARLES GOBIN, ROBERT BIGGER
8/28	MORRISON, GEORGE	ELINOR MORRISON	JACOB FOLLMER, JOHN MARTIN
10/7	DELONCCHAMP, CHAS. J.	MORDECAI OWEN	CHARLES GOBIN, JOHN LYON
10/15	STRAWYER, LUDWIG	HANNAH & JOHN STRAWYER	MART, KERSTETTER, EWING SEILER
10/29	KINKEAD, JOHN	JAMES GREER	BRITTAIN CALDWELL, MATT. WILSON
11/14	KERN, GEORGE	BARBARA & JOHN KERN	SIMON SNYDER, JOSEPH LORENTZ

1794

Date	Name	Column 3	Column 4
3/8	FISHER, WILLIAM	MARY FISHER & WM. REED	JAMES MCMAHAN, SAMUEL SCOTT
3/13	FOX, ANDREW	EVA FOX & JOHN REZNOR	WILLIAM MCADAM, JACOB WEITNER
3/28	JAMES, ISAAC	EZEKIEL JAMES	JAMES MASTERS
4/1	BARNHART, MATTHEW	MARGARET & WM. HENRY BARNHART	JOHN AURAND, PAUL BALDY
4/29	NEEL, ROBERT	ANN NEEL & WM. GALLIHER	CHARLES STEWART, URIAH BARBER
4/30	TATE, EDWARD	ANDREW & DAVID TATE	ADAM LAUGHLIN, WILLIAM BLACK
5/9	SANDOS, JOHN	THOMAS GASKINS	JOHN KIDD, JEREMIAH SIMPSON
6/3	MARKLEY, ELIZABETH	JACOB MARKLEY & MICHAEL MILLER	BALTZER MITTERLING LEONARD WINKLEBLECH
6/11	CAMPBELL, JAMES	JEAN CAMPBELL	ROBERT MARTIN, JOHN WINTER
8/2	TUTTLE, DANIEL	MARY & JAMES TUTTLE	ISAIAH VORIS, WM, VANDERBELT
8/13	TONNER, JOHN	DEB. TONNER & MAT. WILSON	WILLIAM HEPBURN
8/15	BLACK, SARAH	THOMAS BLACK	GARRETT COURT
8/25	MCCLASKEY, FELIX	RACHEL MCCLASKEY	JOHN MCKINNEY, NATHAN EVANS
9/3	SMITH, MATTHEW	AGNES & ROBERT SMITH	JOHN LYTLE, JOHN LYON
10/2	HURLEY, MARGARET	FREDERICK LAZARUS	DANIEL HURLEY, JACOB WEITNER
10/4	SASSAMAN, HENRY	CATHERINE SASSAMAN	MICHAEL DENNIS, JACOB YONER
10/13	MCFALL, JAMES	NANCY MCFALL, JAS. WATSON	GABRIEL LOUN, JACOB WEITNER
10/24	FOUST, JACOB, SR.	FRENIGAR, SEBASTIAN & JACOB FOUST, JR.	GEORGE HUGHES, DANIEL BOGER
11/4	LIVINGOOD, JACOB	PETER LIVINGOOD	JOHN CUMMINGS, D. STONEBRAKER
12/2	SWENGLE, MICHAEL	ELIZABETH SWENGLE	JOHN HOUSEL, MATHIAS SPOTZ
12/20	BOYD, ARCHIBALD	MARGARET & JOHN BOYD	ROBERT TEMPLE, JOHN LYON
10/11	RODY (RUDY?), PETER	CATHERINE RODY	FLAVEL ROAD, WILLIAM MCKELVEY

1795

Date	Name	Column 3	Column 4
1/7	NEELSON, GEORGE	WILLIAM BELL	HENRY SHOEMAKER, JR., WM, GRAY
3/20	BOLLENDER, HENRY	CATH. & GEO. BOLLENDER	GEORGE FREDERICKS, PAUL BALDY
4/20	GABLE, FREDERICK	ELIZABETH GABLE & FRED DRIONE	PETER APPLE, MICHAEL NEWMAN
4/29	KRANKS, JAMES	HENRY MITCHELL	GEORGE MITCHELL, BEN FOWLER
6/9	DODDERER, PHILIP	ABRAHAM DODDERER	H. SHOEMAKER, JR., DAN MCHENRY
6/30	DORNSIFE, JOHN	ELIZABETH DORNSIFE	M. KERSTETTER, JOHN DUNKELBERGER
9/5	WEIRICK, WILLIAM, JR.	CATH. & JOHN WEIRICK	WM. WEIRICK, SR., FRED STINE

7

1795

Date	Name		
9/6	HUGHES, GEORGE	MARTHA & JOHN HUGHES	BENJAMIN FINCHER, WM. HAWK
9/23	WALLIS, JOSEPH	SAM WALLIS, DAN SMITH	JOHN WEITZEL, JOHN BUYERS
10/3	RODMAN, WILLIAM	HUGH RODMAN	JAMES RODMAN, ISAAC IDDINGS
10/7	LEE, JESSE	SARAH LEE	NATHAN LEE
10/13	POLLOCK, CHARLES	AGNES POLLOCK	WALTER & WILLIAM CLARK
10/14	SHAFFER, GEORGE	CATHERINE & GEO. SHAFFER	HENRY DREISBACH, JOHN GRAYBILL
10/20	ROW, JACOB	JACOB PREISINGER	DANIEL BOGAR, JOHN HAAS
10/24	THORNBAUGH, JOHN	WM. GRAY & JOHN BOYD	ABRAHAM SCOTT, WM. STEEDMAN
11/7	SHULL, DAVID	CHRISTINA SHULL	HENRY LIGHT, CASPER REED
11/13	BEATTY, JAMES	HUGH & JOHN BEATTY	SAMUEL TEMPLETON
11/17	GROVER, MICHAEL	ELIZABETH GROVER	POWELL GROVER, EDWARD THORNTON
11/19	YOCUM, PETER	MARGARET YOCUM	JONAS YOCUM
11/26	MEYER, CHRISTOPHER	MARGARET MEYER	ANDREW LOVE, WILLIAM WHITE
12/8	LEFFLER, GOTTLIEB	JOHN LEFFLER	ADAM, HENRY & GOTT. LEFFLER, JR.

1796

Date	Name		
1/27	HASLET, ROBERT	REBECCA HASLET	NICHOLAS SHIPMAN, JOSEPH BRADY
1/28	JORDON, WILLIAM	JANE & WM. JORDON, JR.	JAMES MURRAY, JOHN LYON
2/27	CARTER, RICHARD	MARY CARTER	ROBERT SMITH
2/20	HAGER, JOHN	ELIZ. & FRED. HAGER	GEORGE OTT, MATHIAS APP
2/29	MCCAM, JONATHAN	MARY MCCAM	PETER KERLIN
3/12	SANDOZ, JOHN	JOSEPH LORENTZ	CHARLES GOBIN, WENDEL LORENTZ
3/19	HENNING (HANEY?), HIRONIMUS	PEACOCK MAJOR	FREDERICK ANTES, JACOB MARKLEY
5/2	ROCKEY, JOHN	WM. ROCKEY & WM. BAKER	GEO. YOUNGMAN, WENDELL BAKER
6/15	KLINE, LUDWIG	CATHERINE KLINE	MATHIAS SPOTZ, NICHOLAS MILLER
7/16	FOUST, ABRAHAM	FRONICA FOUST	JACOB YONER, JACOB PREISINGER
9/19	MARR, JOSEPH	SARAH & DAVID MARR	JOHN TIETSWORTH, BETHUEL VINCENT
10/18	GIBSON, DAVID	WILLIAM GIBSON	JOHN BLACK, DANIEL BASTIAN
11/10	CAMERON, DUNCAN	JANET CAMERON	JACOB WITTNER, HEN. VANDERSLICE
11/11	MOORE, MOSES	ELINOR MOORE	JAMES COLLIER, WILLIAM GRAY
11/11	TAYLOR, JOHN	MARG. TAYLOR, JAC. FOLLMER	WILLIAM HESLET, WILLIAM DEWART
11/15	SNYDER, JOHN	GEORGE SNYDER	WENDEL & JOSEPH LORENTZ

1797

Date	Name		
1/6	PEELER, PAUL	CHARLOTTE & JACOB PEELER	DANIEL GOODEN, WILLIAM PARK
3/7	GOBIN, CHARLES	ANN GOBIN	JOS. LORENTZ, JACOB PREISINGER
3/8	HOUSEL, PETER	JOHN HOUSEL	WILLIAM HOUSEL, JOHN HOUSEL
4/4	PLUNKETT, THOMAS	SAMUEL SUMMERS	JOHN BRADY, JOHN KIDD
5/10	SECHRIST, CHRISTIAN, SR.	NANCY & CHRIST. SECHRIST	JOHN & ABRAHAM WITMER
5/16	LENKER, MICHAEL	CATHERINE & JACOB LENKER	NICHOLAS BOBB, DANIEL SHAFFER
6/12	MORTER, JACOB	CATHERINE MORTER	JACOB KEISER, JOHN JOHNSON
6/21	HELMAN, HERMAN	MAGDALENE HELMAN	JOHN AURAND, NICHOLAS MILLER
8/7	SHERMON, SIMON, SR.	MARY & SIMON SHERMON, JR.	MARTIN HOYLE, JOHN HARTER
8/21	WELKER, MICHAEL	WILLIAM RITTENHOUSE	JOSEPH LORENTZ, JOHN HOUSEWORTH
9/2	MCWHORTER, JOHN	HUGH MCWHORTER	JOHN COOK
9/10	WATERS, JAMES	HANNAH WATERS	GEORGE HUNT, ANDREW CRAVELING
10/2	HOW, SAMUEL	ELIZ. HOW & AARON FURMAN	JACOB DEPUY, DAVID DAVIS
10/9	HUGHES, GARRETT	SUSANNA HUGHES & PETER WITHINGTON	CHAS. GEMBERLING, MART. WITHINGTON
10/23	AUCHMUTY, ARTHUR	SAMUEL AUCHMUTY	JOHN REWALT, GEORGE HILTEBITLE
10/31	RICHTER, CHRISTIAN	JULIANA RICHTER	JACOB WEIAND, MICH. DIERSTEIN
11/6	BISHOP, CORNELIUS	REBECCA BISHOP	DAN. MONTGOMERY, CHRIST. DERING
11/19	WEAVER, SEBASTIAN	ANNA MARY & ANTHONY WEAVER	JOHN TROXEL, CASPER WANNAMAKER
11/30	KRAMER, GEO. ADAM	JACOB KRAMER	JOS. LORENTZ, GEO. ZIMMERMAN

1798

Date	Name		
1/12	STRAPHON, JOSEPH	MARY STRAPHON	ALEX. MCDONALD, DAN. MONTGOMERY
2/11	MILLER, CHRISTIAN	MARY MILLER	JAMES PARKS, ANDREW WAGNER
3/12	GIBSON, GEORGE	GOWEN HENRY	DAVID HARRISON, THOMAS WILSON
3/17	WALKER, ROBERT	ANN & HENRY WALKER	JAMES SMITH
4/26	KABEL (KOBEL?), ISAAC	CASPER KABEL	PETER KESTER, SAMUEL BLOOM

1798			
5/18	BARRETT, ELIJAH	CATHERINE BARRETT	WILLIAM DEWART, DANIEL LEBO
5/22	BROWN, JAMES	MARY, CHARLES & JOHN BROWN	JOHN STILLWELL
5/23	STOCK, PETER	PETER APPLE	JACOB BISHOP, ANDREW LIST
5/25	JORDAN, GEORGE	WILLIAM JORDAN	HAMILTON SHAW, HUGH MARTIN
7/16	MILES, JAMES	SUSAN MILES	ABIEZER MILES, SAMUEL MILES
8/4	THOMAS, JOB	THOMAS THOMAS	JAMES SMITH, JACOB WEIDNER
8/28	MOORE, WILLIAM, SR.	WILLIAM MOORE, JR.	SAMUEL FORESMAN, SAM MCKINNEY
8/28	BASTIAN, GEO. MICHAEL	MARY MAGDALENE BASTIAN	MICHAEL WERLINE, MARTIN EPLY
8/30	TAYLOR, JAMES	JAS. TAYLOR, TOM RUFFMAN	PETER SORTER, JOHN JACOBY
8/31	ALLISON, JAMES	ISAIAH WILLETTS	HEZEKIAH BOONE, STACY MARGARUM
9/18	HANNA, WILLIAM	SUSAN HANNA, RICH. MARR	CHARLES IRWIN, DAVID MARR
10/3	SCOTT, ABRAHAM	ALEXANDER SCOTT	THOMAS GRANT, ALEXANDER HENRY
10/7	HENNY (HANEY?), JOHN	ADAM HENNY	PETER OVERMIRE, JACOB HUBLER
10/21	WHEELER, BENJAMIN	LEVI WHEELER	JOSEPH SALMON, JOHN LYON
10/30	WATSON, JAMES	MARY WATSON, SAM MATHIAS	JOHN MAPHER, ISAIAH WILLETTS
10/30	MCFALL, JAMES	SAM MATHIAS	WILLIAM BRADY, JACOB SINTON
12/26	MCCULLY, ALEXANDER	GEORGE MCCULLY	DANIEL MCRAY, WM. MONTGOMERY
1799			
2/1	GODDARD, JOHN	JOHN FRETCHY	LEONARD RUPERT, WM. MCCARTER
2/2	TRUCKENMILLER, JOHN	MICHAEL MEISER	JOHN HAAS, JOSEPH LORENTZ
3/4	NELSON, ABRAHAM	JOHN MCFARRON, JR.	SAMUEL MCFARRON, WM. COOK
3/7	HASSINGER, JOHN	CATHERINE HASSINGER	DAVID NEYHART, GEORGE HUMMEL
3/12	SHOCK (SCHOCH), JOHN (S/O MATHIAS)	BARBARA SHOCK & PHILIP MOSSER	ADAM HARPER, JACOB WERTMAN
3/21	WILSON, THOMAS, SR.	HUGH, WILLIAM & THOMAS WILSON	WILLIAM GRAY, WILLIAM MCADAM
3/30	ANTOINE, PAUL	GOD. KRAMER & AD. SLICK	NICHOLAS MILLER, JOHN HOUSEL
4/4	MCCALLA, ALEXANDER	SARAH & JOHN MCCALLA	JOHN KLECKNER, JACOB WEIDNER
4/25	GETZ, PETER	MAGDALENE GETZ	JOHN SIERER, JACOB PREISINGER
5/13	FREEMAN, NATHANIEL	ANN FREEMAN	HUGH WILSON, JAMES CUMMINGS
5/27	MAGER, GEORGE	RACHEL MAGER	DANIEL STIMELING, NICH. MILLER
8/16	STRAEHLE, CASPER	JOHN & JOS. STRAEHLE	JOSEPH HAMPTON, NATHANIEL LEE
11/12	DEAL, PHILIP	SOPHIA & MICHAEL DEAL	PETER FORSTER, NICH. SCHNEIDER
12/7	ZARTMAN, MICHAEL	HENRY ZARTMAN	" " M. DUNKELBERGER
12/10	DERR, FREDERICK	ADAM & JOHN DERR	ROBERT CLARK, SAMUEL POLLOCK
1800			
1/1	ZIMMERMAN, CHRISTIAN	JACOB GRAYBILL	CHRISTIAN & JOHN GRAYBILL
1/20	SEILER, VALENTINE	HANNAH MARIA SEILER	GEORGE REINER, GEORGE BEYER
1/22	WEITZEL, JOHN	ELIZ. & JOHN WEITZEL	SAMUEL ROBERTS, WILLIAM GRAY
2/3	HOOD, JOHN	ROSE HOOD	JOHN HOOD
2/7	HECKERT, JOHN	PETER & MICHAEL HECKERT	ABRAHAM SNYDER, SEB. SPADE
4/29	OWEN, ROBERT	HENRY HIDLEY	JOSEPH SALMON, PETER MELICK
5/13	CROTZER, JOHN	MARGARET CROTZER	WILLIAM & JOHN FORSTER
7/3	YERGER, ANDREW	ELIZ. YERGER & JAC. SACHS	MATT. LAIRD, GEORGE RENNINGER
7/13	EMERY, DAVID	JACOB MOCK	HENRY RICHARDS, GEORGE SCHOCH
8/16	FERSTER, PETER	LEONARD FERSTER	MICHAEL SHAFFER, MICHAEL REITZ
10/9	HEIDENRICH, JOHN	SUSAN HEIDENRICH & GEO. KNOPPENBERGER	DANIEL BOGER, JAC. PREISINGER
10/16	MILLER, NICHOLAS	TIMOTHY B. MILLER	" " WM. MCADAM
10/28	STINE, MICHAEL	REBECCA STINE	HERMAN YOST, CONRAD MINICH
11/27	LAVERTY, ISAAC	JEAN & ALEX. LAVERTY	HUGH & ROBERT MARTIN
12/27	WALDRON, CORNELIUS, SR.	SARAH, LAFFERT & CORNELIUS WALDORN, JR.	ADAM KIMBLE, JOSEPH HAMMOND
1801			
1/13	HUGHES, MARY	URIAH HUGHES	WILLIAM HAWK, JONAS WEAVER
1/15	MINICH, MARY	CONRAD MINICH	HENRY SHAFFER, HENRY GOODHART
1/29	JACKSON, JEREMIAH	WILLIAM P. BRADY	WILLIAM MCADAM, WILLIAM GRAY

9

1801			
2/19	GINGLES, JAMES	MARTHA & JOHN GINGLES	JOSEPH McCORD
3/17	MERTZ, NICHOLAS	CATHERINE & ISAAC MERTZ	JOHN BOLLENDER, DANIEL BOGER
6/5	BODINE, WILLIAM	JACOB BODINE	JACOB SHIPMAN, AARON THOMAS
6/15	BROOK, SAMUEL	ELIZ. & DAVID BROOK	ELIJAH STARR, B. HAYHURST
6/15	FITZSIMMONS, JOHN	WM. FITZSIMMONS	JOHN MURRAY, JAMES FORSTER
6/22	RENTZ, ANDREW	BARBARA & JOHN RENTZ	FRED & PHILIP RENTZ
8/26	WELSH, JAMES, JR.	JAMES WELSH, SR.	DANIEL VINCENT, DAVID MCKNIGHT
9/15	ALBRIGHT, JACOB, SR.	MARY & JACOB ALBRIGHT	THOMAS SHIPTON, ADAM SMITH
10/7	WANNEMAKER, CASPER	MARY WANNEMAKER & ADAM REGAR	HERMAN OBERDORF, JOSEPH ROMIG
10/8	BARGER, ISAAC	THOS. & ELIZ. BARGER	JOHN CLARK, JOHN CLINE
10/12	DEWITT, PAUL	MARGARET DEWITT	PETER COLOREN, FRANCIS KUNTZ
10/14	APPLEMAN, MATHIAS	BALTHIS & MATHIAS APPLEMAN	PETER APPLEMAN, JAMES HARRIS
10/21	VANBOSKIRK, THOMAS, SR.	THOMAS & MORRIS VANBOSKIRK	JAMES SMITH, JONAS WEAVER
11/3	BREON, GEORGE	MARY ELIZ. BREON	GEORGE KESSLER, GEORGE SCHOCH
11/24	BOWER, MOSES	JACOB BOWER, ADAM FOLLMER	ADAM CHRIST, JAC. PREISINGER
11/25	MILLER, JOHN	GEO. MILLER, CHAS. DRUM	CONRAD WEISER, CONRAD HAIN
12/11	JOHNSTON, ROBERT	NEAL SINCLAIR	SAMUEL HUGH, JOHN MCPHERSON
12/14	WATSON, JAMES, SR.	JAMES WATSON	ALEX. STEWART, DAVID FRAZIER
1802			
1/23	HEPBURN, SAMUEL	JAS. & WM. HEPBURN	WM. COOK, JOHN COWDEN
1/27	DRUM, CATHERINE	CHARLES DRUM	JAMES WHITE, WILLIAM GRAY
2/20	KITCHEN, JACOB	ELIAS KITCHEN	THEO. KIEHL, DANIEL BOGAR
3/2	LONG, JOSEPH	JOHN LONG, JOS. DRAKE	JOHN DRAKE, ELIAS BETRICH
3/23	EPLY, MARTIN	LOEN, EPLY, HENRY BUCHER	JOHN KENDIG, JACOB PREISINGER
4/5	SHAWVER, PHILIP	SIMON BICKEL	MATHIAS SPOTZ, GEORGE ULRICH
4/18	MILLER, JACOB	JACOB MEYER	HENRY ERTLEY, FRED EVANS
4/30	CATIN, IGNATIUS	JAMES SMITH	TOM & MORRIS VANBUSKIRK
5/10	BRADY, JOHN	MARY & WALTER BRADY	PETER COLOREN, GEO. HILTEBITLE
5/18	LATCHA, JOHN	ANDREW LATCHA	ANDREW KENNEDY, JACOB WALKER
5/19	RABUCK, VALENTINE	MICHAEL RABUCK	LEONARD REITZ, GEO. BROSIUS
5/20	SHETTERLY, DAVID	GEO. SHETTERLY & ADAM LIGHT	GEORGE KEEN, GEORGE MOYER
6/2	LANTZ, JOHN	HENRY LANTZ, CASP. SNYDER	JACOB KAIL, DANIEL BOGER
6/21	ADAIR, GILBERT	RACHEL ADAIR	JAMES & SILVANUS BIRD
6/25	GROSSCUP, SAMUEL	HIRONIMUS AUGUSTINE	JOSEPH ROMIG, JOHN MOCK
6/26	HUMMEL, JOHN	HENRY HUMMEL	GEORGE HUMMEL, JAMES SMITH
8/16	WEITZEL, PAUL	JOHN WEITZEL	WM. MCADAM, SIMON SNYDER, JR.
8/25	TIETSWORTH, JOHN	JOHN & WM. TIETSWORTH	GEORGE ELY, JAMES SMITH
9/20	FRY, JACOB	ABRAHAM FRY (SON)	ADAM REGAR, HERMAN OBERDORF
10/2	RAKER, MARTIN	MARY, MARTIN & JACOB RAKER	WM. PEEBER, LEONARD CRISSINGER
10/5	LANTZ, HENRY, SR.	MARGARET, JACOB & HENRY LANTZ	GEORGE BRIGHT, JACOB MARTZ
10/5	HEWITT, EDWARD	JAMES SMITH	JOHN KENDIG, GEORGE RENNINGER
10/11	BROUSE, ADAM	CATHERINE & ABE BROUSE	GEORGE BENFER, PETER KLINGLER
10/11	CLEMENS, PETER	ELIZABETH CLEMENS	JAMES SMITH, JOHN HAAS
10/19	GLENN, JOHN	ROBERT & JAMES GLENN	JOHN CRAIG, WILLIAM MATHER
11/10	BENDER, JACOB, SR.	JACOB BENDER	CHRISTIAN ZERBE, JAMES SMITH
11/15	YODER, BENJAMIN	MARY & JOHN YODER	MELCHOIR YODER, MATHIAS SCHOCH
11/19	HUTCHINSON, THOMAS	MARY & JOHN HUTCHINSON	WM. JOHNSON, GEORGE MARTIN
11/29	JACKSON, JEREMIAH	WM. & LYDIA NORTH	JOS. RICHARDSON, BEN VASTINE
12/8	MACHAMER, PHILIP	ANN & DANIEL MACHAMER	SAMUEL ANDERSON, CONRAD REEDY
12/13	WENTZEL, CHRISTOPHER	ABE & JOHN WENTZEL	HENRY ZARTMAN, MARTIN HEIL
1803			
1/12	NORTH, WILLIAM	LYDIA NORTH	SAMUEL ROBERTS, JAS. SILVERWOOD
1/12	FURY, PATRICK	" "	JOS. LORENTZ " "

10

Date			
1/15	WERLEIN, MICHAEL	MAGDALENE & GEO. BOSSLER	JOSEPH LORENTZ
1/26	WAGNER, JACOB	JOHN WAGNER	PETER HELPESEL, DAN KUNTZMAN
1/31	BILLMAN, VALENTINE	CATHERINE BILLMAN	JOSEPH & JACOB LINTON
2/7	FREDERICK, GEORGE	ELIZ. & GEO. FREDERICK	BENJAMIN MILLER, HOWARD REEDY
2/15	BARBER, MATHIAS	SARAH BARBER	NICH. SHIPMAN, PETER COLDREN
2/21	WEISER, CONRAD	BARBARA & BENJ. WEISER	NICH. GAUGLER, JACOB HUMMEL
2/21	CHAPMAN, JOHN	MARY CHAPMAN	JARED IRWIN, JOSEPH LORENTZ
3/2	PARSON, CATHERINE	LUDWIG LONG	ANDREW & DAVID LIST
3/4	VANDEVENDER, RICHARD	LOVINA VANDEVENDER	GEO. DAUGHERTY, ROB. CAMPBELL
3/8	JENKINS, JAMES	JOHN BOYD	JOHN COYDEN, EVAN R. EVANS
3/10	MEYER, DAVID	JACOB & MARY MEYER	DAVID BIRD, DANIEL WINTER
3/26	YOUNG, BENJAMIN F.	SARAH YOUNG	JOHN BRILL, JOHN BOYD
3/28	GETTIG, FREDERICK	MATHIAS SPOTZ	CHARLES DRUM, PHILIP MORR
3/30	HUNTER, WILLIAM	TOM WALLACE, ROB. MCKEE	ROBERT CLARK, JOHN BEARD
4/8	FRANTZ, MICHAEL	SUSAN FRANTZ, ROB. SMITH	STEPHEN GIRL, JOS. RICHARDSON
4/21	HUNT, WILSON	KEZIAH HUNT	JONAS WEHR, JOHN GULICK
4/26	SCHULTZ, JACOB	MARY & PHILIP SCHULTZ	SAMUEL PEGG, JACOB ABEL
4/26	MORRISON, JOHN	ISABEL MORRISON & THOS. SILLIMAN	EPH. MCCULLOM, FRED FOLLMER
5/2	AURAND, JACOB	MARY WALKER, JOHN AURAND	PETER BASTIAN, CONRAD MINNICH
5/3	DEWITT, ISAAC	MARG. & JOHN DEWITT	STEPHEN BIRD, WILLIAM KASE
5/31	WATSON, DR. ANTHONY	PEGGY WATSON, JOHN TREMBLY	PETER BLUE, JAMES SUTPHEN
6/7	KERN, NICHOLAS, SR.	NICHOLAS KERN, JR.	SIMON SNYDER, LAWRENCE KERN
6/4	FOX, JOHN	PETER FOX	GEORGE RAY, JAMES SMITH
6/5	FORSTER, THOMAS	JAMES FORSTER	ROBERT & ANDREW FORSTER
8/13	HAAS, LAWRENCE	DAVID & JOHN HAAS	HENRY SHAFFER, GEORGE BRIGHT
8/26	ZERN, MARIA ELIZABETH	WILLIAM HEIM	" KREBS, ADAM BOLLENDER
9/10	GULICK, SAMUEL	JOHN GULICK	THOMAS TAYLOR, JAMES SMITH
9/19	LAUVER, BALTZER	ROSINA & JOHN LAUVER	JOHN THOMAS, HENRY MILLER
9/19	HUMPHREY, JOHN (WIFE, ELIZA)	JOHN P. DEQUEECHY	JOHN BOYD, EDWARD LYON
10/15	LEFFLER, GOTTLIEB	MAGDALENE & HENRY LEFFLER	MICHAEL SHAFFER, J. BINGAMAN
11/5	SWARTZ, PETER, SR.	PETER SWARTZ, JR.	JOHN LAWSHE, HENRY SHAFFER
11/21	CLAWSON, JOSIAH	RICHARD DENOT	ENOCH SMITH, JAS. ALEXANDER
12/1	BEGGS, MARY	WILLIAM MCADAM	JOHN HILL, JOHN RICHARDSON
12/3	FISHER, MARY	SAMUEL FISHER	JAMES COLLIER, JAMES SMITH

Date			
1/20	MARTIN, JOHN LUDWIG	MARY MARTIN, JOHN EPLY	LEONARD EPLY, HENRY BUCHER
1/7	KANNELL, MARK	GEORGE SWINEFORD	CONRAD MINNICH, PETER GARMAN
1/25	MATHER, SAMUEL	WM., JAS. & JESSE MATHER	PASCHALL LEWIS, SAMUEL MATHER
1/30	MARCH, JACOB	CONRAD GEIST	PHILIP BOWER, JONAS WEAVER
2/4	BRIGHT, GEORGE	ESTHER BRIGHT, DAN LEBO	JAC. GRISSINGER, HENRY BUCHER
2/7	COCH (KOCH), ADAM	WILLIAM P. BRADY	WILLIAM MCADAM, EVAN R. EVANS
2/9	NORTH, WILLIAM	HENRY VANDERSLICE	AND. ALBRIGHT, JAC. VANDERSLICE
2/9	JACKSON, JEREMIAH	" "	CHRISTIAN MILLER, JONAS WEAVER
2/10	LAWSON, MATHIAS	THEODORUS KIEHLE	JOHN YOUNG
2/26	EVANS, NATHAN	DAVID BROOK	BEN. BROOK, ABNER EVANS
2/27	FOLWEILER, HENRY	JOHN FOLWEILER, JR.	JACOB DORST, JOHN SCHNEIDER
3/8	DOUGHERTY, JOHN	JOHN COWDEN	JOHN BOYD, THOMAS HAMILTON
3/8	MCCURDY, THOMAS	AGNES MCCURDY	SAM OAKES, SAM OAKES, JR.
3/15	WERLEIN, ABRAHAM	PHILIP WOLF	MICHAEL WOLF
3/15	HURSH, PHILIP	JOHN & MARTIN HURSH	PHILIP & MARTIN WEAVER
4/2	BENNER, CHRISTIAN	BARBARA & JOHN BENNER	JOHN DINGES, ADAM SHOUT
4/14	TIETSWORTH, JOHN	JARED IRWIN	DANIEL LEBO, JAMES SMITH
4/24	DREISBACH, MARTIN, SR.	HENRY DREISBACH	JACOB & DANIEL DREISBACH
5/9	GEIST, CONRAD	JOHN GEIST	MICHAEL WERLEIN, JOSEPH ALTER
5/18	MARCH, JACOB	" "	" "
6/11	TAYLOR, FREDERICK	NANCY & ROBERT TAYLOR	WM. TAYLOR, ALEXANDER GUFFY
6/13	WEYMAN, FREDERICK	JOHN WEYMAN	JOS. LORENTZ, JOSEPH ALTER

11

1804

Date	Name		
6/13	WHITEMAN, ABRAHAM	ESTHER WHITEMAN	JERE KULY, JACOB MOYER
7/28	GARY, WILLIAM	MARY GRAY, WM. P. BRADY	JOHN HAYES, JAMES SMITH
8/18	ROBINSON, JAMES	BARBARA ROBINSON	ROB. SIMONTON, JAMES WILSON
8/18	RHODES, JACOB	JACOB GABLE	ANDREW BOSTIAN, MICH. BARTGES
8/25	GLASGOW, WILLIAM	MISHAEL LINCOLN	JAS. THOMPSON, MICHAEL BARTGES
8/29	RICHARDS, JAMES	DANIEL MONTGOMERY	RICH. ROBINSON, JESSE SIMPSON
9/14	BOWER, JOHN	JAC. HIGH, DAN NORGONG	JACOB LOTZ (LUTZ)
9/26	MEYER, ABSALON	CATH. & HERMAN KLINE	ISAAC KLINE, THOS. VANBUSKIRK
10/5	SCHNEIDER, JOHN, SR.	MARY & JOHN SCHNEIDER	JOSEPH ALTER, JOHN KENDIG
10/10	MORRISON, HUGH	JOHN BUYERS, JAS. HEPBURN	JOHN BOYD, THOMAS GRANT
10/11	GIBSON, DAVID	SUSAN GIBSON, G. LUDWIG	JOHN FOLLMER, JACOB JOHNSON
10/21	DEVORS, JOHN	JAMES MCANULTY	JAS. PATTERSON, JOHN BRYSON
10/22	FREY, JACOB	AND. FREY, JOHN ROTH	HUGH HUGHES, JONAS WEAVER
10/22	PETTIT, WILLIAM, SR.	WILLIAM PETTIT, JR.	ISAAC WIGGINS, EDWARD HUGHES
10/25	WERLEIN, MICHAEL	SOLOMON WERLEIN	JACOB & PETER BASTIAN
10/25	FOLTZ, FRANCIS	MARY FOLTZ	PETER GARMAN, PETER HACKENBERG
10/31	MICHAEL, GEORGE	GEORGE MICHAEL, JR.	GEORGE GOOD, JACOB WEIDNER
11/5	IDDINGS, WILLIAM	SAMUEL IDDINGS	BENJAMIN DOAN, REUBEN BURR
11/6	MUSSELMAN, JACOB	MARY KRATZER MUSSELMAN	GEORGE KESSLER, ANDREW BERGER
11/12	CHENEY, JAMES	JOHSTON & CHARLES CHENEY	JAMES MCCUNE
11/12	MOYER, MARY	JOHN MOYER	SAMUEL BLOOM, BERNARD RENN
11/13	ESPY, GEORGE	RUTH & JOHN SMITH	ALEXANDER HUNTER, JOS. MCCLURE
11/15	SECHLER, JOSEPH	ELIZ. & RUDOLPH SECHLER	JACOB & JOHN SECHLER
11/15	ROBINSON, RICHARD	ZILLAH ROBINSON	DANIEL MONTGOMERY
11/16	GINGLES, WILLIAM	SUSAN GINGLES, JAS. MCBRIDE	WILLIAM GINGLES, GEORGE DERR
11/17	PATTON, ANDREW	JOHN DAVIS	ARTHUR MCKESSON, JAMES SMITH
11/19	FELKER, JOHN	ELIZABETH FELKER & CHRISTIAN ROYER	JOHN GORSS, CHRISTOPHER ROYER
11/19	REICHLEY, CONRAD	CATHERINE REICHLEY	JACOB BICKEL, GEORGE SCHOCH
11/19	SWINEHART, ANDREW	ADAM LONG	MICHAEL KUNTZ, JAMES SMITH
11/19	HEDDEN, WILLIAM, SR.	WILLIAM & JAMES HEDDEN	JOHN PAINTER, DANIEL REESE
11/20	THOMAS, DAVID	AGNES THOMAS	MORDECAI MCKINNEY, JOHN SLATER
11/21	FREES, PETER, SR.	JACOB WEIDNER	THEO. KIEHLE, JESSE SIMPSON
11/28	RYAN, WILLIAM	JOSEPH FERGUSON	WILLIAM REED
12/3	KERSHNER, GEORGE	CATHERINE KERSHNER	JOHN HAAS, THEODORE KIEHLE
12/5	SHAPEL (CHAPPEL?), DAN.	JOHN REBER	ANDREW BILLMEYER, BEN MILLER
12/5	MEYER, MANEVAL	ANDREW BILLMEYER	JOHN REBER " "
12/6	MILLER, JOHN	SOLOMON BETZ	ANDREW ALBRIGHT
12/24	MOYER, LEONARD	PHIL. MOYER, PETER FISHER	JACOB HUMMEL, JOHN HARTMAN

1805

Date	Name		
1/14	YEAGLE, CONRAD	CATHERINE & JACOB YEAGLE	JACOB SHAFFER, ADAM LENKER
1/21	RIHLE, FREDERICK	ANDREW GROVE	SOLOMON MARKLEY, LEONARD EPLY
1/25	HUMMEL, JOHN	ROSINA HUMMEL, JERE KLOP	JERE KLOP, SR., JACOB DIETRICH
1/28	FRANTZ, LEWIS	STEPHEN & JOHN FRANTZ	BEN MILLER, CHRISTOPHER BALDY
1/28	TOMLINSON, THOMAS	SUSAN TOMLINSON	JOHN PATTON, SAMUEL BOONE, JR.
2/2	MEYER, CHRISTINA	PETER RICHTER & JOHN HOUSEWORTH	HENRY SHAFFER, THEODORE KIEHLE
1/30	HAAS, HENRY	ABRAHAM & JOHN HAAS	GEORGE & PETER BASTIAN
2/6	SWINEFORD, JOHN	THOMAS SHIPTON	GEORGE & PETER SWINEFORD
2/20	BOWER, JOHN	CATH. BOWER, JOHN CLARK	THOS. MOREHEAD, CON. DIFFENBACHER
3/5	WAY, NECOMA	BENJAMIN FORTNER	DAVID GITTING, JONAS WEAVER
3/19	WOOLEHEVER, JOHN	ELIZABETH WOOLEHEVER	ABRAHAM WITMER, PETER SECHRIST
3/19	SINCLAIR, NEAL	MARY SINCLAIR, SAM HUNTER	JAMES BOVARD, SAMUEL STEWART
3/20	REUBENDALL, JACOB	ROSINA REUBENDALL	CHRISTIAN WILL, WM. DEWART, JR.
3/25	BILLMEYER, JACOB	ANDREW BILLMEYER	JOHN REBER
3/29	LEHMAN, TOBIAS, JR.	TOBIAS LEHMAN, SR.	JAMES SMITH, ANDREW ALBRIGHT
3/30	RIEHLE, JOHN	HENRY & MARIA RIEHLE	MICHAEL WEAVER
4/23	MILLER, GEORGE	HANNAH MILLER, PETER APPLE	PHILIP DIEHL, JOHN DREESE
4/24	RUCKMAN, THOMAS	ALEXANDER FORESMAN	JOHN JACOBY, JOS. HUTCHINSON
4/26	HOSTERMAN, COL. PETER	JAC. HOSTERMAN, JOHN FISHER	SIMON SNYDER, SIMON HERROLD

Date	Name		
5/14	PORTER, WILLIAM, SR.	WILLIAM PORTER, JR.	JOSIAH MCCLURE, JOSIAH WILLETTS
5/22	BOSLER (BASSLER), GEO.	MARIA M. BOSLER	GEORGE SCHOCH, GEORGE KESSLER
6/7	NEVEL, NICHOLAS	CATH. NEVEL, JOHN ZETLER	COL. HENRY ANTES
6/12	BLACK, ELINOR	JAMES BLACK	WILLIAM GIBSON, JOHN BRADY
6/28	GOODLANDER, CHRISTIAN	GEORGE BELLMAN	JAMES SMITH, ANDREW ALBRIGHT
6/29	FREES, PETER, SR.	PETER FREES	" " WILLIAM LOGUE
7/31	KESSLER, PETER	ELIZ. & PETER KESSLER	" " JOS. LORENTZ
8/26	CULP, TILMAN	MARGARET CULP	JOHN TREMBLEY
9/3	MCGEE, JOHN	HENRY MCGEE	BEN MCGEE, PATRICK BRANNEN
9/5	JORDON, PETER	MARTHA JORDON	SAMUEL FORSYTH, FRANCIS JORDON
9/13	DISLER, DAVID	ELIZABETH DISLER (WIFE)	- - - - - - - - - - - - - - -
9/23	HARRISON, GEORGE	GEORGE HARRISON	DANIEL BOGAR, JACOB YONER
10/9	PARKS, WILLIAM	SARAH PARKS	NATHAN PEGG
11/1	ANTES, COL. HENRY	SUSAN ANTES, D. TAGGART	JOHN SHREINER, SIMON SNYDER
11/13	KOCHER, JOHN	CATH. & JOHN KOCHER	JOHN SIGLER, SR., M. KERSTETTER
11/15	HARRIS, LAIRD	JAMES HARRIS	ROBERT HARRIS
11/25	SCHOUFLER, CHRISTIAN	JOHN HOFFA	ANDREW ALBRIGHT, WM. LEEGER
11/30	MCMONIGAL, ALEXANDER	JEAN MCMONIGAL	WILLIAM & JOHN MONTGOMERY
12/14	CHRISTMAN, MICHAEL	DAVID MARTZ, AND. HIME	CASPER REED, JONAS WEAVER
12/16	WITHINGTON, MARTIN	MARY WITHINGTON	HENRY SHAFFER, DANIEL BOGAR
12/16	BUOY, EDWARD	TOAL BUOY	MANUS & HENRY MCGEE
12/28	MUSSER, JOSEPH	MAGD. & JACOB MUSSER	WILLIAM GRAY, ANDREW ALBRIGHT

Date	Name		
1/9	WALLIS, WILLIAM	JEAN & ROBERT WALLIS	GEORGE CLARK, THOMAS HAMILTON
1/10	HULL, PHINEAS	MARY & JOHN WOLVERTON	WILLIAM & NICHOLAS SHIPMAN
1/27	SMITH, JOHN	SUSAN SMITH (MOTHER)	JOHN DREISBACH
1/30	RUNYAN, BONHAM	JACOB GEARHART	ALEXANDER MOORE
3/5	KRAUSE, CHRISTIAN	MAGDALENE & HENRY KRAUSE	HENRY ERDLY, GEORGE MILLER
3/7	BOWERSOX, PAUL	GEO. BOWERSOX, GEO. SPADE	MICH. BOWERSOX, PHILIP ALTER
3/19	EPLER, JOHN	PETER EPLER	GEORGE ROUPP
4/5	VAN BUSKIRK, MORRIS	MARGARET & THOMAS VANBUSKIRK	JAMES SMITH, JOHN KENDIG
4/22	SCHWARTZ, PHILIP	JOHN EPLY	PETER GRAHL
4/22	MCLAUGHLIN, JAMES	HUGH MCLAUGHLIN	JAMES MCGEE
5/1	ULTZ, JOSEPH	GEO. ULTZ, FRED GUTELIUS	CONRAD STRUBLE, STEP. EILERT
5/20	WERTMAN, JACOB	SUSAN WERTMAN & MATHIAS APP	PETER FISHER, HENRY SHAFFER
5/27	LAUDENSLAGER, VALENTINE	HENRY & GEORGE LAUDENSLAGER	GEORGE KESSLER, GEORGE OTT
5/29	TAYLOR, THOMAS	JOSEPH FORESMAN	THEODORE KIEHLE, JAS. SMITH
6/11	MCMAUREN, JAMES	RACHEL MCMAUREN	HANCE POTTS, THOMAS DUGAN
6/12	FORCE, JACOB	PRUDENCE & WM. FORCE	WILLIAM EVES, JACOB LANGS
6/13	BELLES, MATHIAS	MARY BELLES	JOHN BROWN, POWELL GROVER
8/18	ANTES, FREDERICK	FREDERICK EVANS	SIMON SNYDER, DAVID TAGGART
8/26	MILLER, GEORGE	ALBERT MILLER	PETER FISHER, DAVID GETTIG
9/30	CRAIG, ROBERT	SAM CRAIG, JAS. HAMMOND	WILLIAM SCOTT, JOHN SNYDER
10/1	STEEL, WILLIAM	HANNAH STEEL, JOHN KELLY	JOSEPH MOORE, JOSEPH ADAMS
10/7	LEHMAN, TOBIAS	JOHN LEHMAN (NORTH'D.CO.) HENRY " (DAUPHIN CO.)	HENRY SPYKER, ADAM CHRIST
10/8	HAMMER, THOMAS	WILLIAM DALE (WIFE, ELINOR; CHILDREN, JAMES & ELIZABETH HAMMER)	JOHN ALEXANDER, JAMES DALE
10/9	HENDRICKSON, PETER	ABRAHAM HENDRICKSON	ROB. MCWILLIAMS, JAMES CURRY
10/11	ASPY, RUTH	JOHN SMITH	ALEX. SMITH, SAMUEL BOONE
10/20	MOWRER, PETER	HUGH HUGHES	ADAM SCHLEICH, GODFREY KRAMER
10/20	MCCORMICK, WILLIAM	MARY MCCORMICK	JOHN SAMPLE, JOHN BUCHANAN
11/10	SHRINER, MICHAEL	CATHERINE SHRINER	JACOB SHRINER, JOHN SHRINER
11/25	HARE, JOSEPH	REBECCA HARE	JOHN HANNA, THOMAS CLYDE
11/26	CATHERMAN, DAVID	ADAM MCLAUGHLIN & SOLOMON HEISE	ROBERT BARBER, JOHN DEWART
12/23	DONMEYER, JOHN	CATHERINE DONMEYER	JOHN KNARR, JOHN EISENHUTH

Date	Name		
12/27	MEYER, HENRY	ELIZABETH & JOHN MEYER	ADAM CHRIST, CHRISTOPHER GUNDY
1807			
1/9	HEILMAN, JACOB	MARY & MICHAEL HEILMAN	JACOB & MICHAEL SANDERS
2/23	GAUGLER, NICHOLAS	GEORGE GAUGLER	JOHN GEIST, JACOB HUMMEL
3/11	FORESMAN, SARAH	JOSEPH FORESMAN	JEREMIAH & JESSE SIMPSON
3/25	SHOLLY, LUCAS	CATHERINE SHOLLY	ADAM & CHRISTIAN FISHER
3/25	ROW, LEWIS	JOHN RUSSELL, STEPHEN BREARLY	ANDREW CATHCART, CHARLES CLARK
3/30	EPLY, CHRISTIAN	PETER GOODHART	JOHN EPLY, THOMAS ROBBINS
4/23	CALDWELL, EDWARD	WILLIAM HASLET	ROBERT MCKEE
4/25	FRANKLIN, DANIEL	JANE FRANKLIN	HENRY SHAFFER, WILLIAM MCADAM
5/1	ALLISON, RICHARD	MARY ALLISON, JOHN MCKEAN	JAS. MCKEAN, ALEXANDER DUNBAR
5/22	COOK, JOHN	JAMES MONTGOMERY	DANIEL ROBBINS, GEORGE MCKEE
6/1	WILSON, NATHANIEL	GEORGE MCKEE	JAN. MONTGOMERY, ROBERT FINNEY
6/1	MCKIM, WILLIAM	ROBERT MCKIM	JAMES DOUGAL
6/5	WALES, JOSEPH	CATHERINE & JAMES WALES	HENRY REARICK, DAVID OVERMIRE
8/24	SCHAUFFLER, CHRISTIAN	JACOB LAYMAN	ADAM WOLF, WILLIAM RESSER
9/5	REICHSTONE, PETER	CHRISTINA REICHSTONE	PETER SPOTZ
9/10	FLICKINGER, PETER	PETER FLICKINGER, JR.	PETER BROUSE
9/10	METZGER, DANIEL	EVE METZGER, WM. HAYS	ANDREW ALBRIGHT, JARED IRWIN
9/16	HUGHES, THOMAS	MARY HUGHES	TUNIS GEARHART, DANIEL BOGER
9/28	WILSON, SAMUEL	GEO. HOGE, J. HUTCHINSON	JOHN WILSON, JAMES SMITH
9/28	ROENSKER, JOSEPH	JOHN BROWN	WILLIAM HOFFMAN
10/15	KIEHL, PETER	JACOB CLOUGH	SOLOMON REED, MICHEAL REITZ
10/17	LYMAN, JOHN	SUSAN LYMAN & JACOB BREYVOGEL	PETER BOWMAN, GEORGE WORMLEY
10/29	CORNELIUS, JOHN	JEAN CORNELIUS	WILLIAM REYNOLDS
12/4	MENICH, CHRISTINA (NEE HAVERLING)	CONRAD MENICH	JOSEPH ALTER, JOHN GEIST
12/9	IKELER, WILLIAM	ANDREW IKLER, RICH. DEMOT	WILLIAM KITCHEN, WILLIAM MILLER
12/24	SINDLEY, WILLIAM	MARG. SINDLEY, WM. SEARS	DAN. LEBO, HENRY VANDERSLICE
1808			
1/9	MAXWELL, WILLIAM	JANE MAXWELL	JAMES MADDEN, NATHAN SPENCE
1/30	THOMAS, DAVID	JAMES SMITH	JOHN WATSON, AND. ARMSTRONG
2/3	FREALEY, PHILIP	MICHAEL WEHR	JOHN WOLF, JACOB GEARHART
2/24	MEYER (MOYER), JACOB	VALENTINE HAAS	JOHN & SAMUEL HAAS
3/1	HOOVER, JOHN (SON OF ISAAC)	CHRISTOPHER EILERT & SOLOMON KLECKNER	JOHN BOSS, WEST BUFFALO TWP. JOHN CROOST, BUFFALO TWP.
3/4	BOEVARD, CAPT. JAMES	HANNAH BOEVARD, WIDOW	CHARLES SLEAR, JOHN FREELY
3/7	MARTIN, JAMES	DARIUS SHERWIN	JOHN MCEWEN, JACOB SEIDEL
3/22	HENNABACH, DANIEL (WIFE, BARBARA)	VALENTINE HENNABACH & DAVID MARTZ	JOSEPH LORENTZ, DANIEL LEBO
4/26	MCBATH, ANN	JOHN LINN	GIDEON SMITH, AND. MCCLANAHAN
5/13	DUNNING, SAMUEL	HUGH MARTIN, JR.	HUGH MARTIN, SR.
5/16	LEBO, PAUL	JOHN SHRINER	ANDREW ALBRIGHT, JOHN BUCHER
5/17	DUNNING, CATHERINE	JOHN BLACKNEY	JARED IRWIN
5/25	BOWER, THOMAS	JOHN BOWER	JOHN DETRICH, THOMAS DAVIS
5/27	BALLIET, NICHOLAS	JOHN BALLIET	DAN LEBO, JOHN DIFFENBACHER
6/1	JODON, PETER	MARTHA JODON SAIRLES	CHRISTOPHER JOHNSON
6/11	BARTON, DANIEL	SAMUEL & THOMAS BARTON	ROBERT & JOHN MOORE
8/1	RINE, GEORGE (LATE OF LANCASTER CO.)	CHARLES HIGGINS	CHARLES DRUM, WILLIAM MCADAM
8/15	BODDORF, HENRY	ADAM BODDORF	CHRISTIAN THOMAS, NICH. REBUCK
8/15	STACKHOUSE, JOSEPH	ANN STACKHOUSE	JACOB GEARHART, HUGH THOMPSON
8/16	BLITT, REV. FREDERICK	CHRISTIAN BROBST	HENRY FISHER, JERE SIMPSON
8/18	HODGE (HOGE?), JOSEPH	CATHERINE HODGE	RICHARD DEMOT, JOHN MCDONALD
8/19	POLLOCK, ALEXANDER	WILLIAM SHERIFF	JOHN GULICK, ALEXANDER COLT
8/30	DUNNING, SAMUEL	JOHN BLACKNEY	MATTHEW LORD, JOSEPH SPOTZ
9/9	FOULK, OWEN	CALEB FOULK	EVAN R. EVANS, MICHAEL KUTZNER

Date	Name		
9/10	MADDEN, NEAL	MARY & JAMES MADDEN	WM. CHAMBERLIAN, JR., A. ALBRIGHT
9/10	WHITE, JAMES	CHARLOTTE WHITE & HUGH BRONSON	WILLIAM MCADAM, JOHN WEITZEL
10/17	EVERETT, OBED	JAS. EVERETT, PETER BOUGLER	ROB. MOORE, JACOB BOUDEMAN
10/21	THOMAS, JOHN	JAMES SMITH	WILLIAM WITHINGTON
10/27	HARRIS, ROBERT	MARY HARRIS, WM. HAYES	ROAN MCCLURE, MICH. KUTZNER
10/28	BELLMAN, GEORGE, JR.	JOHN GEORGE CONSER	JOHN & GEORGE MARTIN, JR.
11/3	DEVER, JOHN	JOHN MCEWEN	CHARLES HIGGINS

1809

Date	Name		
1/11	MCBRIDE, HUGH	WM. MCBRIDE, ISAC. BOUDEMAN	JACOB BOUDEMAN, ROBERT MOORE
1/17	BRADY, JOHN	WILLIAM PIATT	JOHN SANDERS, WILLIAM MCADAM
1/24	WITMER, SARAH	JOHN & SAMUEL	JEREMIAH SIMPSON
2/9	ROBINS, ZACHRIAH	JOHN ROBINS	ENOCH SMITH, GILBERT ROBINS
2/14	DREESE, JOHN, SR. (BEAVER TWP.)	ANNA MARIA & PETER DREESE	JOHN DREESE, STOPHEL ROYER
2/17	BOB, CONRAD (BEAVER TWP.)	JACOB BOBB, STOPHEL ROYER	SEB. ROYER, JACOB KLOSE
2/22	POH, GEORGE	EVE POH	SOLOMON BEST, JOSEPH LORENTZ
2/33	ELLIOTT, JOHN	ALEXANDER ELLIOTT	WILLIAM LOGUE
2/25	MCFAIN, JOHN	CATH. MCFAIN, DAVID WASSER	JOHN STENGER, JAC, DIFFENBACHER
2/28	KNEIB, JACOB (PENN TWP.)	MICHAEL WEAVER	PETER FISHER, MATHIAN APP
3/1	ZELLER, JOHN (MAHANTANGO TWP.)	ADAM WILT, ADAM LIGHT	FRED HAINS, CHRIST. SECHRIST
3/16	WILKINSON, WILLIAM (MAHANTANGO TWP.)	JOHN BERGSTRESSER	CHARLES STRAUB, JERE SIMPSON
3/17	GOSSLER, ANDREW	CATHERINE & JOHN GOSSLER	JOHN DORST, ABRAHAM KIEHLE
4/17	LINN, JOHN	ANN LINN, THOMAS HOWARD	WM. CLINGAN, WM. MCCALLAHAN
4/18	TWEED, JOHN	SARAH & DAVID TWEED	THOMAS RUCKMAN, JOHN WILSON
5/6	BARE (BEAR), JACOB (CENTER TWP.)	ISAAC BARE & GEORGE ADAM BOWERSOX	JACOB & PHILIP WALTER
5/6	HOOK, STEPHEN (CENTER TWP.)	DANIEL STIMELY (STIMELING)	ISAAC MERTS, GEO. A. BOWERSOX
5/16	HEFFER, ELIZABETH (PENN TWP.)	JACOB MEYER (MOYER)	JOHN NAUGLE, JOHN MARTIN
5/17	SLEAR, CHARLES, SR. (BUFFALO TWP.)	JACOB HUMMEL, WM. KESSLER	GEORGE MILLER, JOHN HUMMEL
6/26	IRWIN, JACOB	CATH. IRWIN, THOMAS WILSON	MICHAEL HEILMAN, ROBERT MOORE
7/3	LILLEY, LEONARD	CATHERINE & JOHN LILLEY	HENRY OHL, JACOB SANDERS
8/4	CUMMINGS, JOHN (EAST BUFFALO TWP.)	JANE CUMMINGS	PETER FLICKINGER, C. HIGGINS
8/5	SHAFFER, JOHN (MAHANOY TWP.)	CHRISTOPHER ROTH	JACOB SHAFFER, ADAM LENKER
8/21	RUSHER, JACOB (BEAVER TWP.)	HENRY RUSHER, FRED WISE	CHRISTOPHER WISE, JAC, FRYER
8/21	LEMON, JOHN (GREENWOOD TWP.)	ELIZABETH & JOSEPH LEMON	RICHARD DEMOT, WM. MATHER
8/30	OHL (EHL, EEL, ETC), HENRY	CATHERINE & HENRY OHL	AND. LARRISH, JOHN RENTZ
9/30	DONAT, PETER (TURBOT TWP.)	EVE DONAT, ADAM FOLLMER	HENRY LENTZ, CONRAD MENGES
10/17	ROYER, JOHN (WEST BUFFALO TWP.)	EVE ROYER	MICHAEL PETERS, THEO. KIEHLE
10/22	DISSLER, DAVID (SEE 9/13/1805)	ELIZABETH DISSLER	JOHN HAFLEY

1810

Date	Name		
1/22	SUMMERS, JOB (POINT TWP.)	JAMES HEPBURN	WILLIAM MCADAM, MICH, KUTZNER
1/27	LONG, SIDNEY (NEE DEWITT)	ADAM LONG (AUGUSTA TWP.)	GEORGE LONG, JAMES MCCUNE

DATE 1810	THE DECEASED	TOWN OR TOWNSHIP	LETTERS TO	SURETIES FOR ADMINISTRATOR
2/12	THORNTON, MICHAEL	CATAWISSA	MICH. THORNTON, JR.	CHRIST. BROBST, MICH. KUTZNER
2/26	DRESHER, SAMUEL	MIFFLIN	GEORGE DRESHER	DAVID MERTZ, FRED HAAS
2/27	MUSSER, JOSEPH	CHILLIS- QUAQUE	CATHERINE MUSSER (WIDOW OF JOSEPH)	SAM JONES, HENRY SHAFFER
2/28	MANTZ, NICHOLAS (WIDOW, MARY)	SUNBURY	ADAM HEILMAN	JOHN BRIGHT, AND. ALBRIGHT
3/27	SMITH, PETER	MAHANOY	JAC. SMITH, LEON. FERST	WM. HEIM, MICHAEL REITZ
4/9	PATTON, JOHN	BLOOM	SAMUEL WEBB, JR.	EPH. LEWIS, PHIL. ACHENBACH
4/20	REARICK, MARY	?	WILLIAM WISE	JOHN WEBB, MICHAEL SCHOCH
5/5	KREBS, HENRY	TURBOT	RACHEL KREBS, J. HOWER	JAMES LOCK, HENRY SHAFFER
5/5	LANGS, GEORGE	DERRY	WILLIAM MARSHALL	PETER GRAHL, STEP. BREARLY
5/10	HENDRICKS, SAMUEL	PENN	JOHN HENDRICKS	PETER GOTSHALL, JOHN EPLY
5/15	MILLER, ELIZABETH	E. BUFFALO	JOHN EPLY	JOHN GEIST, WM. GRAHAM
5/23	SMITH, JOHN	TURBOT	SUSAN, DAN & WM. SMITH	GEO. MCKEE, GEORGE EVELAND
5/24	FREY, ANDREW	SHAMOKIN	MARG. FREY, C. ADAMS	ANDREW RUGART, JONAS WEAVER
6/1	WALLIS, JOS, JACOB	SUNBURY	EVAN R. EVANS	ENOCH, SMITH, MICH. KUTZNER
6/9	WEIRICK, JOHN (S/O CAPT. WM.)	CENTER	HENRY WEIRICK, J. WALES	PHIL. OVERMIRE, CHAS. MEYER
8/21	TOMLINSON, JAMES	BLOOM	JOHN TOMLINSON, SR.	CHRIST. BROBST, LAW. MILLER
8/21	TOMLINSON, ANN	BLOOM	JOHN TOMLINSON, JR.	CHRIST. BROBST, LAW. MILLER
9/15	BOYER, GEORGE	PENN	JOHN & SAMUEL BOYER	HENRY ERDLY, GEO. KESSLER
9/15	SWINEHART, GEORGE	UPPER	BARBARA SWINEHART	LEONARD FERSTER, S. BLOOM
10/19	ZIMMERMAN, PETER	W. BUFFALO	MARY ZIMMERMAN	GEORGE WILT, AMOS HARRIS
10/29	FAIRWEATHER, ED- MOND	POINT	DAVID TAGGART	HENRY SHAFFER, HUGH BELLAS
11/21	BROWN, JANE	TURBOT	WILLIAM HASLET	JOSEPH BROWN, JOHN SNYDER
12/1	DOUGLASS, WILLIAM	CENTER	WM. DOUGLASS, JR.	SOL. HEISE, SAMUEL STOFFER
12/14	SIMPSON, RACHEL (NEE MONTGOMERY)	?	THOS. STEVENSON	ALEX. CAMPBELL, J. SIMPSON
12/15	PETERS, JOHN	SHAMOKIN	JOHN PETERS, JR.	JOHN KELLY, JOHN CAMPBELL
1811				
1/1	STEEDMAN, CHARLES	?	EDWARD GOBIN	EBENEZER GREENO, J. SMITH
1/30	MEYER, CHARLES	PENN	PETER RICHTER	JOHN GEIST, ANDREW BASTIAN
4/12	BRUNNER, ULRICH	SHAMOKIN	JOHN EVERT	HENRY SHAFFER, AND. ALBRIGHT
4/17	MCCORD, WILLIAM	POINT	JOHN MCPHERSON	WM. MCADAM, DAVID STEEL
4/23	EPLY, JOHN	PENN	A. ALBRIGHT, P. GOOD- HART	JAMES SMITH, GEORGE MARTIN
4/23	HUNTER, ALEX.	AUGUSTA	JOHN MCPHERSON	WM. MCADAM, HENRY MASSER
6/14	KREIDLER, DANIEL	FISHING CREEK	FREDERICK KREIDLER & ADAM COODER	DANIEL PEELER, GEO. COODER
6/28	ROSS, ADAM	NORTHUMB ERLAND	ELIZABETH ROSS	JAMES HEPBURN, CHAS. HIGGINS
7/8	STEESE, BARBARA (NEE MORR)	PENN	HON. FRED. STEESE (HUSBAND OF BARBARA)	HENRY SHAFFER, HENRY MASSER
7/30	LEEPORT, JOHN	FISHING CREEK	MATTHEW RHONE	JOHN KEELER
8/1	EICHENMOYER, AND.	L. MAHANOY	JOHN EICHENMOYER	JOHN MASSER, STEPHEN NASH
8/10	BODIE, DR. CHAS. H.	BUFFALO	JAC. STERN, SIM. SNYDER	JOHN CUMMINGS, JAC. LECHNER
8/19	WELKER, JACOB	W. BUFFALO	FREDERICK WELKER	CHRIST. WELKER, FRED DUNBAR
8/30	KUNTZ, PETER	DERRY	CATHERINE KUNTZ	JOHN LANGS, PHIL. REIFSNYDER
8/31	SHANNON, DAVID	TURBOT	JAMES & JOHN SHANNON	DAVE TAGGART, JOHN COWDEN
10/14	ANDREWS, PHILIP	AUGUSTA	ELIZABETH & CHRIST- OPHER ANDREWS	JOHN FORRESTER JOHN ALSPAUGH
10/19	ANDREWS, MARTIN	SHAMOKIN	LENAH ANDREWS	EDW. PRICE, JOHN FARNSWORTH
10/21	HAMILTON, JAMES	MAHONING	WILLIAM B. SULLIVAN	WILLIAM COOK, WILLIAM MCADAM
10/29	MILLER, GEORGE	MIFFLIN	CHRISTIAN MILLER	JOHN BROWN, GEO. STICHER
11/13	CLARK, WILLIAM	HEMLOCK	JOHN CLARK	WM. & THOS. STARTMAN
11/16	DRUM, MAJ. CHAS.	PENN	HENRY VANDERSLICE	SOLOMON MACLAY, CHAS. HIGGINS

DATE	THE DECEASED	TOWN OR TOWNSHIP	LETTERS GRANTED TO	SURETIES FOR THE ADMINISTRATOR
1811				
11/19	HOGE, GEORGE	TURBOT	ROBERT MCKEE	WM. HASLET, JARED IRWIN
11/23	STUTZ, MARGARET	AUGUSTA	DAVID STUTZ	JAS. SMITH, FRED KIEHLE
12/14	EVANS, EVAN R.	SUNBURY	ANDREW ALBRIGHT	ENOCH SMITH, JOHN COWDEN
12/20	STIDLER, JOHN, SR.	MIFFLIN	JOHN & GEORGE STIDLER	GEO. PLANK, PHILIP HENRY
1812				
1/10	HOFFMAN, PETER	L. MAHANOY	MARY HOFFMAN	SOL. MARKLEY, JACOB FURMAN
1/21	YOUNGMAN, THOMAS	W. BUFFALO	GEORGE YOUNGMAN	JOHN WILSON, ADAM WILT
2/4	BRINER, PHILIP	BEAVER	JACOB WOMMER	JOHN DELPH
2/14	BORRELL, PHILIP	U. MAHANOY	ABRAHAM MCKINNEY	LEON. REITZ, LEON. FERSTER
2/19	DINIUS, JOHN	NEW BERLIN	HENRY & JACOB DINIUS	JOHN DINIUS, JOSEPH WISE
2/22	BURLEW, ALEXANDER	POINT	ELIZABETH VANOVER	ALEX. STEWART, SAM DEARMOND
2/27	MACKLEHENNY, TOM	?	ELIZ. MACKLEHENNY	JOSEPH WALLIS, WM. VANOVER
3/5	YOCUM, HENRY (WIFE, ELIZ. SNYDER)	AUGUSTA	ELIZABETH YOCUM & JOHN SNYDER	HENRY HAMMEL, HENRY MASSER
3/9	SAX, JACOB	HARTLEY	ANNA & JOSEPH SAX	B. KLINESMITH, DIETER ROYER
3/21	SHIVELY, MARTIN	CHILLIS-QUAQUE	JOHN GOTTSHALL	J. DENTLER, HENRY SHAFFER
3/23	MONTGOMERY, ROBT.	?	THOMAS PAINTER	WILLIAM GRANT
3/27	ARMSTRONG, ANDREW	POINT	JOHN ARMSTRONG	JACOB HAINES, WM. HASLET
4/3	SHULER, VALENTINE	L. MAHANOY	J. VALENTINE SHULER	HENRY LATSHA, P. ROUSHKALP
4/20	HUGHES, ELLIS	?	BEN SHARPLESS, TOM ELLIS	JOHN CLARK, CHRIST. BROBST
4/20	FROAS (OR TROAS, HENRY	BLOOM	GEORGE HEPLER	JAS. SMITH, LAWRENCE RUCH
5/9	NEIMAN, JOHN	MAHANTANGO	PETER DEVORE	ADAM HILBISH, J. ARBOGAST
5/10	BAUGHMAN, LAWR.	?	CATHERINE BAUGHMAN	DAN BOGER, JOHN BARTHOLOMEW
5/12	SCHOCH, MATHIAS	PENN	MICH. & JACOB SCHOCH	HENRY SHAFFER, P. GOTSHALL
5/12	UMBENHOWER, JONAS	CENTER	GEORGE AURAND	HENRY SHAFFER, ISAAC MERTZ
5/22	TAYLOR, WILLIAM	TURBOT	HENRY GRAHAM & ALEXANDER DUFFY	A. ARMSTRONG, JOHN QUIGLEY
6/4	SWINEFORD, JOHN	CENTER	THOMAS SHIPTON	JACOB FRY, PHILIP BECHTEL
6/11	TAGGART, DAVID	POINT	HUGH BELLAS, H. GROSS	HENRY MASSER, JOHN GROSS
6/15	MARSHALL, JOHN	CENTER	THOMAS SHIPTON	JOHN GROSS, HENRY REARICK
6/16	GEARHART, ISAAC	SHAMOKIN	NELLY & GEO. GEARHART	JAS. SMITH, ALEX. MOORE
6/29	ROBERTS, HIRAM	?	SOPHIA ROBERTS & JOHN JONES	JOHN ORR, JOHN MCKESSON
7/28	EICHINGER, HENRY	CENTER	ISAAC MERTZ	GEO. AURAND, LEON. SMITH
8/8	RISHEL, HENRY	MAHONING	CATH. & MICH. RISHEL	JAC. SANDERS, MICH. HINOMAN
8/13	MECONKEY, JOHN	POINT	JOHN COWDEN, WM. FORSYTH	ENOCH SMITH, JOHN BOYD
8/17	LONGBAUCH, HENRY	HARTLEY	MARY LONGBAUCH	JOHN YARGER, JOSEPH MILLER
8/19	BARBER, PHINEAS	DERRY	JAMES BARBER	JOHN FUNSTON, ANDREW HASLET
8/28	MCCALLA, JOHN	NORTHUMBERLAND	GEORGE KRAMER	WILLIAM CLARK, JOHN HANNA
8/31	SHAFFER, JOHN	MAHANTANGO	CHRISTINA SHAFFER	JOHN SWARTZ, PHILIP MILLER
9/8	HAMMOND, GEORGE	TURBOT	JAMES & JOS. HAMMOND	AND. ALBRIGHT, ABE KEIHL
9/15	CAUSERT, JAMES	POINT	ROBERT MCWILLIAMS	D. MONTGOMERY, HENRY SHAFFER
9/19	CAMP, HENRY	SHAMOKIN	C. FEGLEY, WM. HAAS	JACOB KISNER, MICHAEL ZERN
10/16	SNYDER, WILLIAM	MAHANOY	NICHOLAS SNYDER	GEO. BOYER, LEONARD REITZ
11/7	BUNDY, WILLIAM	L. MAHANOY	PHEBE BUNDY	JOHN SPOTZ, C. WITMER
11/17	MINIGER, MICHAEL	NEW YORK STATE	SAM SUNDERLAND & JOHN DAVIS	ABRAHAM TENBROOK CALEB FARLEY
11/19	ZELLER, DUBOIS	MANANTANGO	ADAM LIGHT	VAL. HAAS, HENRY RAHMSTEIN
11/23	PATTRIDGE, JOHN	DERRY	WILLIAM HASLET	JAMES SMITH, JAS. ARMSTRONG

1812

11/27	FAIRWEATHER, ED-MUND	NORTHUMBER-LAND	JOHN SLATER	THOMAS PAINTER
11/27	WEISER, ELIZABETH	L. MAHANOY	JACOB WEISER	PHIL. WEISER, CON. BACHMAN

1813

1/1	JACOBY, MARY	TURBOT	ROBERT FORESMAN	JAS. SMITH, JOS. FORESMAN
1/18	TURNER, JOSEPH	BUFFALO	DANIEL CHRIST	GEO. CONSER, MATH. SHEFFER
1/19	BLUE, SAMUEL	MAHONING	DAN MONTGOMERY	ALEM MARR, HENRY SHAFFER
1/21	STEWART, ALEX.	TURBOT	SAM C. STEWART & SAMUEL PHERRIN	MATTHEW CORRY
1/22	LINDEMUTH, MICH.	CATAWISSA	CONRAD HARMON	JONAS WEAVER, P. LEISENRING
1/25	CLENDENIN, WM. SR.	W. BUFFALO	JANE & WM. CLENDENIN	JOHN WEBB, HENRY KOHN
1/25	IRWIN, ROBERT	NORTH'MB-ERLAND	JARED IRWIN	JOHN IRWIN, GEO. GREEN SR.
1/29	GEIST, JOHN	NORTHUMB-ERLAND	JAMES SMITH	JAMES HULL, JOSEPH ALTER
2/1	MYERS, WILLIAM	NORTHUMB-ERLAND	LEVI MYERS	WILLIAM LONG, JAMES SMITH
2/4	BAILEY, JOHN	TURBOT	NANCY BAILEY	DAVID DERKSON, JAC. SEIDEL
2/4	CLARK, SAMUEL	TURBOT	JOHN CLARK, R. MCKEE	ISAAC VINCENT, S. IREDELL
2/4	GASTEN, JOHN	?	JOHN MURRAY	JARED IRWIN, JAMES MCCORD
2/8	BUTLER, ROBERT	DERRY	THOS. BUTLER, JR.	JOHN BUTLER, NATHL. SPENCER
2/8	ROBERTS, HIRAM	MILTON	JOHN MCKESSON	JOHN ORR, JOHN JONES
2/10	MUNDAY, BENJAMIN	SHAMOKIN	MARY & HENRY MUNDAY	D. WOLVERTON, J. WILKINSON
2/15	MOORE, STEPHEN	CHILLISQUAQUE	JOHN & ABNER MOORE	JOHN GASKINS, ROB. MCCOY
2/15	KING, JAMES	POINT	PERSIFOR LEMON	JOHN GASKINS, ROB. MOORE
2/16	ESCHBACH, JOHN	TURBOT	PHIL. & ANTHONY ESCHBACH	ADAM FOLLMER JACOB SECHLER
2/18	WILLIAMS, HUDSON	WHITE DEER	NANCY & JOS. WILLIAMS	JOHN HAYES, JAMES SMITH
2/20	CLARK, WILLIAM	WHITE DEER	ROAN CLARK, J. BOAL	WM. CLINGAM, JOHN GUIDER
2/23	MARKLEY, DR. SOL.	SUNBURY	HENRY SHAFFER	HENRY MASSER, HENRY BUCHER
2/24	SIERER, JOHN	E. BUFFALO	JACOB SIERER	JACOB YOUNG, ANDREW REEDY
2/26	LAMPHLEY, SARAH	MILTON	SAMUEL STADDON	HENRY DONNELL, WM. STADDON
3/1	KESSLER, GEORGE	PENN	WM. & JOHN KESSLER	JOHN HUMMEL, ANDREW BARGER
3/8	ECKENROT, ADAM	CHILLISQUAQUE	JOHN DOUTY	ADAM KREITZ, PETER ECKENROTE
3/9	KELLY, EDWARD	MAHONING	JAMES DONALDSON	H. VANDERSLICE, WM. MCBRIDE
3/9	ZIMMERMAN, ABE	HARTLEY	ELIZ. & LEVI ZIMMERMAN	ADAM WILY, J. ZIMMERMAN
3/11	LUNGER, MARTIN	BLOOM	THOMAS ROBINS	ROB. GARDNER, MICH KUTZNER
3/11	MCBRIDGE, JAMES	DERRY	WILLIAM MCBRIDGE	ISAAC WAGNER, DANIEL LEBO
3/11	GULICK, MINIE	AUGUSTA	ABRAHAM GULICK & JOHN HAUGHAWAUT	DANIEL LEBO HENRY VANDERSLICE
3/13	SEELEY, ROBERT	SUNBURY	ANDREW ALBRIGHT	DAN LEBO, HEN. VANDERSLICE
3/15	CAMPBELL, ALEX.	MAHONING	DAVID PETREKIN	HUGH FLACK, CHAS. MAUS
3/18	AIKMAN, WILLIAM	BLOOM	ALEX. AIKMAN	J. HUTCHINSON, CON. LAMBERSON
3/22	GRAY, ROBERT	DERRY	MARY & SAMUEL GRAY	SAM SHANNON, ENOCH SMITH
3/23	MARTIN, DR. JAMES	?	ELIZABETH MARTIN	JOHN BOYD, WILLIAM MCADAM
3/24	BIGGS, RICHARD	BLOOM	SAMUEL WEBB, JR.	PHIL. MEHRLING, ANDREW CROUSE
3/25	HOLLENBACH, JACOB	PENN	JOHN MAUCK & DANIEL PENNABAKER	PHILIP MOOR, PETER HILBISH
3/26	CLARK, JOHN	HARTLEY	JAMES JAMES	ADAM WILT, PHILIP HEHN
3/27	HUNTER, JAMES	TURBOT	SAMUEL RUSSELL	SAMUEL AWL, AND. ALBRIGHT
3/31	FALLS, JAMES	DERRY	JOHN FALLS	ENOCH SMITH, WILLIAM MCADAM
3/31	WATSON, DAVID	W. BUFFALO	ROB. BARBER, P. LEWIS	JAC. BROBST, ROBT. FORSTER
3/31	DEAL, JOHN	W. BUFFALO	JACOB MAIZE	JAC. BROBST, ROBT. FORSTER
3/31	DEAL, HENRY	W. BUFFALO	JACOB MAIZE	JAC. BROBST, ROBT. FORSTER
4/6	BENNER, MICHAEL	E. BUFFALO	CONRAD SCHROYER	JACOB KLINE, JOHN BENNER
4/12	KESSLER, PETER	AUGUSTA	PETER STROUSE	JAS. SMITH, MICHAEL KUTZNER
4/13	RHOADS, PETER	PENN	ABRAHAM HAAS & MATH-IAS DUNBACH	DANIEL LEBO, PAUL BOGER
4/14	WOLVERTON, JON.	SHAMOKIN	CASSIAH WOLVERTON	R. FARNSWORTH, JOHN CAMPBELL
4/14	KARSNER, PETER	MAHANTANGO	CATH. & JOHN KARSNER	JOHN NAGLE, GEORGE GAMBY

18

Date	Name	Township	Relatives	Bondsmen/Witnesses
4/15	GAUGLER, GEORGE	MAHANTANGO	DOROTHY GAUGLER & JACOB REICH	PETER BEISTEL
4/19	HAFFLICH, JOHN	MAHANTANGO	GEORGE HEIMBACH	ADAM LIGHT, MICH. RATHFON
4/19	DONALDSON, JOHN	MAHONING	JAMES DONALDSON	JESSE SIMPSON, IRW. HASLET
4/20	WORRELL, JONATHAN	CATAWISSA	THOMAS FESTER	WM. MEARS, CHRIST. BROBST
4/21	PITTINGER, ABE	TURBOT	CORNELIUS VANFLEET	DAN VINCENT, ROBERT MILLER
4/27	MARTZ, PETER, SR.	CHILLISQUAQUE	PETER MARTZ, JR.	JAS. SMITH, ARCHIBALD GRAY
4/28	NOGLE, CHARLES	?	JOHN NOGLE	HENRY REECE, CONRAD NOGLE
5/8	SEVERSON, ERNEST	MAHONING OR MAHANTANGO	MARGARET SEVERSON & JOHN BENDER	LEONARD SMITH CHRISTIAN GRAYBILL
5/10	BAKER, DR. JACOB	AUGUSTA	ELIZABETH BAKER	HEN. BUCHER, PETER DIMMICK
5/10	CORL, JOHN	HARTLEY	JOSEPH CORL	JOHN & SAMUEL ZIMMERMAN
5/10	THORNTON, JAMES	BLOOM	ELIZABETH THORNTON	HEN. TREMBLY, JOHN WERTMAN
5/11	YOUNGAN, DANIEL (NEGRO)	PENN	KILLIAN FOUST	GEORGE GAUGLER, ADAM EWIG

END OF NORTHUMBERLAND COUNTY LETTERS OF ADMINISTRATION

WILLS OF NORTHUMBERLAND COUNTY, PENNSYLVANIA
(COUNTY ORGANIZED IN 1772)
COUNTY SEAT, SUNBURY, PA.

WILL DATE PROBATED	THE DECEASED	TOWN OR TOWNSHIP	HEIRS
5/16/1774 8/24/1774	ROTTAN, JOSEPH	BUFFALO	WIFE, MARY, CH. THOMAS, ROGER, ELIZABETH
7/4/1774 8/3/1774	PARKS, DAVID (NATIVE OF N. J.)	PENN	CH. WILLIAM, JOSEPH, ABNER, SARAH, ABIGAIL, JANE.
7/9/1772 6/1/1774	MCQUIRE, THOMAS	?	WF. JEAN. CH. FRANCIS AND A POSTHUMUS CHILD
5/23/1777 6/9/1777	GEIGER, VALENTINE	AUGUSTA	WF. MARGARET, CH. JACOB, VALENTINE, JR., GEORGE, SARAH, CATHERINE ELIZABETH. BRO. CHRISTOPHER.
5/1/1777 6/13/1777	FLEMING, JOHN	BALD EAGLE	CH. ROBERT, JOSEPH, ROSANNA, JAMES, ELIZABETH, JOHN, MARY, EZEKIEL, DAVID.
4/19/1777 11/24/1777	BROWN, MATTHEW	WHITE DEER	WF. ELINOR, CH. 4 SONS AND 4 DAUGHTERS, NOT NAMED
11/15/1777 5/23/1778	DUNLAP, JOHN	LYCOMING	WF. ELIZABETH, CH. JOHN, MARGARET BOONE (WHO HAD A SON, JOHN) ANN WIELLY (WHO HAD A SON, JOSEPH); ELIZABETH, MARTHA.
3/20/1779 3/27/1779	CALHOON, CAPT. GEO.	AUGUSTA	BRO. WILLIAM OF DRUMMONTOLEN, IRELAND. NEPH. GEORGE, S/O WILLIAM ABOVE. COUSINS; JAMES AND ELIZABETH MCCLEARY. FRIENDS, CAPTS. WM. GRAY & GEORGE GRANT.
2/11/1777 4/20/1779	BONCER, JOS. (OR JAS.)	?	WIFE AND CHILDREN, NO NAMES GIVEN.
5/5/1779 5/20/1779	ALLEN, SAMUEL, SR.	WHITE DEER	WF. AGNES, CH. RUTH REYNOLDS, AGNES, MARGARET RIPPEY, EPHRAIM, SAMUEL, JAMES, MARY ANN, JOSEPH, JOHN, ROBERT.
6/3/1779 6/5/1779	BALL, THOMOND	SUNBURY	WIFE AND CHILD, NO NAMES GIVEN.
2/9/1779 8/16/1779	WEEKS, JOSEPH	WHITE DEER	WF. RACHEL. CH. JESSE, HANNAH TRAVERS, JEMIMA SUNDERLIN, NAOMI HIGGINBOTTOM.
1/7/1780 6/26/1780	BOMBACH, GEORGE	PENN	WIFE & CHILDREN, NO NAMES GIVEN
7/25/1780 10/21/1780	PFEIFFER, JOHN	?	CH. JOHN, GEORGE, CATHERINE, MARGARET, ELIZA-BETH, BARBARA, SUSANNA.
8/2/1780 10/25/1780	ROBINS, WILLIAM	SUNBURY	BRO. ZACHARIAS. SIS. MARABE. A CHILD OF MARY EVERHART
4/2/1781 5/18/1781	YOST, MAJ. CASPER	PENN	WIVE AND CHILDREN, NO NAMES GIVEN.
2/11/1783 9/20/1783	MCCANDLISH, WM. SR.	BUFFALO	WF. MARY. CH. PETER, JOHN, GEORGE, GRIZELL, JANET, ALEXANDER, MARTIN, WILLIAM, JR.
---------- 9/25/1783	ARMSTRONG, THOMAS	MAHONING	WF. MAGDALENE. CH. JAMES, JOHN, MARY, HAMILTON, NANCY MCADAMS, ELIZABETH WILSON.
3/25/1777 12/2/1783	MILES, JOHN	?	CH. ROBERT, JAMES, WILLIAM, MARGARET, JEAN, ANN, THOMAS, JOHN.
3/17/1784 4/18/1784	WOLF, JOHN	MAHONING	HEIRS, HIS BROTHER GEORGE'S CHILDREN; HENRY, JOHN, GEORGE, PHILIP.
10/8/1782 4/19/1784	VANDIKE, HENRY (LATE OF LANCASTER CO.)	DERRY	WF. ELIZABETH. CH. LAMBERT, JOHN, ELIZABETH, HANNAH, MARY, SARAH.
3/21/1784 4/24/1784	KERR, ABRAHAM	?	WF. MAGDALENE. CH. DAVID, JACOB.
3/29/1784 6/21/1784	HUNTER, COL. SAMUEL	AUGUSTA	WF. SUSAN. CH. NANCY, POLLY. BROTHERS, JOHN, WILLIAM.
---------- 6/25/1784	MCCLANAHAN, JAMES	WHITE DEER	WF. SARAH, CH. MARGARET, WILLIAM, ROBERT, DAVID ANDREW, ELIZABETH, SARAH, JAMES.

————— 10/1/1784	HARRISON, JOHN	AUGUSTA	CH. MARY (MRS. JACOB LAMESON), JOHN ELIZA- BETH, HANNAH, SARAH.
9/13/1783 10/24/1784	FORSTER, JOHN	BUFFALO	WF. MARGARET. CH. THOMAS, ANDREW, ROBERT, JANE, ELIZABETH GRAY, REBECCA MCFARLAND, CHRIST- INA (MRS. JOHN MONTGOMERY), MARGARET.
8/11/1778 5/28/1785	MOODIE, ROBERT	TURBOT	WF. ABIGAIL. CH. JAMES, LUCY, AGNES, EUPHEMIA.
4/30/1785 6/10/1785	MCGINLEY, HUGH (WEAVER)	BALD EAGLE	CH. HUGH, ISABELLA SMITH, JANE.
5/23/1777 6/11/1785	CARSON, ADAM	BALD EAGLE	CH. JOHN, JAMES, ADAM, SAMUEL, MARY MCFADDEN. ELIZABETH, JANE DAVIS, AGNES HARE.
3/5/1785 6/24/1785	REILLY, FRED	SUNBURY	WF. ROSINA.
11/23/1780 11/29/1785	FAULKNER, JOHN	?	BROTHER, ROBERT, OF NEW YORK STATE
9/10/1785 12/23/1785	GAUGH, CHARLES	AUGUSTA	WF. CATHERINE. CH. JOHN, CATHERINE.
10/21/1784 3/15/1786	ROBINSON, ISAAC	MAHONING	CH. NO NAMES GIVEN. BROTHER, JAMES.
————— 3/20/1786	ARMOND, J. GEORGE	?	WF. ELIZABETH. HEIR, WILLIAM BAYLIES.
5/1/1776 4/3/1786	BURK, HENRY	?	BROTHER, JOHN.
2/10/1786 5/26/1786	FORSTER, JOHN	BUFFALO	WF. JANE. CH. JAMES, JOHN, AGNES, MARGARET, WILLIAM, MARY.
2/22/1787 3/7/1787	MCCULLY, ELIZABETH	?	HEIRS; ARTHUR MCGILL AND DAUGHTER, ANN. NEPHEWS; HUGH & ROBERT LOGUE. ROBERT KING.
2/16/1787 3/20/1787	KERSTETTER, SABAS.	PENN	WF. MARY. CH. MARTIN, LEONARD, PETER, SEBASTIAN, FRANCES, CATHERINE, MARGARET.
6/12/1783 5/1/1787	MCCLUNG, JOHN	BUFFALO	CH. JAMES. MATTHEW, JOHN, CHARLES, WILLIAM (WHO) WAS DEAD AND LEFT SARAH, REBECCA, WILLIAM), SARAH CLARK, AND 3 OTHER DAUGHTERS.
4/9/1787 6/19/1787	GERMAN, JACOB (NOW GARMAN) OWNED LAND IN YORK AND CUMBERLAND COS.	PENN	WF. ANNA. CH. CHRISTIAN, JOHN, CATHERINE FOULK (WHO HAD A SON NAMED CHRISTIAN), ROSINA WARD, REGINA (MRS. JOHN HAMMERSLY).
5/17/1787 6/19/1787	NEWMAN, THOMAS (BORN 1699)	MUNCY	WF. WINIFRED. CH. MARY (WD/O JAS. HOGELAND), SARAH (WD/O GEO. SILVERTHORN), SUSAN (WD/O JAS. HAMILTON), WINIFRED (WD/O JOHN MOORE), JOANNA (MRS. THOS. SILVERTHORN). GCH. JONA- THAN, JAMES & THOMAS HAMPTON, AND ARTHUR MOORE. HEIR; WILLIAM S/O JACOB NEWMAN.
5/21/1787 6/25/1787	BEATTY, ALEX, SR.	BUFFALO	WF. AGNES. CH. JANE, AGNES, HANNAH, SARAH, HUGH, JOHN, ALEXANDER, JAMES.
3/22/1787 8/10/1787	YOUNG, MATTHEW	BUFFALO	CH. JOHN, MARGARET, SARAH, ROBERT D., AGNES.
6/9/1787 11/21/1787	MCKEE, SAMUEL	TURBOT	WF. MARY ANN. CH. THOMAS, JOHN, JAMES, DAVID, SAMUEL, JEAN, MARGARET HOOD (WHO HAD DAUGHTER, ELIZABETH), GEORGE, ROBERT.
4/1/1788 4/28/1788	RADDICK, JOHN	?	WF. ELIZABETH. GRANDSON, JOHN ALEXANDER
6/2/1788 6/18/1788	SHAFFER, JOHN	MAHANOY	WF. MARIA. CH. JOHN ADAM, JOHN NICHOLAS, JOHN MICHAEL, ANDREW, JOHN GEORGE, CATHERINE (DEAD), ELIZABETH, MAGDALENE.
6/11/1786 6/27/1788	CLELAND, WILLIAM (CHESTER COUNTY)	LONDON- DERRY	WF. ELIZABETH. CH. WILLIAM, ROBERT, ————.
2/22/1788 9/22/1788	HAYNES, BARTHOLOMEW	DERRY	WF. JANE. CH. JOSEPH, JOHN, HANNAH, MARY, MARG- ARET, JANE, JONATHAN, & AN UNNAMED SON.

4/8/1777 10/14/1788	MCCLURE, JAMES	WYOMING	WF. MARY. CH. PRISCILLA, JOSEPH, JAMES, ———,
3/23/1786 12/10/1788	GRONINGER, LEONARD	BUFFALO	WF. ELIZABETH. CH. DANIEL, LEONARD, JACOB, JOSEPH, ELIZABETH, MOLLY, SUSAN, MARGARET.
8/27/1777 2/12/1789	KIRK, MOSES	TURBOT	WF. MARY. CH. WILLIAM, JAMES, SEVERAL DAUGHTERS NOT NAMED.
1/27/1789 2/23/1789	BINKLEY, JOHN	PENN	WF. CATHERINE. CH. CATHERINE, JACOB, ADAM, MARIA, MARY ELIZABETH.
3/6/1789 6/25/1789	MELICK, PETER, SR.	WYOMING	WF. MARY. CH. CHRISTINA, CHARITY, PETER, MICHAEL, MARGARET, HENRY, JOHN, DAVID.
9/10/1789 11/3/1789	FORSTER, JAMES	LYCOMING	WF. DORCAS. CH. LOVINA, ELIZABETH.
10/16/1784 3/10/1790	BICKEL, TOBIAS, SR.	PENN	CH. HENRY (DEAD), TOBIAS, JOHN, SIMON, THOMAS, JACOB, CATHERINE, MARY, ELIZABETH, MARY MARGARET, ANNA MARY, ROSINA.
2/24/1790 3/29/1790	DRUCKENMILLER, FREDERICK	PENN	WF. CHRISTINA. CH. JOHN FREDERICK, PETER, MARY, ELIZABETH, MARGARET, CHRISTINA, CATH- ERINE, MAGDALENA, BARBARA.
6/9/1789 6/18/1790	LUTZ (LOTZ), ULRICH	?	WF. ELIZABETH. CH. JOHN JACOB, JOHN, CATHERINE, ANNA MARIA.
7/8/1790 7/10/1790	BRITTAIN, ZEBOETH (NORTHAMPTON CO)	MT. BETHEL	WF. ELIZABETH. CH. WILLIAM, AND OTHERS, NOT NAMED.
6/8/1790 7/12/1790	GETTIG, CHRISTOPHER	SUNBURY	WF. ANNA DOROTHEA. CH. MAUDELENA, FREDERICK, BARBARA (MRS. PAUL LEBO), ELIZABETH (MRS. JOHN BUCHER), CHRISTOPHER, CATHERINE, JOSEPH.
1/29/1787 8/7/1790	FOCHT (VOGT), JAMAS	BUFFALO	CH. MICHAEL, BARBARA, EVE, ANN, ELIZABETH.
11/27/1787 8/25/1790	DOCK (DUCK), NINEVEH	TURBOT	CH. JOHN, HUGH, WILLIAM, MARGARET, MARTHA.
3/20/1782 8/26/1790	DRUCKENMILLER, PETER	PENN	WF. ANNA MARY. CH. FREDERICK, ELIZABETH (MRS. ANDREW HAFFER, OR HAFER).
9/22/1790 10/26/1790	HANEY, CHRISTOPHER SR.	HAINES	CH. HIRONIMUS, CHRISTOPHER, ADAM, FREDERICK, JOHN, EVE, MARGARET, ELIZABETH.
11/2/1782 11/22/1790	WHEELER, JOSEPH	WYOMING	WF. MARY. CH. JOHN, SAMUEL, LEVI, ELLEN, ELIZ- ABETH, ANN, MARY, PHOEBE.
9/4/1790 12/6/1790	BLACK, JOHN	SUNBURY	BROS. DAVID (WHO HAD JOHN, ANNA, HANNAH), JAMES (WHO HAD DAVID & JEAN), WILLIA, SISTER, SUSAN, IN IRELAND. NEPH. JAMES OF LEWISBURG, PA.
1/3/1789 1/3/1791	BROSIUS, SEBASTIAN	MAHANOY	CH. NICHOLAS, GEORGE DANIEL, JOHN GEORGE, MAGDALENE (MRS. NICHOLAS BOBB), JACOB, CATHERINE KREIGER, JULIANA SHAFFER, MARG- ARET REITZ, MARY.
10/25/1784 2/25/1791	BORN, PETER	BUFFALO	WF. BARBARA. CH. PETER, HENRY, JOHN, SUSAN, CATHERINE, ELIZABETH, BARBARA, CHRISTINA.
3/1/1791 5/25/1791	PLUNKETT, WILLIAM	?	CH. ELIZABETH (MRS. SAMUEL MACLAY), ISABEL (MRS. WILLIAM BELL), MARGARET RICHARDSON.
7/9/1791 8/25/1791	STRAYER, MATHIAS	BEAVER	WF. MARY MARGARET. CH. ANDREW, AND OTHERS NOT NAMED.
5/11/1791 8/31/1791	IRWIN, JOHN	?	SON, ANDREW.
4/15/1791 10/10/1791	PONTIUS, MARCUS	SUNBURY	WF. MARY ELIZABETH. CH. ELIZABETH.
3/7/1791 12/21/1791	NEWMAN, JACOB	PENN	CH. MICHAEL, WIANT, EVE, GERTRUDE, ELIZABETH (MRS. JACOB KOPY), SUSAN (MRS. JACOB THOMAS), ANN.
11/12/1791 1/24/1792	FLEMING, JAMES	BUFFALO	STEPCHILDREN; SAMUEL, BENJAMINE, AND JANE RODMAN.
12/31/1791 1/24/1792	FORSTER, MARGARET	BUFFALO	CH. MARGARET (MRS. BEN. WELLS), ANDREW AND OTHERS. SEE J. FORSTER WILL 10/24/1784

5/9/1792 5/17/1792	MCGRADY, ALEX, SR.	BUFFALO	WF. MARGARET. CH. ALEXANDER, WILLIAM, AGNES (MRS. ELI HOLEMAN), JANE (MRS. JAMES JOHNS- TON), SAMUEL.
7/2/1792 8/11/1792	GRUBER, JOHN GEO.	MAHANOY	WF. ELIZABETH. CH. HENRY, CATHERINE, ELIZABETH, SUSAN, ROSINA.
7/28/1782 9/10/1792	SMITH, JOHN	NIPPENOSE	WF. ELIZABETH. CH. JOHN, ABRAHAM, CHRISTIAN, JACOB, MARY.
2/21/1786 12/12/1792	BAIRD, WILLIAM	PINE CREEK	CH. WILLIAM, ZEBULON, BENJAMIN, JOSEPH, PHEBE (MRS. SAM SEELEY), MARY ANN, SARAH DIL- LEW, ANN DUNN, LYDIA DUNN.
12/10/1792 12/28/1792	SLACK, JOHN	MUNCY	WF. ANNA. CH. RALPH, EZEKIEL, HENRY, ANNA, SARAH, MILLICENT.
1/1/1793	SHANNON, ROBERT	TURBOT	WF. SARAH. SON, SAMUEL.
10/15/1792 1/4/1793	MILLER, HENRY	HAINES	CH. JACOB, HENRY, JOHN, DANIEL, MARTIN, JOSEPH, DAVID, ABRAHAM.
1/22/1793 3/12/1793	COCHRAN, JAMES	CHILLISQUAQUE	WF. CATHERINE. CH. JAMES, JOHN, MARGARET, REBECCA.
5/22/1777 3/20/1793	SNYDER, ABRAHAM (BERKS COUNTY)	TULPEHOCKEN	WF. NO NAME. CH. JACOB, ABRAHAM, JOHN, GEORGE, THOMAS, MARIA.
2/11/1793 3/30/1793	ZARTMAN, JACOB	MAHANOY	WF. ANNA MARGARET. CH. HENRY, JACOB, MARTIN, PETER, MARGARET, MARIA, SUSAN.
4/7/1786 5/8/1793	FORSTER, SARAH (LANCASTER CO.)	UPPER PAXTON	CH. THOMAS, DORCAS, ISABEL, MARGARET, ELIZABETH, GRANDAUGHTER, SARAH SPENCER.
5/6/1793 6/8/1793	MCCURDY, WILLIAM	CHILLISQUAQUE	WF. MARY.
———— 8/3/1793	WITMER, PETER, SR.	PENN	WF. SALOME. CH. PETER, MRS. JOHN THORNTON, MRS. JOHN MOTZ, SAMUEL, JOHN, SUSANNA.
9/29/1793 10/5/1793	DUSING, NICHOLAS	PENN	WF. DOROTHY. CH. JOHN, ELIZABETH (MRS. JOHN HARTMAN).
8/14/1793 10/5/1793	SHAFFER, CHRISTOPHER	PENN	WF. MARIA EVA ROSINA. CH. CHRISTOPHER, CATHERINE (MRS. PAUL HEIM), BARBARA (MRS. ABRAHAM MARKLEY), ELIZABETH (MRS. PHILIP FOULKROD), JOHN, PHILIP, ANDREW, JACOB, ROS- INA, DANIEL, MAGDALENA, ANNA MARIA.
8/1/1793 10/12/1793	GASTON, ROBERT	TURBOT	CH. DANIEL, GEORGE W., JOHN, JOSEPH, GRACE (MRS. HUGH GASTON), MARGARET MALICK, MARY BARKLEY, ANNA.
4/2/1793 4/24/1793	WILSON, WILLIAM	WHITE DEER	HAD CHILDREN, DID NOT NAME THEM. BROTHERS; NATHANIEL, JAMES.
12/12/1783 5/3/1793	FERGUSON, JAMES	BUFFALO	CH. MARY (MRS. WM. THOMPSON), ELIZABETH (MRS. CHAS. HOMMEL), MRS. HUGH MCCONNELL, JOHN, WHO MARRIED A DAUGHTER OF DAVID HANNA.
10/7/1793 11/4/1793	FOLLMER, MICHAEL	TURBOT	CH. JOHN, GEORGE, ADAM, FRED, MICHAEL, ELIZA- BETH (MRS. ADAM CHRIST), HENRY, MARY MAGDALENE.
6/8/1792 11/11/1793	MCCORLEY, ROBERT	WHITE DEER	WF. ANN. CH. ROBERT, JAMES, ISABELLE, MARY, ROLAND, JACOB.
———— 11/16/1793	ROBB, JOHN	?	CH. JOHN, MARY, BROTHER, DAVID.
6/15/1772 1/28/1794	MCFADDEN, JOHN	?	BROTHER, HUGH, IN IRELAND, NEPHEW, BERNARD FERRILL.
8/15/1793 2/8/1794	HARRIS, SAMUEL	LOYALSOCK	CH. SAMUEL, JOHN, WILLIAM, BENJAMIN, THOMAS, JOSEPH, GEORGE, NANCY, ELIZABETH, SARAH, MARY (MRS. GIDEON PERVIEL).
2/12/1794 4/14/1794	DREESE, JACOB	BEAVER	WF. NO NAME. CH. JOHN, JACOB, MARY MAGDALENE, PETER, MARY ELIZABETH, CHRISTINA. BROTHER, JOHN.
6/16/1792 5/27/1794	PONTIUS, JOHN	BUFFALO	CH. MARY (MRS. JACOB WELKER), HENRY, ANDREW.
3/31/1794 7/15/1794	SHIRK, JOHN	MAHANTANGO	WF. CATHERINE. CH. HAD CHILDREN, NOT NAMED.

Date	Name	Township	Family/Heirs
6/18/1794 8/2/1794	WINTER, WILLIAM	LOYALSOCK	WF. ELINOR. CH. HANNAH (MRS. HENRY MILLER), JANE CAMPBELL, PHEBE JONES, WILLIAM, JOHN, SARAH, MARY, JAMES, ELIAS, ARCHIBALD, ELIZABETH, ELINOR, LUCY ANN (MRS. GEO. CRAWFORD) SON-IN-LAW, THOMAS LINKHORN.
5/12/1794 8/5/1794	SMITH, GEORGE	BUFFALO	WF. ANNA MARGARET. CH. JOHN. SISTER, MARGARET GILLMAN (WHO HAD SUSAN & JOHN). BROTHERS, ADAM (HAD SON GEORGE), MICHAEL (HAD SON GEO. MICHAEL).
7/9/1794 8/26/1794	BOWER, CASPER	EAST BUFFALO	CH. HENRY, MARGARET HOLTER, SUSAN DRESLER, BARBAR SMITH, CATHERINE SANDERS, MARIA FLICKINGER, MARIA MAGDALENE.
7/26/1794 10/5/1794	FISHER, JOHN	WHITE DEER	WF. ELIZABETH. CH. HENRY, PAUL, JOHN, MICHAEL, GEORGE, MARY, ELIZABETH DAUGHERTY, CATHERINE ULEY
7/17/1794 11/24/1794	LUNGER, JACOB	CHILLISQUAQUE	WF. JULIA. CH. ELIZABETH, AND OTHERS, NOT NAMED.
11/29/1794 1/1/1795	WILKINSON, EDWARD	SHAMOKIN	CH. REBECCA, EUNICE, ELIZABETH, JANE, MARY, ALLEN JOHN, JOSEPH, JAMES AZARIAH (WHO HAD CATHERINE, EDWARD, WILLIAM, BROOKS). OTHER GRANDCHILDREN; GIDEON, MOSES, MARY, KEZIAN, MARTHA, DEBORAH, WHO WERE PROBABLY THE CHILDREN OF SON, JOSEPH.)
11/16/1794 1/5/1795	DOEBLER, JOSEPH	BUFFALO	SISTERS; CATHERINE, BARBARA, ELIZABETH SHENK, BROTHER; CHRISTOPHER (STOPHEL)
1/30/1795 3/2/1795	IRWIN, WILLIAM	BUFFALO	WF. JANE. CH. SARAH CHARTERS (WHO HAD WM., MARGARET, ELIZABETH), CATHERINE WILSON, ELIZABETH MARY, NANCY.
3/24/1795 4/10/1795	KELLER, HENRY	?	CH. GEORGE, LEONARD, PETER, HENRY, JOHN, ANTHONY, FRED, JACOB, MAGDALENE, MARGARET, JUDY, MARY.
11/17/1794 4/27/1795	HOCK, STEPHEN	PENN	WF. CHRISTINA. CH. MARY (MRS. ANTHONY HULL), MARGARET, CHRISTINA (MRS. ARTHUR BAILEY), ELIZABETH, CONRAD, BARBARA (MRS. DANIEL STIMELING, STIMELY), ANDREW, HENRY.
3/19/1795 4/30/1795	FLIN (FLYNN), LAWRENCE	FISHING CREEK	WF. ELIZABETH. CH. EDITH (MRS. ISAAC PHILLIPS, WHO HAD DAUGHTER, ELIZABETH). FRIEND; TOM EVES, (WHO HAD DAUGHTER, EDITH).
- - - - - 6/22/1795	HAINES, JOSIAH	NORTHUMBERLAND	MENTIONS WIFE AND CHILDREN, BUT GIVES NO NAMES. HE FORMERLY LIVED IN PHILADELPHIA.
8/10/1795 8/15/1795	BLOOM, STEPHEN	AUGUSTA	WF. MARY. CH. DANIEL, CATHERINE, SAMUEL, AND PROBABLY OTHERS.
1/29/1795 9/25/1795	PFILE, JACOB	PENN	MOTHER; NOT NAMED. BROTHERS; GEORGE, HENRY.
8/12/1795 11/1/1795	SMITH, ANNA MARY	?	HEIRS; SUSAN D/O HENRY GILMAN. A SON, NOT NAMED. SISTER; ELIZABETH. MOTHER, NOT NAMED. JOHN AURAND, JR.
8/14/1795 11/19/1795	MEISER, JOHN	PENN	CH. JOHN, GEORGE & ANOTHER SON. MARGARET (MRS. PETER STOKE, WHO HAD 2 DAUGHTERS, BARBARA & MRS. GEO. COYTSEWILE), AND TWO OTHER DAUGHTERS, NOT NAMED.
3/4/1794 11/20/1795	MARTIN, REV. JAMES	?	WF. ELINOR. CH. JOHN, MARGARET, JAMES, ROBERT, MARY ANN, SAMUEL, ELIZABETH (MRS. DAVID STEWART).
5/6/1790 12/—/1795	KEISTER, GEORGE	BUFFALO	WIFE, NOT NAMED. CH. PETER, ELIZABETH, JOHN HENRY, CHRISTINA. MAYBE A SON NAMED GEO.
7/10/1795 1/27/1796	WILSON, JOHN	MAHONING	WF. PHEBE. CH. THOMAS, JOHN, MARY, HANNAH, RACHEL, PHEBE, SARAH FRAZIER (SON CHARLES).
2/6/1796 2/12/1796	FRICKEY, CHRISTIAN	?	1ST WIFE, CHRISTINA KETTERLY. 2ND WIFE, ANNA MADALINE. CH. CATHERINE, GEORGE.
9/5/1795 2/13/1796	OPP, PHILIP (S/O JOHN)	MAHONING	CH. PHILIP, EVE, MARY (MRS. JOHN BOGERT)
1/23/1795 2/22/1796	RUSH, JOHN	PENN	CH. DANIEL, CATHERINE MEYERS, PETER, JACOB, ELIZABETH, SALOME (MRS. JOHN SHALLENBERGER)

Date	Name	Township	Details
9/29/1792 2/23/1796	ESPY, JAMES	TURBOT	WF. MARTHA. NO CHILDREN MENTIONED.
2/8/1796 2/23/1796	IRWIN, JOHN	?	WF. MARY. CH. JOHN, ELIZABETH, ANN, JAMES, GEORGE, SAMUEL, ROSANNA, OTHERS; WELCH, ANDREW, ALEXANDER & GAVIN IRWIN.
6/18/1795 3/7/1796	SMITH, PETER	MAHONEY	CH. JOHN GEORGE, PETER, ANDREW, MARY ELIZABETH, MARY, JOHN, JACOB.
3/14/1796 3/24/1796	RIDDLE, GEORGE	FAIRVIEW	WF. NOT NAMED. CH. MARY ANN, ELIZA, BROTHER, JOHN, OF IRELAND, WHO HAD SON, JAMES.
3/24/1796 3/29/1796	HAVERLING, JACOB	SUNBURY	WF. CHRISTINA. NO CHILDREN MENTIONED.
6/14/1790 4/6/1796	HOOD, JOHN	TURBOT	WF. NOT NAMED. CH. GEORGE, WILLIAM, ROBERT, JOHN, ANDREW, ELIZABETH, MARY HAYNES, GRAND-DAUGHTER, RACHEL MAGILL.
12/12/1794 4/9/1796	SMITH, BALTHASER	MAHONEY	CH. MARY ELIZABETH, MARY MARGARET, JACOB, PETER, ADAM (DEAD), LEAVING JOHN, NICHOLAS, CATHERINE, MARGARET ELIZABETH.
11/17/1794 5/17/1796	OVERDORF, HENRY (MAYBE ORNDORF)	HAINES (CENTRE CO.)	WF. CATHERINE. CH. JOHN, ELIZABETH.
11/24/1794 - - - - -1796	WEISER, SAMUEL	MAHONEY	WF. JUDITH. CH. BENJAMIN, MARY MARGARET. GODSON; SAMUEL, S/O PETER FETTER, READING, PA. (PETER, OR SAMUEL, HAD A BROTHER, JAC.)
- - - - - 6/6/1796	STACKHOUSE, THOS.	FISHING CREEK	WF. MARTHA. CH. THOMAS, MARTHA CAWLEY, PARTHENIA PARKER, MARGARET MITCHELL, SARAH MITCHELL, JAMES (DEAD, LEFT MARTHA).
8/23/1796 8/26/1796	PAXTON, JONAS	?	WF. MARY. CH. JOHN, SAMUEL, MARY, HANNAH, JOSEPH, REBECCA, RUTH.
9/6/1794 8/30/1796	ROUSHER, NICHOLAS	SUNBURY	WF. BARBARA. CH. BURKHART, NICHOLAS, CATHERINE, MARGARET, BARBARA.
8/23/1796 10/17/1796	COURSIN, JAMES	TURBOT	WF. JANE. CH. BENJAMIN, DERICK, POLLY, FRANCIS
7/27/1793 10/26/1796	LUTZ, JOHN	HAINES	WF. ELIZABETH. CH. JOHN, GEORGE, JACOB, ELEANOR, ELIZABETH, CATHERINE, SUSAN, SARAH.
10/17/1796 11/30/1796	LEISENRING, AND.	?	WF. ELIZABETH. CH. HANNAH, MARY, ELIZABETH.
11/16/1796 4/3/1797	KIEHL (OR KIEHLE), JOHN	AUGUSTA	WF. MARIA. NO CHILDREN. VARIOUS HEIRS NAMED RENN, AND ADAM KLES.
- - - - - 4/24/1797	NEIDIG, SOLOMON	HAINES	WF. MARIA ELIZABETH. CH. JOHN ADAM, JOHN, JACOB, ELIZABETH.
12/6/1794 6/7/1797	GODHART, JOHN (LATE OF NORTH-AMPTON COUNTY)	MAHONING	CH. ELIZABETH (MRS. HENRY DEBERGLER), CATHERINE (MRS. WM. HESS). GRANDCHILDREN; JOHN FRUCKY, MARY (MRS. CHRISTIAN LAUBACH), SOPIHA (MRS. ABRAHAM TRONSON).
6/14/1797 7/7/1797	LETTERMAN, PETER, JR.	NORTHUMBER-LAND	WF. PHILIPINA. CH. THREEN, NOT NAMED
6/8/1797 7/31/1787	COLLINGS, WILLIAM	CATAWISSA	WF. ELINOR. NEPHEW, NICHOLAS FRANCE.
8/2/1797 9/6/1797	GETTIG, CHRISTOPHER	SUNBURY	WF. ELIZABETH. CH. CHRISTOPHER, HENRY, ELIZABETH, JOHN.
10/16/1797 11/29/1797	PETER, HENRY	EAST BUFFALO	WF. MARIA SOPHIA. CH. ANNA CATHERINE, MARY SUSAN, ANNA MARGARET, BARBARA.
- - - - - 2/2/1798	STADDON, THOMAS	TURBOT	WF. MARGARET. CH. NANCY, ELIZABETH, WM., ISAAC, JOHN, POLLY (MRS. WM. MOODY), SARAH
11/10/1797 2/3/1798	LOWDEN, MAJ. JOHN	WEST BUFFALO	WF. ANN. CH. JOHN, SUSAN WRIGHT, CATHERINE, GCH. CHARLOTTE & CATHERINE STAKE, JAMES WRIGHT, BROTHER, RICHARD.
12/26/1797 3/1/1798	HUDSON, JOSEPH	TURBOT	WF. ANN. CH. JAMES, WILLIAM, MARY, ANN.

Dates	Name	Township	Details
12/25/1797 5/5/1798	STOCK, MELCHOIR, SR.	PENN	2ND WIFE, ANNA MARY. CH. GEORGE, PETER (DEAD), MELCHOIR (WHO HAD PETER & ELIZABETH), MICHAEL MATHIAS, AND SEVERAL DAUGHTERS.
3/20/1798 5/17/1798	LITTLE, THOMAS	CHILLISQUAQUE	HEIRS; MARGARET, BETSY, AND MARY, DAUGHTERS OF JAMES STEEDMAN.
3/19/1798 5/22/1798	STILWELL, DANIEL	WHITE DEER	WF. ELIZABETH. CH. SAMUEL, JOHN, JOSEPH, JAMES, ANDREW, MARGARET.
12/23/1797 5/31/1798	CLARK, ROBERT	WHITE DEER	WF. JEAN. CH. ELINOR (MRS. ROBERT FRUIT), MARGARET, AGNES, ROBERT, GEORGE, CHAS., JOHN.
3/26/1798 6/17/1798	DREBS, JOHN HENRY	MAHANOY	WF. CHRISTINA MARGARET. CH. JOHN HENRY, JOHN GEORGE, ELIZABETH, CHRISTINA, CATHERINE, MARY ELIZABETH, SUSAN (DIED 1792).
8/12/1797 6/26/1798	WHITE, JOHN	MAHANOY	WF. ELIZABETH. CH. JAMES, JOHN, THOMAS, MARY, ELIZABETH AND 5 YOUNGER CHILDREN, UNNAMED.
5/24/1798 6/28/1798	MURPHY, JOHN	LEWISBURG	CH. BENJAMIN, JOHN, HENRY, MARY, NANCY, SALLY.
8/12/1783 8/26/1789	HAIN, GEORGE	BUFFALO	WF. MAGDALENE ELIZABETH. CH. JOHN, CONRAD, ANNA MARIA LONG, PHILIP, ELIZABETH WAREHEIM, MARGARET (MRS. PHILIP KRICK) DEAD, JOHN GEORGE (DEAD), LEAVING JOHN GEORGE & MAGDELENE.
9/20/1798 11/2/1798	TEMPLETON, ROBERT	DERRY	WF. MARY. CH. MARY, AGNES, SARAH, NEPHEWS; ROBERT TEMPLETON, S/O JOHN; ROBERT CLARK, S/O WILLIAM; ROBERT SINCLAIR, S/O DUNCAN.
9/19/1798 11/24/1798	DERSTETTER, MARTIN	MAHANOY	WF. ELIZABETH. CH. JOHN ADAM, JOHN, RUDOLPH, MARGARET, ELIZABETH, BARBARA, CATHERINE, ANN.
11/9/1798 11/29/1798	BEAVER, HENRY	MILTON	WF. ELIZABETH. CH. NONE MENTIONED.
11/22/1798 12/12/1798	WALES, JOHN	PENN	WF. ANNA MARY. CH. JAMES, JOHN, JACOB, JOSEPH, SARAH, SUSAN, AND PROBABLY OTHERS.
1/24/1799	ALLEN, ROBERT	MILES	WF. ELIZABETH. CH. NONE MENTIONED.
4/25/1798 3/30/1799	WEARY, CHRISTIAN	MAHANOY	CH. ANTHONY, JOHN, JACOB, MICHAEL, MARY.
1/17/1799 4/12/1799	KADERMAN, PHILIP (CATHERMAN)	MAHANOY	CH. MICHAEL.
8/18/1798 6/17/1799	DOUGHERTY, ELINOR	NORTHUMB- ERLAND	CH. JANE CAMPBELL, RICHARD, ELIZABETH, CATHERINE, EZILA.
3/10/1794 9/25/1799	ALBERT, PETER	MAHANOY	WF. ANNA REGINE. CH. JOHN PETER & 5 OTHER CHILDREN, NOT NAMED. SON-IN-LAW, JOHN DURK.
---------- 10/19/1799	ROSEBURY, JOSEPH	BLOOM	CH. JOSEPH, MARY (MRS. EDMOND CRAWFORD), HANNAH, DEBORAH (MRS. JOHN DAVIS), G'CHILDREN, JOSEPH ROSEBURY, SARAH STOCKLEY (MRS. CORNELIUS COOPER.)
9/19/1799 10/13/1799	STAHL, PHILIP	BUFFALO	CH. JOHN, JACOB, PHILIP, PETER, CATHERINE, MARY, ELIZABETH, MARGARET, SUSAN.
11/1/1799 11/7/1799	TOMLINSON, HENRY	BLOOM	WF. MARTHA. CH. MOLLIE, ANN, SAMUEL, ELIZABETH.
8/16/1797 11/26/1799	PENROSE, RICHARD	CATAWISSA	WF. MARGARET. CH. RICHARD (DEAD), HIS WIDOW MARRIED JOHN WILLIAMS. SAM HUGHES, SON-IN-LAW. HANNAH (MRS. JESSE YARNOLD), MARGARET, THOMAS.
10/16/1799 11/30/1799	WHITENIGHT, MATTHIAS	MAHONING	WF. NOT NAMED. CH. PHILIP, DANIEL, ELIZABETH, MARY, ROSANNA, MATHIAS, MICHAEL, GEORGE, CHRISTIAN, JOHN.
1/3/1800 2/11/1800	OBERDORF, GEORGE	AUGUSTA	MOTHER, CATHERINE, NOW MARRIED TO MARTIN WERFEL, BROS., PETER & JACOB, AUGUSTA TWP., & JOHN, BERKS CO. SISTERS; MAGDALENE (MRS. JACOB CARL), LONGSWAMP TWP., BERKS CO., CATHERINE (MRS. JOHN HOFFMAN), RUSCOMB TWP., BERKS CO.
2/8/1800 3/3/1800	LONG, JOSEPH	BLOOM	WF. SARAH. CH. CATHERINE DYER, SARAH DRAKE, MARY STENGER, JOHN, HENRY, MARGARET, ELIZABETH, ANNA, WILLIAM.

2/24/1800 3/11/1800	MEYER, CHARLES, SR.	PENN	WF. CHRISTINA. CH. FREDERICK, JACOB, CHARLES, AND OTHERS, NOT NAMED.
5/1/1798 3/12/1800	KEMPEL, JOHN ADAM	MAHANOY	WF. CATHERINE. CH. JOHN, ADAM, 2 OTHERS, AND ONE UNBORN.
8/3/1792 3/25/1800	COCHRAN, JAMES	MAHONING	CH. WILLIAM, ANDREW (WHO HAD JUNE & MARGARET) MRS. JAMES BLACK (WHO HAD SON, JOHN).
1/20/1800 4/1/1800	WITTENMIRE, ANDREW	PENN	WF. NOT NAMED. CH. ANNA, MARY, JACOB, CATHERINE MILER, BARBARA (DEAD) (MRS. JACOB ROUSH), SUSAN APPLE, MAGDALENE.
1/26/1800 4/3/1800	YOUNG, JACOB	BUFFALO	WF. MARIA. CH. HAD CHILDREN, DID NOT NAME.
9/3/1784 4/9/1800	MCCORD, WILLIAM	NORTHUMB-LAND.	WF. NOT NAMED. NO CHILDREN.
9/20/1798 8/20/1800	HUGHES, ELLIS	CATAWISSA	WF. NOT NAMED. CH. URIAH, ISSACHER, THEOPOLIS, ELLIS, JUDITH FOSTER, PHILA LOUNT (OR LORENT), MARY (MRS. JOHN CLEAVER)
9/19/1800 9/30/1800	WATERS, JONATHAN	SHAMOKIN	WF. MARY. CH. JACOB, WILLIAM, MARY, JOHN, ELIZABETH, NEHEMAIH, JONATHAN, BENJAMIN, SAMUEL, AARON, DENNIS.
10/6/1800 10/11/1800	ANDERSON, JACOB	PENN	WF. JANEY. CH. SUSAN, ELIZABETH.
9/18/1800 10/18/1800	TOMLINSON, JAMES	BLOOM	WF. SARAH. CH. MENTIONS CHILDREN, DOES NOT NAME THEM.
--------- 12/6/1800	EWING, JASPER	?	SISTER; WIFE OF GEN EDWARD HAND, THEIR CHILDREN, JESSE, JOHN, SARAH, DOLLY AND TWO OTHER DAUGHTERS.
5/28/1793 12/18/1800	MCKNIGHT, WILLIAM	TURBOT	CH. JANE (MRS. WILLIAM IRELAND), ELIZABETH, MARY, JAMES.
6/18/1798 1/6/1801	HARTER, JOHN	MAHANOY	WF. ANNA MARIA. CH. JOHN, ANDREW, MATHIAS, JACOB, ANNA MARIA (MRS. PETER SMITH), CATHERINE (MRS. JOHN HEIM).
--------- 1/13/1801	LYON, JOHN	SUNBURY	WF. MARY. CH. JOHN, JAMES, REBECCA, ELIZABETH,
8/16/1797 2/20/1801	MURRAY, JOHN	CHILLISQUAQUE	CH. THOMAS, MARY, ANN, JEAN (MRS. MCMAHON). G'SON, JOHN MURRAY. SON-IN-LAW JOHN REZNOR.
12/19/1800 2/20/1801	MURRAY, MARY (D/O JOHN, ABOVE)	CHILLISQUAQUE	BROTHER, THOMAS. SISTERS; JEAN MCMAHON, ANN REZNOR, CHARITY MURRAY.
1/19/1801 2/26/1801	CONRAD, ADAM	BRIER CREEK	WF. SARAH. CH. ELIZABETH, ELINOR, EVE, BENJAMIN, SAMUEL, HENRY, CATHERINE, JACOB.
1/19/1801 3/7/1801	STEEDMAN, JAMES	CHILLISQUAQUE	CH. MARGARET, ELIZABETH, MARY, WILLIAM. DAUGHTER-IN-LAW, REBECCA.
3/8/1800 4/1/1801	GOUGH, CATHERINE	SUNBURY	CH. CATHERINE (MRS. JAMES ALEXANDER, WHOSE CHILDREN WERE; CATHERINE, HANNAH, ANN, LYDIA).
4/28/1800 4/8/1801	HAHN, MICHAEL, SR.	MAHANTANGO	CH. MICHAEL, VERONICA(MRS. HENRY SHETTERLY), JACOB, MAGDALENE (MRS. GEORGE WEIAND), CATHERINE (MRS. JOHN SHADLE), ANDREW, AND ELIZABETH, A MINOR.
4/15/1801 5/21/1801	OCHSENREITER, JACOB	MAHANOY	WF. BARBARA. CH. MICHAEL, JACOB, PETER, ANDREW, GERHART, HENRY, BARBARA, ELIZABETH.
4/15/1801 5/14/1801	STEINBRUCH, ABRAHAM	PENN	WF. EVE. CH. JACOB, BARBARA, MARY, CATHERINE, FREDERICK, ABRAHAM, PETER.
4/30/1801 5/21/1801	BERKHOUS, CHRISTOPHER	MAHANOY	WF. GERTRUDE. CH. JOHN, JACOB, GEORGE, MARY MAGDALENE.
10/9/1796 5/27/1801	HAMMOND, DAVID	TURBOT	WF. JANE. NO CHILDREN MENTIONED.
8/27/1800 8/7/1801	MEISER, HENRY	MAHANTANGO	WF. NOT NAMED. CH. MARY ELIZABETH, CATHERINE, BARBARA, JOHN, MICHAEL, HENRY, GEORGE, FREDERICK, ANDREW.
7/5/1801 8/25/1801	HECKERT, ANN ELIZA-BETH CATHERINE	MAHANOY	CH. PETER, CASPER, MICHAEL, FREDERICK, STEPDAUGHTER, ELIZABETH SILER.

--------- 8/18/1801	MORR, ANDREW	PENN	2ND WF. MARY. CH. JOHN GEORGE, PHILIP, CHRISTINA (MRS. JOHN GEORGE ROUSH, DEAD), MARGARET (MRS. PHILIP MOYER), MAGDALENE (MRS. ADAM BOLLENDER, DEAD), CATHERINE ELIZABETH (MRS. MICHAEL WEAVER, JR.), JULIANA (MRS. JACOB MOYER, JR.), BARBARA (MRS. FREDERICK STEESE)
8/15/1801 9/26/1801	SMITH, DAVID	MAHANTANGO	WF. REBECCA. CH. JOSEPH, DAVID, JAMES, ABRAHAM, DANIEL, SOLOMON, ELIZABETH, BARBARA.
4/28/1801 10/5/1801	THMPSON, JOHN	WEST BUFFALO	CH. JAMES, BENJAMIN, RACHEL LINCOLN, SUSAN PATTERSON, SARAH PIPER.
8/13/1798 10/5/1801	REZNOR, JOHN, SR.	WEST BUFFALO	WF. UNNAMED. CH. JOHN, GEORGE, HUGH, SUSAN, SAMUEL, DAVID.
---------- 10/--/1801	MACKEY, JOHN	NORTHUMBERLAND	COUSINS; JAMES & WILLIAM MACKEY. NEPHEWS; JOHN, S/O DAVID MACKEY, WILLIAM, S/O WILLIAM. NIECE; NANCY, D/O WILLIAM MACKEY.
7/18/1799 10/14/1801	HOWER, JOHN FRED	TURBOT	WF. BARBARA. CH. JOHN, MARY (MRS. TOBIAS SHIRTZ) MARIA, RACHEL, HANNAH.
5/1/1799 12/5/1801	HUNTER, AGNES	WHITE DEER	CH. JAMES, JANE, POLLY, NANCY, ROSANNA, ELIZABETH, LYDIA. G'SON, GEORGE WILSON.
10/18/1801 1/9/1802	THOMPSON, MICHAEL	SHAMOKIN	WF. LYDIA. CH. ELIZABETH, JESSE, MICHAEL, JOHN, JOSEPH, MARY ANN (MRS. FRED WHITEHEAD). GRANDDAUGHTER, HANNAH MCKEW (MCHUGH?).
11/4/1801 1/2/1802	HOLTZAPPLE, HENRY	MAHANTANGO	WF. BARBARA. CH. JOHN, JACOB.
8/13/1800 1/16/1802	WATSON, ALEXANDER	DERRY	WF. JEAN. CH. THOMAS, MARGARET STEWART, ELIZABETH FRAZIER, JOHN, ALEXANDER, ROBERT, JANE, ANN.
2/16/1802 4/8/1802	RAY, GEORGE	W. BUFFALO	WF. MARGARET. CH. JOHN, GEORGE, WILLIAM, BARBARA, MARGARET, SARAH, MARY, CATHERINE.
12/27/1801 3/4/1802	ZIMMERMAN, GEORGE	AUGUSTA	CH. HENRY, CATHERINE, MAGDALENE, GEORGE, SUSAN, MARY, JOHN, SARAH.
2/16/1802 3/11/1802	BECK, CONRAD	AUGUSTA	WF. ELIZABETH. CH. DOROTHY (MRS. JACOB DORST), ELIZABETH (MRS. ABRAHAM KIEHLE), JACOB, DANIEL, MARIA, SARAH.
12/25/1801 3/17/1802	EWIG, ADAM, SR.	PENN	CH. JOHN, MICHAEL, GEORGE, ADAM, ELIZABETH HEHN, CHRISTINA (MRS. JOHN ADAMS), CATHERINE (BORN 1774) (MRS. MICH. WARTMAN, OF OHIO).
1/9/1802 3/30/1802	GETTIG, CHRISTOPHER, JR.	SUNBURY	WF. BARBARA. HEIR, SUSAN D/O OF BROTHER, HENRY GETTIG.
10/11/1800 R/10/1802	HOAR, BENJAMIN	CATAWISSA	WF. PRUDENCE. CH. DAVID.
4/2/1802 4/26/1802	CHENEY, JOHN	?	WF. ELIZABETH. CH. JOHN, WILLIAM, JAMES, CHARLES.
2/2/1802 4/26/1802	SPADE, SEBASTIAN	MAHANOY	WF. ANN ELIZABETH. CH. HENRY, SEBASTIAN, ELIZABETH, CATHERINE, JOHN, JACOB, GEORGE, MAGDALENE.
5/25/1802 6/7/1802	EASTERLY, GEORGE	HUGHESBURG	WF. CHARITY (WHOSE FIRST HUSBAND WAS JOHN BARNET FOSTER). DAUGHTER, BETSY.
5/31/1802 6/15/1802	MAZE, ELIZABETH (WID/O JOHN)	BUFFALO	CH. MICHAEL, MRS. MICHAEL MOYER.
10/3/1794 6/22/1802	VANBUSKIRK, THOMAS	?	WF. ESTHER. CH. THOMAS, MORRIS, MARY, ELIZABETH, JEAN.
----1799 6/22/1802	WITMER, CHRISTOPHER	MAHANOY	CH. CHRISTOPHER, JR., AND OTHERS, NOT NAMED.
4/30/1800 7/12/1802	EVES, JOHN	DERRY	WF. ELIZABETH. CH. THOMAS, JOHN, JOSEPH, WILLIAM, CHANDLEE, ANDREW, EDITH, ELIZABETH, SARAH, MARY, PRISCILLA, ANN.
10/10/1801 7/13/1802	THOMPSON, JOSEPH	POINT	WF. MARGARET. NO CHILDREN. SISTER, ELIZABETH (MRS. HENRY BENNETT, LANCASTER CO., PA.) SISTER, ANN SHARP. CHILDREN OF BROTHERS, JOSHUA, JOHN, AND ABRAHAM.

1/6/1798 8/9/1802	REED, CAPT, CASPER	MAHANTANGO	WF, ANNA, CH, HANNAH (MRS, CHRISTOPHER WITMER), FREDERICK, MARY (MRS, JACOB WITMER), EVE (MRS, SIMON ROHRBACH, DEAD, LEAVING HANNAH, CATHERINE, JOHN, ELIZABETH, DAVID ROHRBACH,)
8/13/1802 8/16/1802	PONTIUS, ELIZABETH	SUNBURY	STEP-DAUGHTER, ELIZABETH PONTIUS, PRESBYTERIAN CHURCH, SUNBURY, PA, GRACE BRANDON, JOHN, S/O DANIEL BOGER,
12/18/1801 8/17/1802	HASSINGER, JACOB	BEAVER	WF, ELIZABETH, CH, DANIEL, JACOB, VALENTINE, GEORGE, ABRAHAM, FREDERICK, JEREMIAH, JOHN, ELIZABETH, SUSAN, PHILIP,
7/2/1802 8/24/1802.	CLARK, WILLIAM	SHAMOKIN	WF, ELIZABETH, CH, WILLIAM, JOHN, ELIZABETH (MRS, ABRAHAM DEWITT), MARGARET (MRS, GEORGE PEARSON), SARAH (MRS, CHRISTOPHER REED), ANN (MRS, JONATHAN FARNCWORTH), ELINOR (MRS, JOHN WATERS), THOMAS (DEAD, LEFT SON WM,)
12/1/1801 8/25/1802	MOORE, JOHN	MAHONING	WF, MARGARET, CH, ROBERT, JOHN, JAMES, ISABEL, JEAN,
10/6/1782 8/25/1802	WILSON, ROBERT	TURBOT	NEPHEW, JOSEPH WILSON,
10/24/1796 8/27/1802	JENKINS, PHEBE	EAST BUFFALO	CH, WILLIAM, JAMES (WHO HAD THOMAS, MARY, SARAH), RICHARD, DAUGHTER-IN-LAW, SARAH,
12/10/1799 11/26/1802	GLASS, JOHN GEORGE	PENN	WF, EVE ALBRIGHT, CH, CHRISTIAN, GEORGE, JOHN, EVA, SALOME, BARBARA,
2/24/1802 12/23/1802	HAMPTON, JOSEPH	CATAWISSA	WF, MARY, CH, DAVID, JOHN, JOSEPH, ABRAHAM, SAMUEL, MARY, HANNAH, ANN, AMOS, ESTHER, JONATHAN,
1/20/1803 2/3/1803	WELKER, JACOB	NORTHUMB- ERLAND	WF, ELIZABETH, CH, JACOB (WHO HAD JOHN, ELIZABETH, AND MARGARET),
1/30/1803 2/22/1803	MARTZ, JACOB	AUGUSTA	WF, MARGARET, CH, DAVID, AND OTHERS, NOT NAMED,
1/12/1802 2/23/1803	ROBERTS, DAVID	MAHONING	WF, BETSY, CH, MARY, ANN, OWEN,
11/2/1801 3/2/1803	CREECE, JOHN	MIFFLIN	WF, MARY, CH, JOHN, HENRY, ADAM, BENJAMIN, ANN, ELIZABETH, ELSIE, MARY,
2/4/1802 3/12/1803	LONG, PETER	FREEBURG	WF, CATHERINE HACKENBERG, D/O PETER, SR, CH, ELIZABETH, PETER, HANNAH, CATHERINE, AND OTHERS,
3/9/1803 3/25/1803	WERTZ, DIETRICH	WHITE DEER	WF, MARY, CH, JACOB, ADAM, ELIZABETH GOODLANDER (WHO HAD PAUL, CATHERINE, BENJAMIN, AND CHRISTIAN GOODLANDER), FOUR OTHERS, NOT NAMED,
9/22/1803 10/17/1803	NERHOOD, HENRY	BEAVER	WF, MARY, CH, JACOB, ADAM, MICHAEL, CATHERINE, MARIE, MARGARET,
8/26/1802 10/31/1803	EVANS, CALEB	PENN	BROTHER, LEWIS,
8/17/1802 11/12/1803	HERROLD, J, GEORGE	MAHANTANGO	CH, SIMON, FREDERICK, SUSAN BOTHER, ELIZABETH WINKLEMAN, CATHERINE, ANNA MARIA (MRS, CASPER ARNOLD,
9/6/1802 12/7/1803	KRATZER, FREDERICK	PENN	WF, ELIZABETH, CH, LUDWIG, DANIEL, ELIZABETH KEIPER, MAGDALENE PLANK, CHRISTINA SNYDER, JOHN (DEAD),
12/19/1803 1/4/1804	MERTZ, PHILIP	PENN	WF, EVA, CH, PETER, HENRY, CATHERINE (MRS, JOHN WEIAND), SUSAN (MRS, PETER REEVES), EVE (MRS, NICHOLAS ARBOGAST), ELIZABETH (MRS, ADAM HOLTZ-APPLE), MARGARET, GERTRUDE, MARY, SARAH,
1/10/1802 2/21/1804	PRIESTLY, DR, JOS, (OXYGEN DISCOVERER)	NORTHUMB- ERLAND	BROS, TIMOTHY & JOSHUA, OF ENGLAND, SISTER, MARTHA CROUCH, OF ENGLAND, CH, JOSEPH, WILLIAM (WHOSE WIFE WAS MARGARET), SARAH (MRS, WILLIAM FINCH, BIRMINGHAM, ENGLAND),
7/20/1803 2/23/1804	MILLER, JOHN	SHAMOKIN	WF, CATHERINE, CH, ELIZABETH, SARAH, GEORGE, DAVID,

2/18/1804 3/11/1804	REESE, DANIEL	BUFFALO	WF. CATHERINE. CH. GEORGE, AND OTHERS, NOT NAMED.
2/15/1804 3/7/1804	BOTTORF, MICHAEL	WHITE DEER	WF. CATHERINE. MENTIONS 9 CHILDREN, NAMES NONE.
12/2/1802 3/8/1804	GULICK, MINNE	MAHONING	CH. JOHN, SAMUEL, KEZIAH HUNT, ELIZABETH, ZUBA, RENTCHY, MINNIE DONALDSON, SALLY GEARHART, KATE, CHARITY. G'DAUGHTER, ELIZABETH MARLEY.
2/4/1804 3/19/1804	JOHN, ISAAC	CATAWISSA	WF. MARGARET. CH. ABRAHAM, JACOB, ISAAC, GEO., SAMUEL, MARY DAVIS, ANN, SARAH, MARGARET, ELLIS LEE, SON-IN-LAW.
2/1/1802 3/29/1804	MCMONIGAL, ALEX.	MAHONING	WF. JANE. G'DAUGHTER, JEAN, D/O JOHN MONTGOMERY. COUSIN, SALLY MURRAY.
3/8/1804 4/3/1804	SIMPSON, JOHN	SUNBURY	CH. JEREMIAH, JESSE, RACHEL MONTGOMERY, SARAH, THOMAS.
4/16/1804 4/27/1804	COOKE, COL. WM. (12TH PA. REGT. CONT. LINE)	POINT	WF. SARAH. CH. JOHN (WHOSE SONS WERE JACOB, ROBERT), REBECCA STEEDMAN, JANE (MRS. WM. P. BRADY), MARY (MRS. ROBERT BRADY), SARAH MCCLELLAN, WILLIAM (WHO HAD A SON, WM. M.).
12/17/1803 4/4/1804	HENDRICKS, JACOB	MAHANTANGO	WF. PRISCILLA. CH. JOSEPH, JESSE, ISAAC, EPHRAIM, ANDREW, ABRAHAM, HENRY, JACOB, JOHN, VARA (MRS. ANDREW KERNER), JANES NEITZ, ABIGAIL GERL, SUSAN FRANTZ, NANCY, MARGARET.
2/4/1804 5/3/1804	ALLEN, ROBERT	FISHING CREEK	DAU. ELIZABETH. OTHER HEIR, JOHN KIEHLE.
2/22/1804 7/6/1804	WAGNER, PETER	BEAVER	WF. MARIA MARGARET RAGER (D/O ADAM RAGER). CH. PETER, SUSAN. BROTHER, JACOB.
12/6/1803 7/6/1804	MEECK, ANDREW (MECK, MOOK?)	BEAVER	WF. ANNA MARIA. CH. MARGARET, HENRY, ANDREW, JOHN.
7/8/1804 8/11/1804	STITES, JOSEPH	W. BUFFALO	WF. SARAH. CH. GEORGE, JOHN, ELIZABETH.
10/15/1803 8/—/1804	DREISBACH, JACOB	W. BUFFALO	WF. MAGDALENE. CH. MARTIN, JOHN, & 11 OTHERS, NOT NAMED.
8/3/1804 8/27/1804	WAGNER, ELIAS	BEAVER	WF. EVE. CH. JOHN, MRS. DANIEL MUSSER. SIX OTHER SONS & FOUR OTHER DAUGHTERS, NOT NAMED.
7/21/1804 9/7/1804	FULLMER, JACOB (FOLLMER)	?	WF. CATHERINE. CH. JACOB, HENRY, WILLIAM, MICHAEL, DANIEL, ANNA MARGARET (MRS. WM. GAUKER), CATHERINE (MRS. JOHN GORTNER), ANNA MARIA (MRS. FRED. DIEFFENBACHER), ELIZABETH (MRS. JOHN DIEFFENBACHER).
7/30/1804 10/5/1804	SNYDER, JACOB	SHAMOKIN	WF. ESTHER. CH. MARY (WID/O JON. WATERS), LEAH (MRS. JOHN OTT), RACHEL (MRS. JAS. HIXSON), CHARITY (MRS. DAN. STINEMAN), ANN (MRS. HENRY STIRES), REBECCA (MRS. ISAAC SIMESON).
9/24/1804 10/5/1804	PREISINGER, JACOB	SUNBURY	WF. CATHERINE AURAND. MOTHER, ELIZABETH. MOTHER-IN-LAW, APPALONIA AURAND. ESTATE TO POOR OF SUNBURY, AFTER WIFE'S DEATH.
9/28/1802 10/10/1804	HARRISON, JAMES	TURBOT	WF. JANE. CH. POLLY, HETTY, ROBERT, JANE, CARLISLE, JOSEPH, THOMAS, HUGH, AND OTHERS, NOT NAMED.
2/21/1804 10/19/1804	HUTCHINSON, JOSEPH	TURBOT	WF. MARGARET. CH. JOHN, JOSEPH, ELDER, MARY (MRS. MATTHEW HART) WHO HAD A DAUGHTER, MARGARET SWAN & JOHN H. HART), JANE (MRS. ROBERT HUTCHINSON), MARGARET (MRS. ROBERT SHENARD), FLORENCE. G'CH. MARY, D/O JOSEPH, JOSEPH, S/O JOHN.
9/20/1804 10/31/1804	DALE, SAMUEL	BUFFALO	WF. ANN. CH. SAMUEL, RUTH, JANE, JAMES, WILLIAM, ANN, MARY, ELIZABETH, MARGARET.
10/29/1804 11/10/1804	BRUNER, JACOB (BRUNNER)	BUFFALO	WF. MAGDALENE. CH. JOHN, ELIZABETH MOORE, CASPER.

10/24/1804 11/16/1804	KISNER, JOHN	BRIAR CREEK	WF. EVA CATHERINE. CH. MICHAEL, JOHN, JACOB, LEONARD, SEBASTIAN, ANN, MARY, PETER, GEORGE.
1/1/1790 11/19/1804	CHERRY, JAMES (HUNTERDON CO., NEW JERSEY)	SHAMOKIN	WF. ELIZABETH. CH. CHARLES, PHILIP, JOHN, JOSEPH, ABRAHAM, MARY, JAMES, JESSE, REUBEN, ELIZABETH, BURRIS.
10/7/1804 11/19/1804	HOWER, BARBARA	TURBOT	CH. JOHN, MARY (MRS. TOBIAS SHIRTZ), MARTHA (MRS. JOHN DENTLER), RACHEL, HANNAH.
7/16/1804 12/4/1804	KERSEETTER, MAGD- LENE, WID OF SEB.	MAHANTANGO	CH. MARTIN, OTHERS NOT NAMED. GRAND-DAUGHTER, MAGDALENE MILLER.
11/22/1804 12/10/1804	WEARS, THOMAS	CATAWISSA	WF. SUSAN. CH. ELIZABETH, BROTHER, JOHN.
1/10/1805 1/28/1805	MEYER, CHRISTINA (WID. OF CHAS.)	PENN	CH. ANNA MARIA (MRS. PETER RICHTER), MARTIN, CHARLES, JACOB, FREDERICK, CATHERINE (MRS. JOHN HAAS).
12/29/1804 2/13/1805	FULLERTON, WM.	MILTON	SISTER, MARY HAMILTON.
4/15/1805 5/10/1805	MARTIN, ROBT., JR.	WHITE DEER	WF. MARY. CH. JOSEPH.
———————— 6/29/1805	SNYDER, JOHN (CAPT. JOHN?)	MAHANTANGO	WF. SUSANNA. CH. JOHN, GEORGE, MARY NEITZ, ELIZABETH (MRS. GEO. KERSTETTER), JACOB, MARGARET STAHLEY.
6/11/1805 8/8/1805	SMITH, MICHAEL	CHILLISQUAQUE	WF. SUSAN. CH. BENJAMIN, JOHN, MICHAEL, HENRY, CATHERINE (MRS. MICHAEL WOLF), BETSY, POLLY, SUSAN.
10/18/1804 9/2/1805	HOUSEL, MARTIN	W. BUFFALO	WF. NOT NAMED. CH. JACOB, JOSHUA, CATHERINE, MARY, ELIZABETH, SARAH.
8/14/1805 9/7/1805	STACKHOUSE, ELINOR	BRIAR CREEK	CH. JAMES, SALEM TWP., LUZERNE CO. REBECCA BOWMAN, SUSAN CONRAD, ANN STACKHOUSE.
——————— 10/3/1805	IRWIN, FRANCIS	CHILLISQUAQUE	WF. ELIZABETH. CH. JOHN, ANDREW, MARGARET, AGNES, RICHARD, WILLIAM, FRANCIS.
7/24/1805 10/12/1805	BEATTY, SAMUEL	SHAMOKIN	SISTERS, HESTER, JEAN (MRS. JOHN FORESTER).
9/13/1805 10/22/1805	DISLER, DAVID (DISSLER)	MAHANTANGO	WF. ELIZABETH. CH. HAD SOME, DID NOT NAME THEM IN WILL.
8/25/1805 11/21/1805	EMERICH, MICHAEL	MAHANOY	WF. CATHERINE. CH. JOHN, ELIZABETH, GEORGE, SALOME, CATHERINE, MARY, MICHAEL.
———— 1790 11/29/1805	OVERMIRE, J. GEO. (CAPT. IN REV)	BUFFALO	2ND WIFE, BARBARA. CH. GEORGE, PETER, PHILIP, JOHN, DAVID, JACOB, CATHERINE, ELIZABETH, EVE ESTHER, MAGDALENE, BARBARA, MARGARET.
10/31/1805 12/7/1805	SHOWER, ADAM, SR.	CENTER	WF. ELIZABETH. CH. JACOB, FRED, ADAM, JOHN, MAGDALENE, ELIZABETH, ANNA MARY.
11/5/1805 1/11/1806	EMMIT, JOHN, JR.	HEMLOCK	WF. JANE. CH. WILLIAM, ALEXANDER, JAMES, JOHN, SAMUEL, MARY, ELIZABETH, MARGARET.
11/14/1805 1/11/1806	GILBERT, PAUL	BLOOM	WF. ELIZABETH. CH. PAUL.
12/11/1805 1/11/1806	MILLER, JOSEPH	DERRY	WF. MARGARET. CH. LETTY, POLLY. STEPSON, ISAIAH MCCARTNEY.
2/4/1806 2/22/1806	MOTZ, GEO. PETER	PENN	WF. MARY. CH. JOHN, MRS. LAWRENCE HAINES, SUSAN, BARBARA, AND TWO OTHERS NOT NAMED.
8/30/1803 2/25/1806	GRAYBILL, JOHN	MAHANTANGO	WF. BARBARA. CH. CHRISTIAN, JACOB, JOHN, SUSAN (MRS. JOHN SNYDER), BARBARA SHAFFER, MAGDALENE (MRS. HARMAN SNYDER, JR.), CATHERINE (MRS. PETER SECHRIST), ANNA (MRS. JACOB ACKER, OCKER), MARY KNEPLEY.
2/4/1806 3/21/1806	MARTIN, GEORGE	WHITE DEER	2ND WIFE, LEANNA. CH. JEAN, ELIZABETH, JAMES, JOHN, ROBERT, MARTHA, ALEXANDER.
9/15/1805 3/23/1806	GEARHART, PHILIP	MAHANOY	WF. CATHERINE. CH. SUSAN, MARY, MAGDALENE, ELIZABETH, CATHERINE (MRS. HENRY HAUPT).

2/24/1806	JONES, ELIZABETH	CHILLISQUAQUE	2ND HUSBAND, SAMUEL JONES. CH. BY LST HUSBAND,
4/8/1806			JOHN C. IRWIN, CHAS. B., THOMAS H. IRWIN.
1/9/1805	GWYNN, HUGH	PENN	WF. MARGARET. CH. GEORGE, WILLIAM, HUGH, SAM-
4/28/1806			UEL, DANIEL, THOMAS, MARGARET (MRS. JOHN TATE),
			MARY (MRS. JACOB OVERMIRE), DEBORAH (MRS.
			ARCHIBALD MARR.)
1/17/1801	ADAMS, JAMES	WHITE DEER	WF. MARGARET. CH. JAMES, JOHN, MARGARET,
5/13/1806			SARAH, AGNES.
5/3/1806	HETTRICK, NICHOLAS	MAHANOY	WF. ANNA MARY. CH. JULIANA (MRS. GEO. LEON.
5/27/1806			EMERICH), JOHN PETER, MARY ELIZABETH (MRS.
			PETER SMITH), NICHOLAS, CATHERINE (MRS. MICH-
			AEL KADERMAN), BARBARA (MRS. LEONARD FERSTER),
			MARGARET, JOHN PHILIP, GEORGE, MICHAEL, ELIZ-
			ABETH, ROBINA, ANNA MARY.
2/15/1806	GREEN, JOSEPH	HEMLOCK	WF. ANN. CH. ROBERT, WHEELER, JOHN, RICHARD,
6/17/1806			ISAAC, WILLIAM, SARAH, ELIZABETH, ANNA, MARY,
			EVE. SON-IN-LAW, DANIEL PURSEL.
7/24/1806	STRAUB, ANDREW	TURBOT	WF. MARY. CH. JOSEPH, ABRAHAM, ISAAC, ANDREW
8/18/1806	(FOUNDER OF		(WHO HAD A SON, ANDREW), AND PROBABLY OTHER
	FREEBURG, PA.?)		CHILDREN.
8/1/1806	MONTGOMERY, JANE	MILTON	CH. SARAH (MRS. GEO. WHITEHILL), MARY (MRS.
8/18/1806			THOMAS BULL), JANE (MRS. JAMES MOODIE), NANCY,
			PEGGY, DORCAS. SISTER, NANCY POTTER.
2/15/1802	GREEN, CAPT. JOS.	BEAVER	WF. MARY. CH. GEORGE, GEN. ABBOTT, ELIZABETH
8/29/1806			SHIVELY, ALICE MCCOY, JOHN T., JOSEPH, WILLIAM,
			THOMAS.
2/21/1786	DEHAAS, COL. JOHN	PHILADELPHIA	WF. ELINOR. CH. JOHN PHILIP, JR., HENRIETTA
3/8/1787	PHILIP		(MRS. WILLIAM CRAIG)

(A CERTIFIED COPY FROM THE PHILADELPHIA COUNTY RECORDS)

2/16/1803	FOWLER, DAVID	BRIAR CREEK	WF. SARAH. CH. GILBERT, DAVID, ASAHEL, NATHAN,
10/11/1806			DEBORAH.
----------	MAURER, PETER	PENN	WF. CATHERINE. CH. JOHN, PETER, PHILIP, MRS.
10/20/1806			JACOB BILLMAN, AND PROBABLY OTHERS.
6/2/1806	STOTT, ALEXANDER	TURBOT	WF. SRAAH. CH. JOHN, JAMES, JANE, MARIA.
10/30/1806			
9/9/1806	CATHERMAN, DAVID	WEST BUFFALO	WF. BARBARA. CH. JACOB, GEORGE, BARBARA, KATE.
11/10/1806			
11/12/1806	MANN, SAMUEL	DERRY	WF. ELIZABETH. CH. ALLEN, WILLIAM, JANE,
12/15/1806			MARGARET CARNAHAN, ELIZABETH WATSON.
9/11/1806	GEARHART, JACOB	MIFFLIN	WF. MAGDALENE. CH. JACOB, JOHN, MAGDALENE,
12/18/1806			HERMAN, GEORGE, WILLIAM, CHARLES, ISAAC,
			BENJAMIN, ELIZABETH, MARY, CATHERINE. SONS-
			IN-LAW, JOHN PHYPHER, HARMAN DEHAVEN.
----------	STAHL, JACOB	TURBOT	WF. ANN. CH. JOHN, GEORGE, MARY, CATHERINE,
2/24/1807			JACOB, SUSAN, ANN ELIZABETH, MICHAEL, ISAAC,
			PETER, ABRAHAM, SARAH.
7/13/1803	BRENNER, FRANCIS	PENN	WF. MARY. CH. CATHERINE ELIZABETH (MRS. JOHN
2/25/1807	PETER		BERRY), JOHN, DANIEL, FRANCIS LUDWIG (DEAD,
			LEFT DAUGHTER, CATHERINE.)
12/9/1805	HOGE, REV. JOHN	TURBOT	WF. ROSANNA. CH. SAMUEL, EBENEZER, DAVID,
2/26/1807			JONATHAN, ELIZABETH BRICE, MARY REDICK (DEAD),
			PRISCILLA BENNETT, BROTHER, BENJAMIN. G'DAU.
			NANCY LEMON.
2/15/1807	YOUNG, ADAM	BUFFALO	A CHILD LIVING WITH TOBIAS SHECKLER.
3/2/1807			
3/28/1807	CARTER, MARY	SUNBURY	HEIRS: CHILDREN OF HER BROTHER, JAMES DONNELLY.
4/8/1807			
4/2/1807	BLAIN, THOMAS	TURBOT	WF. SARAH. CH. JAMES, JOHN, ELINOR, ELIZABETH,
4/20/1807			MARGARET, THOMAS, JANE (MRS. JAMES BLAIN), MARY,
			(MRS. ALEX. MURRAY), SARAH (MRS. ROB. MURRAY)

Dates	Name	Place	Details
1/26/1807 5/8/1807	WILT, GEORGE	WEST BUFFALO	WF. CATHERINE. CH. ELIZABETH, ADAM, GEORGE, MARY, BARBARA (WHO LEFT CATHERINE & ELIZ.)
1/26/1807 5/27/1807	KERLIN, THOMAS	AUGUSTA	WF. MOLLY. CH. WILLIAM, LETTICE, AND OTHERS, NOT NAMED.
3/27/1807 6/8/1907	NEWMAN, CONRAD	MAHANTANGO	WF. CATHERINE. CH. 3 SONS, NO NAMES GIVEN.
3/14/1806 6/10/1807	HARRIS, WILLIAM	GREENWOOD	WF. ELIZABETH. CH. MARY HILBURN, CATHERINE ROBINS, SARAH NICHOLS, EXPERIENCE ARMSTRONG, HANNAH LOVE, ELIZABETH HITTLE, WILLIAM.
5/15/1807 6/10/1807	CALDWELL, JOHN	MAHONING	WF. MARY. NO CHILDREN MENTIONED.
6/10/1807 7/3/1807	DONALDSON, JOHN (INNKEEPER)	DANVILLE	WF. JEMIMA. CH. SUKEY, BETSY, MARIA, HANNAH. FATHER AND MOTHER.
6/7/1807 7/4/1807	ARTER, JOHN, SR.	SHAMOKIN	WF. MARIA. CH. JOHN, ABRAHAM, PHILIP, WILLIAM, MARIA, ELIZABETH.
7/3/1807 8/9/1807	HAMILTON, THOMAS	NORTHUMBERLAND	WF. ELIZABETH. CH. ANN, BETSY, JEAN, SARAH, GEORGE, JOHN.
5/13/1807 8/19/1807	WILSON, JAMES	DERRY	WF. ANN, HEIRS; CH. OF BRO. WILLIAM, JAMES AND MARY ANN. AMY D/O JAMES JOHNSTON. SISTER'S CH. JOHN AND ANN STRAWBRIDGE.
12/24/1802 9/7/1807	WITMACAR, CONRAD (NORTHAMPTON CO.)	UPPER MILFORD	CH. DAVID, CONRAD, MAGDALENE (MRS. HENRY BORTZ), ANNA (MRS. ADAM BORTZ.)
5/30/1807 9/18/1807	BERGER, THOMAS	CATAWISSA	SISTERS; MARY EDWARDS, ELIZABETH CALENDENIN, REBECCA STRAHL. SIS.-IN-LAW, LYDIA BERGER. BROS. JOSEPH, SIMEON.
3/12/1807 10/1/1807	WILSON, NATHANIEL	CHILLISQUAQUE	CH. HUGH, AGNES, MARY McGUIGAN, RICHARD, ELINOR.
6/12/1807 10/7/1807	BURGET, GEORGE	MAHONING	CH. JOHN, HENRY, DANIEL, ELIZABETH, SAMUEL.
10/15/1806 11/21/1807	CREIGHTON, EDWARD	CHILLISQUAQUE	CH. EDWARD, JOHN, ROBERT, BARBARA, CATHERINE, JEAN (MRS. ROBERT SCOTT), ELIZABETH (MRS. EPHRAIM SCOTT.)
12/2/1802 11/20/1807	WORMLEY, ELIZABETH (CUMBERLAND CO.)	E. PENNSBORO	CH. GEORGE (WHO HAD ELIZABETH AND CATHERINE), ELIZABETH (MRS. GEO. LUTZ), MARY STEIGELMAN, WHO HAD ANNA MARIA, ELIZABET; CATHERINE AND SUSAN LUTZ).
11/28/1807 12/5/1807	GINGLES, JOHN	?	WF. SARAH. BROS. WILLIAM, ANDREW. WILLIAM MEHARD, JOSEPH MEHARD (WHO HAD MARY, JANET, AGNES). MARTHA GINGLES (WHO HAD ROBERT, JOHN, JAMES).
12/5/1807 12/25/1807	SHELLENBERGER, MARTIN, SR.	WASHINGTON	CH. JACOB, JOHN, MARTIN, EPHRAIM, SAMUEL, ISAAC, FANNY, DAVID, NANCY.
10/13/1807 2/29/1808	SANDERSON, EZEKIEL	MILTON	BROS. JAMES, WILLIAM (WHO HAD SON HENRY), SISTER, ELINOR.
2/20/1808 3/7/1808	HUMMEL, GEO. ADAM	CENTER	WF. MAGDALENE. CH. HENRY, JACOB, ELIZABETH, ANNA MARIA, CATHERINE, SUSAN, SOLOMON, BARBARA; MOLLIE, GEORGE; BENJAMIN, JOHN.
2/12/1808 4/15/1808	ERNE, ELIZABETH	EAST BUFFALO	CH. ELIZABETH (MRS. JACOB MOORE), ANNA MARIA, BARBARA, SUSAN CATHERINE. SON-IN-LAW, BERNHARD STICHSTER.
1/13/1808 4/18/1808	AURAND, JOHN, SR.	BUFFALO	CH. HENRY, REV. DIETRICK, PETER, GEORGE (DEAD), JACOB (DEAD), DANIEL, ELIZABETH (MRS. FRANCIS ZELLER). BY 2ND WIFE, JOHN, ABRAHAM, MARY (MRS. JOHN WOLF).
11/25/1807 4/22/1808	THOMPSON, WILLIAM	WHITE DEER	WF. JEAN. CH. JAMES, RUTH (WHO HAD A DAUGHTER, NANCY T. REZNOR).
5/9/1808 5/23/1808	DONALDSON, WM.	MAHONING	WF. ISABELLA. CH. JOHN, ALICE, ELIZABETH, JAMES, WILLIAM.
4/29/1808 5/26/1808	CHRIST, ADAM	BUFFALO	WF. ELIZABETH. CH. HENRY, ELIZABETH, EVE. AND 7 OTHERS, NOT NAMED. BRO-IN-LAW, ADAM FOLLMER. SON-IN-LAW, JOHN SNOOK.

4/13/1806 6/11/1808	AURAND, JOHN, JR.	BUFFALO	WF. CATHERINE. CH. UNNAMED. BROTHERS, HENRY, GEORGE.
7/24/1807 6/28/1808	FREDERICK1, CHARLES S.	MIFFLIN	WF. SARAH. CH. HENRY, SOLOMON, FERDINAND, JOSEPH.
2/12/1808 7/--/1808	MCCURLEY, JAMES	WASHINGTON	WF. MARGARET. CH. ROBERT, JOHN.
4/21/1808 8/17/1808	RICHARDS, ROBERT	GREENWOOD	WF. ELIZABETH. CH. WILLIAM, JOSEPH, MARGARET (MRS. JOHN PATTON), MARY (MRS. EPHRAIM LEWIS), HENRY, VINCENT, JOHN, EBENEZER.
4/5/1802 8/19/1808	MCMAHAN, JOHN	CHILLISQUAQUE	WF. NOT NAMED. CH. JAMES, BENJAMIN, THOMAS, WILLIAM, MARGARET, HANNAH, MARY. BROTHER-IN- LAW, THOMAS MURRAY.
5/1/1808 8/21/1808	DUNNING, SAMUEL	WHITE DEER	WF. CATHERINE. HEIRS; JOHN MCGILL MILLER, WILLIAM DIXON, CATHERINE MUCKLE, JOHN BLACKNEY (STEPSON).
9/2/1808 9/19/1808	DOUGHERTY, GEORGE	SHAMOKIN	WF. MARTHA. CH. ANTHONY, JANE (MRS. SIMON KIPP), BARBARA (MRS. DR. THOMAS BARRETT). G'CH. ANTH- ONY, CATHERINE, AND MARTHA BOONE.
10/19/1808 11/18/1808	WHITE, JOHN	HEMLOCK	WF. CATHERINE. CH. WILLIA, JOHN, SAMUEL, JACOB, SONS-IN-LAW, JOHN SMITH, DANIEL SCHULTZ, JOSEPH BRITTAIN, WILLIAM HADDEN, JOHN RODENBACH, WILLIAM JONES.
11/24/1808 1/4/1809	ESHBACH, WILLIAM	MIFFLIN	WF. PEGGY. MOTHER, CATHERINE. BROS. GEORGE (WHO HAD DAUGHTER, SUSAN), JOHN ADAM (WHO HAD A SON, ADAM),
8/29/1808 1/17/1809	BEAR, PETER, SR.	CATAWISSA	WF. AMELIA. CH. HENRY, PETER, CATHERINE (MRS. GEORGE PITNER).
---------- 2/6/1808	STAHL, JOHN	TURBOT	WF. ELIZABETH. CH. JOHN, GEORGE, PHILIP, SUSAN (MRS. HENRY FOLLMER), SUSAN (MRS. SOLOMON ESHBACH).
1/24/1809 2/18/1809	ROBINSON, ROBERT	TURBOT	CH. MARY (MRS. GEORGE PECK), AGNES NANCY, SARAH DOUGHERTY, ESTHER (MRS. MARTIN SMITH), MARGARET (MRS. GEORGE HAMMOND, DEAD, WHO HAD ----------, ELIZABETH & ROBERT HAMMOND).
12/9/1807 3/9/1809	CLARK, JOHN	WEST BUFFALO	CH. JANE (MRS. DAVID WATSON), JOSEPH (WHO HAD WILLIAM & JANE). HRS. JOHN RAMSEY, AND THE WIDOWS OF PHILIP FISHER, SAM LITTLE AND -------- MCMUTTRY.
2/25/1809 3/22/1809	WOMMER, ADAM	CATAWISSA	WF. JUSTINA. CH. NOT NAMED.
2/12/1809 4/3/1809	TROUTMAN, PETER	MAHANOY	WF. EVE. CH. EIGHT, NONE NAMED.
3/31/1808 4/25/1809	CUTTER, ROBERT	WASHINGTON	CH. ROBERT, MARY, WILLIAM.
2/18/1809 4/3/1809	DIETRICH, JOHN	BLOOM	CH. ELIAS, JAMES, FREDERICK, ANN MARGARET (MRS. HENRY KNORR), SARAH.
5/3/1805 6/30/1809	DAVIS, WILLIAM	TURBOT	WF. SUSAN. CH. HANNAH, ELIZABETH, WILLIAM, AZARIAH, JOHN, PHILIP, PRISCILLA, ELINOR.
1/7/1801 8/14/1809	CARSCADDON, JAMES	CHILLISQUAQUE	WF. LETTICE. CH. JOHN, JAMES, ANNIS, ISABEL, CATHERINE, MARY, HUGH, JANE.
7/25/1809 8/18/1809	LATHY, WM. K.	?	WF. MARY. HEIR, JUDSON MCEWEN.
7/20/1804 9/4/1809	DILDINE, HENRY	FISHING CREEK	CH. CATHERINE, MARY, JOHN, ELIZABETH (MRS. WM. CARTY), HARMON (DEAD), WHOSE WIDOW WAS MARG- ARET, ANDREW (DEAD).
4/15/1808 9/9/1809	RUSSELL, ROBERT	DERRY	WF. MARGARET. CH. JOHN, ANDREW, SAMUEL, MARG- ARET.
9/23/1809 10/9/1809	HUFFMAN, PETER	HEMLOCK	WF. ANNA. CH. WILLIAM, GEORGE, JACOB, (NON-CUPATIVE WILL)

7/19/1809 10/18/1809	FLICK, PETER	HEMLOCK	WF. ANNA MARIA. CH. JOHN, LUDWIG, ANTHONY, DANIEL, MARIA.
————— 10/19/1809	HUTCHINSON, MARY	WHITE DEER	CH. MARY, SARAH, CORNELIUS, ELIZABETH (MRS. JAMES CORNELIUS). G'CH. MARY HUTCHINSON, TOM H. STILWELL, TOM, H. CHAMBERLAIN, TOM H. CARSWELL, TOM H. CORNELIUS.
6/24/1807 11/13/1809	ECKHART, JACOB	MAHANTANGO	WF. CHRISTINA (WIDOW OF FRED DRUCKENMILLER). CH. JACOB, ROSINA MEISER, MARY MEISER, ELIZABETH MILLER, BARBARA EBERHARD, CHRISTINA LIVINGOOD.
7/8/1807 11/20/1809	REEDY, CONRAD	BUFFALO	WF. NOT NAMED. CH. JACOB, ANDREW, AND OTHERS, NOT NAMED.
10/20/1809 11/21/1809	RANK, ADAM	WHITE DEER	WF. CATHERINE. CH. RACHEL, MARY, DANIEL, NOAH, ADAM. BRO. JOHN (WHO HAD A SON, JOHN).
8/13/1807 11/27/1809	SWINEFORD, ALBRIGHT	CENTER	WF. MARGARET. CH. JOHN, GEORGE MICHAEL, PETER, JACOB, CATHERINE (MRS. JOHN CUMMINGS). G'SON. SAMUEL, S/O PETER.
10/—/1809 1/29/1810	EMMETT, JOHN	HEMLOCK	CH. JOHN, JR. (WHOSE CHILDREN WERE, ALEXANDER, MARY, JAMES, ELIZABETH, MARGARET, JOHN, SAMUEL, WILLIAM.
————— 2/26/1810	MCDONALD, JOHN	?	WF. SARAH. CH. NANCY, JEAN, HANNAH, JOHN.
12/13/1809 2/26/1810	HENDERSHOT, MICHAEL	DERRY	WF. SARAH. CH. JOHN, WILLIAM, JESSE, ISAAC, SARAH JOHNSON, MARGARET JOHNSON, CATHERINE DILDINE, MARY WELLIVER, PHEBE EVELAND.
2/16/1810 4/23/1810	LATSHA, JOHN	UPPER MAHANOY	WF. CHATARINA. CH. JOHN, HENRY, FREDERICK, DANIEL, CHATARINA, MAGDALENE, ANN ELIZABETH.
8/21/1809 4/12/1810	SMITH, JOHN	TURBOT	WF. CASSANDRA. CH. SAMUEL J., GRACE S. BROTHER, ENOCH.
2/20/1810 4/17/1810	RUSSELL, ANDREW	TURBOT	WF. ISABELLA. CH. PATRICK K., SAMUEL, JOHN, ANDREW, MARY, MARGARET (MRS. HUGH HARRISON).
7/13/1809 4/19/1810	RICHART, WILLIAM	DERRY	WF. NOT NAMED. CH. JOHN, SAMUEL, MARY, ANN, PATSY, WILLIAM, JAMES, ROBERT.
4/12/1804 4/24/1810	CHILD, JOHN	?	WF. MARY. CH. ANDREW, JOHN, JAMES, ESTHER, NANCY, MARY, RACHEL, MARGARET, ELIZABETH.
3/18/1806 4/28/1810	FRICK, PHILIP	NORTHUMBERLAND	WF. MARGARET. CH. CATHERINE (MRS. ROBERT MONTGOMERY, WHO HAD JOHN, DAVID, CATHERINE, MARGARET, SARAH, CHRISTINA), BROTHER, FREDERICK, HEIR; JASON CHAPEL.
3/5/1810 6/8/1810	HASSINGER, JOHN	CENTER	WF. CATHERINE. CH. A NUMBER OF MINORS, NO NAMES GIVEN, BROTHER, GEORGE.
5/1/1810 6/21/1810	CLARK, JOHN	WHITE DEER	BROS. ROBERT, GEORGE, CHARLES (WHO HAD POLLY, JAMES, CHARLES). SISTERS; ELINOR FRUIT, MARGARET DONNELLY, NANCY FINNEY.
8/10/1805 9/24/1810	REICHENBACH, JOHN, JR.	MAHANTANGO	WF. MARY. CH. JOHN, MARY BOYER. BROTHER, JACOB.
6/27/1810 10/10/1810	MCCALLA, JOHN	POINT	CH. SARAH PATTERSON, MARGARET (MRS. DAVID TAGGART) WILLIAM, TAMER, ELIZABETH HUBLEY, RUTH WELKER, MARTHA, JOHN, NANCY, SUSAN.
5/13/1808 11/1/1810	WOLVERTON, CHARLES	SHAMOKIN	WF. MARY. CH. DENNIS, ROGER, JOHN, RACHEL (MRS. CLEMENT BONSELL), MARY (MRS. PHINEAS HULL), OSEA (MRS. SAMUEL FRY), ELIZABETH (MRS. AMOS HIXON), ISAAC, SARAH, CHARLES. G'SON. PASMESY (MRS. ANNIAS SAXTON).
————— 11/30/1810	OAKES, SAMUEL	WASHINGTON	WF. NOT NAMED. CH. JOSEPH, CHRISTIANA BAILEY, SUSAN, SAMUEL. HEIR, WILLIAM SCHOOLEY.
12/18/1809 1/24/1811	DEWART, WILLIAM, JR.	WEST BUFFALO	WF. NOT NAMED. CH. WILLIAM, JANE, D/O JANE CAMPBELL, BROTHER, LEWIS.
11/6/1809 2/9/1811	DICKSON, JOHN	DERRY	WF. AGNES. CH. ALEXANDER, WILLIAM, AGNES, MORRIS

35

3/2/1811	KESTER, PAUL	DERRY	WF. ANN. CH. RACHEL EVES, BENJAMIN, MARY WOOF, ARNOLD, JOSEPH, SUSAN, ANN.
1/15/1811 3/28/1911	GLASS, JOHN (S/O GEORGE)	PENN	WF. CHRISTINA. CH. MARGARET, JACOB.
2/28/1811 4/13/1811	FRICK, JOHN	SUNBURY	WF. ELIZABETH. CH. GEORGE A., CHARLES, JAMES, CATHERINE, BENJAMIN, JACOB, WILLIAM, HENRY, FRED, JOHN, REBECCA (MRS. JOS. B. NORBURY).
3/25/1811 4/15/1811	HOLSTEIN, GEORGE	SELINSGROVE	WF. MARIA. CH. A NUMBER OF MINORS, NO NAMES GIVEN.
1/12/1809 4/20/1811	RHOADS, CAPT. FRAN-CIS, WILLIAM	SELINSGROVE	WF. HANNAH. CH. FRANCIS, DANIEL, PETER, JACOB, HENRY (DEAD), SUSAN (MRS. GEORGE RHOADS), MARY MAGDALENE (MRS. JOHN GEORGE FISHER). MRS. HENRY MAWHORTER (DEAD, WHO LEFT HANNAH, JOHN, ELIZABETH, SARAH, MARY, HETTY).
4/15/1811 5/14/1811	ARHOGAST, JOHN	PENN	WF. CATHERINE. CH. NICHOLAS, PETER, JOHN, LUDWIG, WILLIAM, CATHERINE (MRS. CHRISTOPHER SHATZBERGER), ANNA MARIA (MRS. JACOB FELMLY), BARBARA (MRS. JOHN ZWALLY).
3/1/1811 0/13/1811	SPRINGER, CONRAD	DERRY	WF. MAGDALENE. CH. JOSEPH, JOHN, SUSAN (MRS. JACOB FARNER), MOLLY (MRS. CHRISTIAN MEHLER), JACOB, ELIZABETH (MRS. PHILIP LONG), CATHERINE, SARAH.
8/3/1811 8/13/1811	SHAW. WILLIAM	TURBOT	WF. ELIZABETH. CH. AGNES (MRS. DAVID MONTGOMERY) MARGARET, MARY (MRS. WILLIAM DAVIS, WHO HAD SON WM. SHAW DAVIS). BROTHER, JAMES (WHO HAD SON WM. SHAW).
3/1/1811 8/23/1811	BOONE, SAMUEL	BLOOM	CH. JAMES, SAMUEL, BENJAMIN, SUSAN, RACHEL. G'DAU. PEGGY MCCLURE, D/O JOSIAH MCCLURE.
6/5/1803 9/11/1811	JOHN, GRIFFITH	SHAMOKIN	CH. REBECCA DAVIES (HAD SON, GRIFFITH JOHN DAVIES), HANNAH, PHILIP (HAD SON, GRIFFITH JOHN), RACHEL BRENHOLTZ, GRACE DAVIES, MARY BENNETT, LEAH MATIS.
6/12/1811 9/16/1811	AIGLER, JOHN JACOB	BEAVER	WF. CHRISTINA. CH. SIMON, JACOB, JOHN SOPHIA, CHRISTINA, ELIZABETH.
10/29/1804 9/26/1811	MACLAY, HON. SAMUEL (U. S. SENATOR)	BUFFALO	WF. ELIZABETH. CH. WILLIAM P., CHARLES, JOHN, ESTHER, JANE, SAMUEL, DAVID, ROBERT.
9/16/1810 10/1/1811	MILLER, ELIZABETH	SUNBURY	CH. HENRY, JACOB, CHRISTINA (MRS. JONAS WEAVER), MARY, ELIZABETH, D/O JACOB FRUTZ.
2/21/1811 11/20/1811	BELLAS, GEORGE	BLOOM	WF. ELIZABETH. CH. NANCY, MURLIN, SARAH, SAM-UEL, JAMES, THOMAS, HUGH, ELIZABETH.
4/16/1811 11/20/1811	EVANS, JOSEPH	BUFFALO	WF. CATHERINE. CH. MARGARET, WILLIAM.
4/13/1810 12/16/1811	GALLAHER, ELIZABETH	MILTON	CH. REBECCA (MRS. NATHAN PATTON), SALLY BENNETT, BETSY TIETSWORTH, THOMAS, WILLIAM. SISTER BETSY.
8/30/1811	MOCKELHENNY, THOS.	?	SISTER, BETSY.
1/21/1812	WOODROW, SIMON	MAHANTANGO	G'CH. REBECCA, REUBEN, AND SARAH FOUTZ, NEPHEW, JOHN WOODROW. HEIR, HANNAH COGAN.
2/6/1810 3/10/1812	STEFFEN, JOHN	MAHANTANGO	WF. ELIZABETH SHADLE, D/O HENRY. CH. DAVID, MARIA, SUSAN.
7/23/1810 3/13/1812	FELKER, JOHN HENRY	MIDDLEBURG	CH. CATHERINE, MARY (MRS. HENRY TITTLE). DAU.-IN-LAW, ELIZABETH. G'CH. HENRY & JOHN.
6/--/1808 8/18/1812	STEEL, JOHN	WHITE DEER	WF. MARY. CH. RICHARD, ALEXANDER, MARGARET, JEAN, MARY, CATHERINE, WILLIAM (HAD MARGARET).
8/19/1811 4/14/1812	FULLER, FREDERICK	WASHINGTON	WF. SUSAN. CH. DANIEL, RACHEL, SUSAN (MRS. JOSEPH MACKEY).
4/3/1812 4/14/1812	FOLLMER, FREDERICK	?	CH. NOT NAMED. BROTHERS, ADAM, HENRY.
3/--/1812 4/15/1812	DIMM, JACOB	TURBOT	WF. NOT NAMED. CH. HENRY, JOHN AND A DAUGHTER. BROTHERS, PHILIP, SIMON, PETER.

8/10/1811 4/22/1812	SHUMAN, RUDOLPH	CATAWISSA	CH. JACOB, JOHN (DEAD).
4/14/1812 4/30/1812	SWINEFORD, GEORGE MICHAEL	CENTER	2ND WF. SUSAN. CH. POLLY (MRS. HENRY SMITH), ELIZABETH (MRS. JOHN BACHMAN), JOHN, GEORGE, ISRAEL, PHILIP, CATHERINE, MARGARET, ————,
4/5/1812 4/30/1812	HUGHES, JOHN	CATAWISSA	WF. ELINOR. HEIR, JOSEPH, S/O SAMUEL NEW.
5/4/1812 5/11/1812	KRITZ, SIMON	MIFFLIN	DAUGHTER, JULIA.
5/18/1812 6/3/1812	NYHART, JACOB	EASY BUFFALO	WF. MARY SOPHIA. CH. NOT NAMED. FATHER, DAVID.
1/14/1812 6/10/1812	NUNGESSER, GEORGE	MIFFLIN	WF. CATHERINE. CH. JONATHAN, GEORGE, MARTIN, MAGDALENE, JOHN, SON-IN-LAW, MARTIN DONAUT.
12/23/1807 6/16/1812	SECHLER, JACOB	MAHONING	BROS. ABE (HAD SON, ABE), JOSEPH (HAD SON, JACOB), JOHN (HAD SON, JACOB), AND DAUGHTERS OF JOSEPH.
6/28/1806 6/18/1812	STEANS, CATHERINE	BUFFALO	CH. ANN (MRS. JOHN WAPLE, OR MAPLE), JOHN, ELIZABETH (MRS. SAMUEL HAIL), SARAH (MRS. JOHN CARTNEY). G'SON. THOMAS WAPLE.
———— 6/22/1812	SHELLENBERGER,	MIFFLIN	WF. MAGDALENE. CH. ELIZABETH, WILLIAM, JACOB, POLLY, HANNAH, SARAH.
5/25/1811 7/7/1812	CONRAD, JACOB	?	CH. NICHOLAS, JACOB, PETER, HENRY, JOHN, MARY, (MRS. DAVID MALICK), ELIZABETH (MRS. JACOB HENBROOK), SUSAN (MRS. GEORGE HALL), CATHERINE (MRS. GEORGE LONG).
4/24/1811 8/6/1812	KRAMER, GEORGE	EAST BUFFALO	WF. SOPHIA. CH. MATHIAS, HARMON, CHRISTIANA ALBERTSON, MORRIS, CHARLES, GEORGE, WILLIAM, ABRAHAM, ELIZABETH, JOSEPH, SAMUEL.
9/4/1812	MCCLINTOCK, SAMUEL	NORTHUMBERLAND	WF. HANNAH. CH. JEAN, ANDREW, JAMES.
8/18/1806 0/21/1812	WALTER, JOHN	TULPEHOCKEN (BERKS CO.)	WF. MARGARET. CH. BENJAMIN, WILLIAM, MAGDALENE, GEORGE, JONATHAN.
6/2/1812 9/14/1812	TREMBLEY, JOHN	BLOOM	CH. HENRY M., JACOB H., JOSEPH, MARY, PHEBE, MATILDA, SARAH, HANNAH, PEGGY.
8/11/1812 9/18/1812	FITMAN, PHILIP	GREENWOOD	WF. MARY. CH. BALTHIS, JOHN, ELISHA.
9/25/1812 10/20/1812	HILTEBRAND, LEVI	W. BUFFALO	WF. MARY. CH. NO NAMES GIVEN.
——— 1812 11/2/1812	WALLIS, LYDIA	TURBOT	CH. HENRY, SAMUEL, CASSANDRA SMITH, MARY (MRS. HUGH BRADY).
———— 11/19/1812	BICKHAM (BICKMAN), GEORGE	PHILADELPHIA	CH. ANNA (MRS. LEWIS NEIL), CHRISTIANA FINNEY, SUSAN, STEPCH. JACOB & MARY REESE. HEIRS, JAMES WHITEHILL, ALEXANDER HENRY.
4/23/1812 11/17/1812	REZNOR, DAVID	WHITE DEER	WF. JEAN. CH. ISABELLA.
4/23/1812 12/19/1812	BRIGGS, JOHN, SR.	MIFFLIN	WF. SARAH. CH. JOHN WILLIAM.
12/25/1812 12/29/1812	SMITH, PETER	SUNBURY	REFORMED CHURCH OF SUNBURY, ½ OF ESTATE. LUTHERAN CHURCH OF SUNBURY, ½ OF ESTATE.
1/4/1813 1/19/1813	NOWLAN, MICHAEL	TURBOT	WF. UNNAMED. CH. ANDREW, WILLIAM, THOMAS, JOHN, JAMES, DAVID, ELIZABETH.
3/25/1811 1/21/1813	HUTCHINSON, MARGARET	DERRY	CH. JOSEPH, JOHN (WHOSE WIFE WAS ANN), ELDER, MARY, SARAH, JANE, FLORENCE, MARGARET.
1/26/1813 2/1/1813	ERWIN, SAMUEL	MAHONING	CH. FRANCIS, SUSAN, JANE, ANN.
11/13/1806 2/9/1813	CASE, PETER	BETHEL TWP., HUNTERDON CO. NEW JERSEY.	WF. CATHERINE, CH. WILLIAM, DANIEL, PETER, JOHN, CHARITY, CATHERINE, ELIZABETH, ABIGAIL, SARAH, SUSAN, MARGARET, JACOB.
1/17/1813 2/13/1813	DURHAM, JAMES	CHILLISQUAQUE	WF. MARGARET, CH. JAMES, WILLIAM, MARY, WILSON, MARGARET, NANCY, JAMES.

1/5/1813 2/24/1813	ROBERTSON, WM.	?	CH. ISABELLA, JANE, JAMES, WILLIAM, MARY, SAMUEL.
---------- 2/15/1813	GASKINS, THOMAS	POINT	WF. ELIZABETH. CH. JOHN, JONATHAN, THOMAS, ELINOR, MARY, RACHEL, BETSY.
10/31/1812 2/16/1813	HARTMAN, THOMAS	FISHING CREEK	WF. ANNA MARY. CH. JOHN, FRED, VALENTINE, SUSAN, CATHERINE, ELIZABETH, ANNA MARY, GEORGE, MARY.
2/10/1813 2/25/1813	WILSON, JOHN	TURBOT	1ST WIFE., JANE. 2ND WIFE, MARGARET. HEIRS; BRO. JOSEPH, WHO HAD JOHN & MARY. NEPH. WM. HUTCHINSON, S/O JOSEPH. JANE WELCH.
2/11/1813 3/1/1813	COLE, WILLIAM, SR.	CHILLISQUAQUE	CH. ABASLON, POLLY, JOHN, LUIGI, THOMAS, JACOB, SAMSON, WILLIAM.
2/8/1813 3/8/1813	CLARK, GEORGE (NON-CUP. WILL)	DERRY	WF. MARY. FATHER, WILLIAM.
8/15/1811 3/8/1813	ECKENROT, CHRISTOPHER	CHILLISQUAQUE	WF. MARGARET. CH. PETER, JOHN, ELIZABETH MILLER.
4/20/1812 3/9/1813	SEEBOLD, CHRISTOPHER	BUFFALO	CH. MARGARET (MRS. ANDREW WAGNER, WHO HAD CATHERINE & WILLIAM), STELLA (MRS. MICHAEL GREENHO, WHO HAD SON, JACOB), JOHN, AND OTHERS.
2/28/1813 3/15/1813	MEARS, SANUEL	CATAWISSA	WF. MARY. CH. SARAH (MRS. MICHAEL HUGHES), NANCY FLEMING, MARY PANCOAST, MARTHA MEARS, ELIZABETH (MRS. CHARLES ENT), ALEXANDER, SAMUEL.
2/25/1813 3/20/1813	MASSER, JOHN	UPPER MAHANOY	WF. MARGARET. CH. SARAH, MARGARET, POLLY, FERDINAND, JOHN, JACOB.
11/11/1812 3/29/1813	GIRTON, WILLIAM	DERRY	WF. LENA. CH. ESAU, JACOB, MARSHALL, GEORGE, JOHN, WILLIAM, STEPHEN, PETER, MARGARET, RACHEL, HANNAH.
2/12/1813 3/20/1813	GEARHART, JACOB	SHAMOKIN	WF. CATHERINE. CH. ELIZABETH DEPUY, JACOB, HARMON, JOHN, TUNIS, GEORGE, MARY GULIXK, WILLIAM, CHARLES, CATHERINE MOORE.
5/29/1809 3/31/1813	GUIGER, MICHAEL	CATAWISSA	CH. DANIEL, CONRAD, ELIZABETH (MRS. GEORGE PFRONG, OR PRONG).
4/3/1813 4/9/1813	BARTHOLOMEW, JOHN	AUGUSTA	WF. CATHERINE. CH. JOHN, ELIZABETH, CHARLES, JACOB, SARAH, PETER, LEAH, DAN, BENJAMIN.
12/22/1801 4/15/1813	KESTER, PETER	GREENWOOD	WF. ELINOR. HEIRS; PETER WEBSTER, PETER PALMER.
4/1/1813 4/16/1813	EGBERT, NICHOLAS	EAST BUFFALO	WF. LYDIA. HAD MINOR CHILDREN, NOT NAMED.
4/8/1813 4/19/1813	BIGGS, JOHN	BLOOM	WF. ELIZABETH. CH. RICHARD, ELIAS, PETER, GEORGE.
4/5/1813 4/19/1813	HARLAN, THOMAS	PENN	WF. NOT NAMED. CH. ISAAC, SARAH W. (MRS. SOLOMON FISHER), AND OTHERS, NOT NAMED.
4/4/1813 4/26/1813	CONNER, JOSEPH	GREENWOOD	WF. CATHERINE, BRO. WILLIAM (WHO HAD SONS, CHARLES & JOSEPH.
11/14/1812 4/27/1813	LIKENS, JOSEPH	DERRY	HEIRS; JAMES JOHNSON, SARAH HESLET JOHNSON, WM. HESLET, SR., DERRY PRESBYTERIAN CHURCH.
3/2/1813 4/28/1813	ALBRIGHT, JACOB, JR.	BEAVER	WF. MARY. CH. NONE MENTIONED. BROS., PETER & CHRISTOPHER. COUSIN, MARY ALBRIGHT.
4/19/1810 5/1/1813	SMITH, ELIZABETH	SUNBURY	1ST HUSBAND, NICHOLAS UNGERMAN, LATE OF 4TH PA. REGT. NICHOLAS UNGERMAN, JR. 2ND HUS. PETER SMITH
4/22/1813 5/3/1813	ZIMMERMAN, JOHN	HARTLEY	CH. LEVI, JOSEPH, HANNAH COVERLY, RACHEL.
2/4/1813 5/12/1813	SMITH, JOHN	LEWISBURG	HEIRS: FANNY BILLMEYER. COUSINS; JONAS, ADAM, MICHAEL SMITH.

END OF NORTHUMBERLAND COUNTY WILLS.

WILLS OF UNION COUNTY, PENNSYLVANIA.
(1813-1818)

UNION COUNTY WAS FORMED FROM PART OF NORTHUMBERLAND COUNTY IN 1813. IN 1855, SNYDER COUNTY FORMED FROM THE SOUTHERN HALF OF UNION COUNTY.

8/24/1813 9/8/1813	MOYER, GEORGE	PENN	WF. MARY. CH. GEORGE, ELIZABETH (MRS. FREDERICK RICHTER), BARBARA (MRS. JACOB HAINS), JULIA, SUSAN, MARY, MARGARET, CHRISTINA, LYDIA, DAVID.
9/28/1813 11/6/1813	WEISER, CHRISTOPHER, JR.	BUFFALO	MOTHER, BARBARA. BROS., GEORGE, DAVID, DANIEL. SISTER, ELIZABETH.
---------- 3/8/1814	OTT, J. GEORGE	PENN	CH. DANIEL, BARBARA (MRS. JOS. FEEHRER), SUSAN (MRS. MICHAEL BEAVER, SR.), CATHERINE (MRS. JACOB JARRETT), FREDERICK, HANNAH (MRS. JOHN LEYMAN), ELIZABETH (MRS. JOHN STEININGER), MARIA (MRS. PETER DREESE).
---------- 3/16/1814	READING, DAVID	CENTER	HAD WIFE AND CHILDREN, NO NAMES GIVEN.
1/31/1814 3/17/1814	IRWIN, RICHARD	WHITE DEER	WF. ANNA. CH. RICHARD, JOSEPH, SAMUEL, JOHN, JAMES, NENIAN.
---------- 4/14/1814	BROWN, CHRISTIAN (POTTER)	WEST BUFFALO	WF. CATHERINE. CH. NO NAMES GIVEN.
---------- 6/3/1814	RINE, HENRY	MAHANTANGO	WF. CHRISTINA. CH. JOHN, MARGARET NEIMAN, ANN ELIZABETH SHETTERLY, CHRISTINA COLEMAN, BARBARA COLEMAN (HAD SON, HENRY), CATHERINE (MRS. PETER LAMBERT), CHRISTINA (MRS. FREDERICK MEISER).
---------- 10/13/1814	SCHNEPP, HENRY (NOW KNEPP)	CENTER	WF. CATHERINE. CH. JOHN, HENRY (M. IDA COTSHALL) CATHERINE, CHRISTINA, ELIZABETH.
6/--/1814 10/18/1814	LAUGHLIN, ADAM	HARTLEY	WF. ESTHER (DEAD). HAL-SISTER, MARGARET (MRS. JAMES TWADDLE) SISTERS, JANE, NANCY, MARY. BROTHER, ANDREW.
6/2/1814 10/18/1814	BAKER, WENDELL	BUFFALO	CH. JOHN, JACOB, ELIZABETH, CATHERINE, ESTHER, CHRISTINA (DEAD, LEAVING ABRAHAM ROCKEY). GCH. JOHN, JACOB, SOLOMON, WILLIAM, GEORGE ALSPACH. JOHN & ANN MIXENER.
7/28/1814 8/31/1814	RENFREW, JACOB	BUFFALO	WF. CATHERINE. CH. ALEXANDER. BROS., ROBERT & JAMES. SISTER, AGNES SHAW.
8/22/1814 10/22/1814	STRUBLE, ADAM	BUFFALO	WF. MARY. CH. NO NAMES GIVE. BRO., CONRAD.
8/31/1813 12/19/1814	LYTLE, ELEANOR	WASHINGTON	CH. JOHN, HANNAH, MARY, SARAH, JEAN. BY FORMER MARRIAGE, WM. BROWN, SARAH SMITH. GDAU., ANNA HAMMOND.
---------- 1/6/1815	MENGES, J. ADAM	PENN	CH. GEORGE, JOHN, PETER, MARGARET (MRS. CHRISTIAN KANTZ), JACOB, MARY ELIZABETH, CATHERINE (MRS. MICH. MILLER), MARY (MRS. REV. J. P. SHINDEL, SR.
---------- 2/9/1815	HAINES, JOHN (HENZ)	MAHANTANGO	WF. REGINA SCHUSTER. CH. GEORGE, LAWRENCE, FRED, PETER, JACOB (M. BARBARA MOYER, D/O GEO.), MARGARET (MRS. PETER FREED), ANNA MARY (MRS. PETER STROUP), CATHERINE (MRS. HENRY HEIMBACH), ELIZABETH (MRS. JOHN SMITH,) CHRISTINA (MRS. HENRY MERTZ).
2/16/1815 2/22/1815	HASLETT, JANE	WHITE DEER	DAU., ELIZABETH RAMSEY. SON, JAMES (WHO HAD MARY P., WM. H., ALICIA). SON-IN-LAW TOM HOOD.
---------- 5/6/1815	MOYER, MICHAEL	CENTER	WF. BARBARA, D/O JACOB KRICK, SR.). SISTER, SUSAN (MRS. HENRY MOYER). SERVANT, BARBARA FISHER. B/LAW, JACOB KRICK, JR. COUSIN, JACOB MOYER, TANNER, BEAVER TOWNSHIP.
4/26/1815 5/26/1815	STERN, JACOB	NEW BERLIN	WF. CATHERINE. CH. LEWIS, WALTINA, AMELIA, CATHERINE.

-------- 5/27/1815	GRUBB, JACOB	CENTER	WF. ELIZABETH. CH. JOHN, HENRY, SUSAN, JACOB, ELIZABETH, CATHERINE.
-------- 7/14/1815	ALBRIGHT, MICHAEL	MAHANTANGO	WF. CATHERINE. CH. EMANUEL, ELIZABETH.
-------- 7/29/1815	LEPLEY, JACOB	CENTER	WF. CATHERINE, CH. JACOB, HENRY, ANTHONY, MARGARET KERN, MICHAEL, JOHN, CATHERINE KERN, ELIZABETH, ADAM, CHRISTIAN, MARY.
-------- 9/1/1815	KERSTETTER, MARTIN	BEAVER	WF. ELIZABETH. CH. TOBIAS (EAST BUFFALO TWP), 3 OTHER SONS, 6 DAUGHTERS, NOT NAMED.
-------- 9/4/1815	BROWN, JOHN	CENTER	SON-IN-LAW, JOHN GEORGE ENGLE.
-------- 9/5/1815	HENDRICKS, JOHN	CENTER	WF. CATHERINE GOTTSHALL. CH. PETER, SAMUEL, JOHN, CATHERINE, ANNA, BARBARA, JACOB, ANDREW, ABRAHAM, ELIZABETH (MRS. JACOB KESSLER), MARIA (MRS. JOSEPH DUCK).
-------- 9/18/1815	ROSE, ADAM	WEST BUFFALO	BRO., LEWIS EIKY. SISTERS, CATHERINE (MRS. JACOB STAHL), SARAH (MRS. GEORGE KUHNS).
8/6/1815 10/3/1815	TRUTT, ANDREW	?	WF. HANNAH. CH. PHILIP.
-------- 10/28/1815	BOYER, SAMUEL	CENTER	CH. GEORGE, SON OF LAST WIFE.
-------- 10/--/1815	LECHNER, JACOB	PENN	WF. MARY, S/O GOV. SIMON SNYDER. CH. WILLIAM M., DR. HENRY A.
10/24/1815 11/25/1815	NEVIUS, CHRISTIAN	WHITE DEER	WF. LUCRETIA. CH. WILLIAM, JOHN, ANNA, RALPH, AARON (AND PROBABLY OTHERS).
9/1/1813 12/6/1815	GRAY, WILLIAM	WHITE DEER	CH. SALLY, MARY DUNLAP, SUSAN (MRS. ANDREW FORSTER), JANE (MRS. SAM HUTCHINSON), ELEANOR (MRS. JOHN ROBINSON), MARGARET (MRS. JOHN HAYES), NANCY (MRS. HUDSON WILLIAMS, WHOSE CHILDREN WERE, MOLLY, WILLIAM, LEWIS, HUDSON, NANCY), JANE (MRS. WM. WALLACE, HER CHILDREN, JOSEPH, JAMES, NANCY, SALLY, ISABEL.).
2/18/1816 2/29/1816	MOYER, JULIANA (D/O GEO. SR.)	FREEBURG	HEIRS; MARIA D/O CHRISTOPHER MEYER. DR. CHAS. BEYER. BROS. & SISTERS, BARBARA HAINES, ELIZABETH, SUSAN, GEORGE, MARY, REBECCA, CHRISTINA, LYDIA, DAVID.
1/16/1816 4/30/1816	BOWER, PHILIP	WEST BUFFALO	WF. BARBARA. CH. MARGARET, FELIX, JOHN.
3/20/1815 6/10/1816	DUNKEL, WILLIAM	BUFFALO	CH. JACOB, PETER, JOHN, GEORGE, ELIZABETH, ROSINA MAGDALENE, EVA CATHERINE.
-------- 7/22/1816	SHAFFER, ANDREW	PENN	WF. CATHERINE. CH. JOHN, CATHERINE (MRS. THOMAS BICKEL).
----1816	YODER, JACOB (BACHELOR)	CENTER	NEPHEWS; JACOB, MELCHOIR, JOHN YODER.
-------- 8/21/1816	GERHART, JACOB	BEAVER	WF. MOLLY. CH. JOHN, OTHERS NOT NAMED.
12/22/1815 10/4/1816	YOUNG, CHRISTIAN	WEST BUFFALO	WF. NO NAME GIVE. NO CHILDREN MENTIONED.
-------- 10/11/1816	HAFFLICH, JACOB	PERRY	WF. MARGARET. CH. PHILIP (M. HANNAH----), JOHN, CHRISTINA (MRS. GEO. HEIMBACH), JACOB (M. ELIZ. ZELLER), BARBARA (MRS. PETER EAGLER), ANNA MARIA (MRS. FRED ROUSH), CATHERINE (MRS. DANIEL RIBLETT), ELIZABETH PEGGY (MRS. PETER SWARTZ).
9/8/1816 10/12/1816	WEISER, DANIEL (S/O CHRISTOPHER)	EAST BUFFALO	MOTHER, BARBARA.
11/6/1815 10/31/1816	SHAFFER, HENRY	WEST "	WF. ANNA MARIA. CH. WILLIAM, JACOB, JOSEPH, SUSAN, CATHERINE.
1/2/1808 12/18/1816	ROCKEY, WILLIAM	" "	WF. MARGARET. CH. GEORGE, WILLIAM, ELIZABETH, MARY, CATHERINE. SON-IN-LAW, HENRY ROUSH.

---------- 12/18/1816	ALBRIGHT, FREDERICK	MAHANTANGO	CH. ELIZABETH (MRS. FRANCIS LUDWIG BRENNER, WHO HAD A DAUGHTER, CATHERINE HELWIG), SUSANNA (MRS. ADAM STAHL).
---------- 2/4/1817	BARNSTEIN, JOHN	PERRY	WF. ELIZABETH. NO CHILDREN MENTIONED.
4/21/1817 5/6/1817	HOFFMAN, GEORGE	WHITE DEER	WF. CATHERINE. CH. MICHAEL, POLLY, JOHN, MARY, SALLY, JACOB.
---------- 5/8/1817	MORR, MARY	PENN	CH. SARAH. SON-IN-LAW, PHILIP G. MORR.
---------- ----1817	MAWHORTER, HENRY (S/O THOMAS)	*	LEFT WIFE AND SEVERAL CHILDREN, DID NOT NAME THEM.
3/18/1812 6/27/1817	ZELLER, PETER	WEST BUFFALO	CH. JOHN, ADAM, HENRY, CATHERINE SHOUDER, ELIZABETH BARTGES (WHO HAD HENRY & SARAH), ANDREW (YOUNGEST SON).
12/10/1809 5/30/1817	IRWIN, RICHARD (SEE 3/17/1814)	WHITE DEER	WF. ANN. CH. RICHARD, JOSEPH, SAMUEL, JOHN, JAMES, NENIAN, ELIZABETH, ROBERT.
---------- 7/5/1817	PUFF, PHILIP	MAHANTANGO	WF. MARY. CH. JOHN, CATHERINE, SUSAN, MARY (MRS. CASPER ARNOLD, JR.), ELIZABETH, ANN.
12/19/1815 7/21/1817	SPYKER, HENRY	LEWISBURG	WF. MARY. CH. PETER, DANIEL, HENRY, JONATHAN, MARGARET, LYDIA, CATHERINE.
11/3/1814 8/30/1817	CHAMBERLIN, COL. WILLIAM	WHITE DEER	4TH WIFE, ANNA MARY. CH. AARON, JOHN, LEWIS, JOSEPH, JAMES, MOSES, NELLY (MRS. JOHN LASHE), ANNA (MRS. JOHN BASS), LUCRETIA (MRS. CHRISTIAN NEVIUS), SARAH, MARY, ELIZABETH (MRS. WILLIAM MCCREARY) GCH. ABRAHAM, JOHN, ELIZABETH, WILLIAM, AND LEWIS LASHE.
11/4/1817 3/10/1818	WOLF, PETER	BUFFALO	WF. ELIZABETH. CH. MOLLY (YOUNGEST), LEONARD & OTHERS, NOT NAMED.
12/21/1817 4/10/1818	WEIDER, CHRIST- OPHER, SR.	EAST BUFFALO	CH. GEORGE, DAVID, ELIZABETH, MARGARET.

END OF UNION COUNTY WILLS

DATE	THE DECEASED	TOWN OR TOWNSHIP	LETTERS TO	SURETIES FOR ADMINISTRATOR
5/21/1813	DRUCKENMILLER, PETER	MAHANTANGO	HENRY RAMSTEIN	JACOB ECKERT, JOHN STEESE
5/--/1813	SHATZBERGER, CHRISTOPHER	"	NICHOLAS ARBOGAST	PETER ARBOGAST, M. RATHFON
6/10/1813	KEEN, GEORGE	"	DANIEL WOMER & GEO. SHETTERLY	CASPER GELNET, FREDERICK GOGIN.
7/20/1813	MILLER, LEWIS	"	ADAM LIGHT	FRED WENDT, GEORGE GAMBY
8/7/1813	SHRADER, HENRY	"	GEO. SHENEBERGER	PAUL KUSTER, JOS. PAWLING
9/18/1813	FORRY, CHRISTIAN	"	JAMES L. FORRY	DAN WOMER, WILLIS GORDON
10/5/1813	BERRY, JOHN	PENN	ELIZABETH BERRY & PETER HACKENBERG	JOHN ROUGH, AND. GOTTSHALL
11/5/1813	REYNOLDS, BENJ.	BUFFALO	DANIEL SECHLER	JACOB MEASE
11/11/1813	SNYDER, DANIEL	"	BALTZER SNYDER & ADAM WILT	DAN WINTER, PETER DAUBERMAN
11/18/1813	SMITH, GIDEON WILSON	WHITE DEER	WM. & JOHN SMITH	GIDEON SMITH, ROBT. BARBER
1/27/1814	TREON, JACOB (TRIAN)	PENN	DAN PENNEBACKER & PETER HACKENBERG	PETER & HENRY GARMAN
3/8/1814	SULTZ, PETER (SHULTZ?)	CENTER	FRED WISE	GEO. FREDERICK, JACOB BEIDLER
3/17/1814	MCLAUGHLIN, HUGH	WHITE DEER	THOMAS WILSON & JOHN BOAL	WM. & JAMES WILSON
4/7/1814	BERGER, CONRAD	WEST BUFFALO	MARY BERGER & GEORGE MITCHELL	CHRIST. SEEBOLD, HEN. SANDERS
4/13/1814	CAMERON, CHARLES	BUFFALO	MARTHA CAMERON	GEORGE KNOX
4/19/1814	BISHOP, JACOB	CENTER	CATHERINE BISHOP & DAVID OVERMIRE	JOHN BISHOP, JOHN STITZER
5/8/1814	SHOWER, ADAM, SR.	MAHANTANGO	ADAM SHOWER, JR.	HENRY GARMAN, GEO. SHETTERLY
6/14/1814	EAGLER, WILLIAM	"	JOHN GRAYBILL, JR.	PHILIP WIRT, CHRIST. GRABILL
7/2/1814	ADAMS, SARAH	WHITE DEER	JAMES MARSHALL	LAZARUS FINNEY
7/11/1814	BARGH, JOHN, JR.	MAHANTANGO	JOHN BARGHE, SR.	MICH. STOCK, JACOB HOFFMAN
7/13/1814	MEYER, ELIZABETH	HARTLEY	VALENTINE MEYER	DANIEL MEYER, HENRY ROYER
8/30/1814	WOLF, JACOB	BUFFALO	CATH. WOLF & ABRAHAM AURAND	JOHN DREISBACH, CHRISTOPHER WAGNER
9/9/1814	FREDERICK, GEORGE	"	JOHN THOMPSON	GEO. YOUNGMAN, JACOB KRATZER
11/15/1814	LONG, JACOB	SELINSGROVE	ABRAHAM HOCH	CONRAD PRICE, DAN BASTIAN
11/24/1814	FERTICH, ADAM	CENTER	ELIZABETH FERTICH	JOHN SOWER, NICHOLAS BAUSE
1/4/1815	MORTON, JAFFETT	BUFFALO	ALEXANDER MORTON	P. HIMMELREICH, URIAH SILSBY
1/21/1815	KLINE, ABRAHAM	"	DANIEL KILNE	GEO. ENGLEHART, J. KAUFFMAN
2/17/1815	AUMILLER, JOHN	PENN	JOHN & GEORGE AUMILLER	ISAAC MERTZ, JOHN COURTNEY
3/20/1815	DARROUGH, JOHN	WHITE DEER	WILLIAM KELLY	WILLIAM ROBINSON
4/17/1815	FETTER, JACOB	PENN	ADAM & PHILIP FETTER	CONRAD WALTER, YOST WAGNER
5/16/1815	MIDDLESWORTH, JOHN	BEAVER	CHRISTOPHER WISE	JOHN WEISER, JOHN MIDDLESWORTH.
5/25/1815	BARGIE, ANDREW (BERGY)	MAHANTANGO	ANDREW SHAFFER	HENRY PFILE, CHRISTIAN GRAYBILL
5/28/1815	SHAMBACH, GEO.	CENTER	REV. JOHN SHAMBACH FREDERICK WISE	PHILIP WALTER, JOHN RENNINGER.
7/10/1815	FRIENDLY, JOHN	BUFFALO	ELIZABETH FRIEDLY	DANIEL NYHART, JOHN BROWN
10/13/1815	SCHMELCHER, JACOB (SMELTZER?)	CENTER	JOHN BOWER	JAS. K. DAVIS, J. STILLWELL
10/24	TROXEL, JOHN	BEAVER	HENRY AURAND & JOHN TROXEL	FREDERICK BINGAMAN, JOHN MOYER

12/15/1815	BOLICH, GEORGE (BOLIG)	CENTER	CHRISTINA BOLICH	NICHOLAS BAUSE, CONRAD SWARTZLANDER
2/12/1816	SNOOK, WILLIAM	HARTLEY	HENRY GOSS	HERY SWARTZ, JACOB HOUSER
3/15/1816	COOK, JAMES	"	AND. & JOS. COOK	JOHN MAUCK, ALEX. MCCORD
3/12/1816	KEPHART, JOHN PHILIP	BUFFALO	JACOB MOSSER	JOHN R——, JOHN HAYES
4/23/1816	MILLER, GEORGE	UNION	MAGDALENE & SOLOMON MILLER	JOHN DREISBACH, CONRAD PHILLIPS
5/13/1816	THORNTON, JOHN (REV. SOLDIER)	MAHANTANGO	MAGDALENE WITKER THORNTON	JOHN THORNTON, JACOB KEISER
5/15/1816	ROBB, WILLIAM	WHITE DEER	JAMES ROBB	WM. JOHNSON, SAMUEL SHAW
6/8/1816	CORNELIUS, WM.	?	JAMES CORNELIUS	J. M. ANDERSON, ISAAC TAYLOR
6/22/1816	SMITH, MELSHOIR	HARTLEY	LEONARD & MELCHOIR SMITH	JAC. SNYDER, LEVI ZIMMERMAN
8/10/1816	HEHN, CONRAD (WF. ELIZABETH)	PENN	JOHN HEHN & JACOB LONG	PHILIP GEMBERLING, JACOB HUMMEL
5/8/1817	GUNDY, BENJAMIN	HARTLEY	ADAM WILT	JOHN HUBER
——1817	DUNKEL, JACOB	BUFFALO	JOHN & CONRAD DUNKEL	JOHN REEDY, JOHN RINGLER
6/4/1817	BERGER, BARBARA	CENTER	ANDREW BERGER OF DERRY TWP., COLUMBIA CO., PA.	WILLIAM KESSLER
5/10/1817	YOUNGMAN, ELIAS	W. BUFFALO	HENRY YEARICK	JACOB MAIZE, GEORGE ROUSH
6/28/1817	STEEL, DAVID	UNION	DAVID & WILLIAM STEEL	JOHN MCPHERSON, ANDREW STEEL
9/2/1817	PHILIPS, CONRAD	UNION	GEORGE PHILIPS	ADAM SHOWER, ABE ALTER
10/25/1817	GLASS, EVE (WID. OF GEO.)	PENN	GEORGE & CHRISTIAN GLASS (SONS)	DANIEL PENNEPACKER, JOHN MOYER
12/24/1817	YOUNGMAN, ELIAS	W. BUFFALO	GEORGE YOUNGMAN & JOHN DREISBACH	JOHN HUMMEL, WILLIAM BETZ
1/5/1818	MORTON, EDWARD	?	ALEX. MORTON	URIAH SILSBY, URIAH INMAN
2/16/1818	CATHERINE, DAVID	W. BUFFALO	CATHERINE & FRED CATHERMAN	BANJAMIN CATHERMAN, DANIEL SPEIGLEMIRE
3/24/1818	SNOOK, PETER	BEAVER	JOHN & PETER SNOOK	JOHN REGAR, LEONARD MANBECK
4/23/1818	PONTIUS, ELIZABETH	BUFFALO	DAVID & GEORGE WEISER	WM. KESSLER, GEORGE BOGAR
4/23/1818	HAGGERTY, JOHN	MAHANTANGO	JOHN GARMAN, JR.	JACOB KEISER, PHIL. BURKHART
6/22/1818	GRUMBACH, GEORGE H.	?	CASPER GELNET	DAN WOMER, GEO SHETTERLY
8/26/1818	MENGES, JOHN	WASHINGTON	JACOB MENGES	DAN KLOSE, CHRISTIAN KANTZ
8/29/1818	KREITZNER, FRED.	CHAPMAN	MICHAEL RATHFON	VALENTINE HAAS, ADAM LIGHT
12/15/1818	FETTER, ELIZABETH (NEE SNYDER)	PENN	PETER FETTER	WILLIAM KESSLER, GEORGE LAUDENSLAGER
12/15/1818	SWINEFORD, JOHN	CENTER	GEORGE SNYDER	JAC. FRYER, PHILIP HASSINGER
12/24/1818	MARTIN, JOHN	MAHANTANGO	DAN. PENNEPACKER	PETER & HENRY GARMAN

END OF UNION COUNTY LETTERS OF ADMINISTRATION

MIFFLIN COUNTY WAS FORMED FROM THE NORTHERN PART OF CUMBERLAND COUNTY IN 1789. PERRY AND JUNIATA COUNTIES WERE LATER FORMED FROM THE SOUTHERN PART OF MIFFLIN COUNTY. THE COUNTY SEAT OF MIFFLIN COUNTY IS LEWISTOWN, PA. NOTE: FIRST DATE, IS DATE OF WILL, SECOND DATE, IS DATE ON WHICH IT WAS PROBATED.

DATES	NAME OF DECEASED	TOWNSHIP	NAMES OF HEIRS.
5/1/1783 12/11/1789	MONTOOTH, WILLIAM	MILFORD	WF, MARY. CH, A DAUGHTER, NOT NAMED. BROTHER, DAVID (WHO HAD MARY, AGNES, ISABEL, ELIZABETH).
11/20/1789 12/12/1789	O'HARRA, CHARLES	MILFORD	HIS PARTNER, WILLIAM MCKINNEY, AND REV. JAMES JOHNSTON OF ARMAGH TOWNSHIP.
9/1/1789 12/12/1789	BROWN, ALEXANDER	ARMAGH	WF, JEAN. CH, MARY, ROSANNA, ELIZABETH, MOTHER MARY.
10/24/1789 12/15/1789	POTTER, JAMES	POTTER	CH, JAMES, AND OTHERS, NOT NAMED.
8/7/1777 12/19/1789	BOWER, JOHN	FERMANAUGH	UNCLE, JOHN KEAVER. JOHN COY, SR., JOHN COY, JR.
12/10/1789 3/9/1790	SIGLER, GEORGE (REV. SOLDIER)	DERRY	WF, ELIZABETH. CH, JOHN, GEORGE, HENRY, JACOB, ADAM, SAMUEL, ELIZABETH. (SAMUEL WAS BORN 1774).
9/5/1789 4/6/1790	COLLINS, JOHN	LACK	WF, CATHERINE. CH, BRUCE, MARGARET (MRS. JOHN MCCUER, OR MCCLUER).
6/5/1790 6/14/1790	MITCHELL, DAVID	WAYNE	WF, SARAH. CH, JOHN, THOMAS, DAVID, MARY, MARGARET, SARAH.
3/9/1789 10/18/1790	HUNTER, CHARLES	MILFORD	CH, ROBERT, MARY, SARAH, MARK, JOHN, JOSEPH, CHARLES. SON-IN-LAW, NATHANIEL HAMLIN.
11/28/1791 1/14/1792	CAMERON, DUNCAN	ARMAGH	WF, CATHERINE. CH, ALEXANDER, JOHN, HUGH, CATHERINE.
1/18/1792 2/4/1792	BUCHANNAN, ARTHUR, JR.	?	WF, ISABELLA. CH, JOHN, WILLIAM, AND AN UNNAMED DAUGHTER.
6/24/1792 7/2/1792	STARK, ZEPHNIAH	DERRY	WF, NANCY. CH, ZEPHNIAH, JR., EXPERIENCE, NANCY, MARY, MARTHA, ROBERT, EBENEZER.
10/20/1792 11/12/1792	DICK, MARY	GREENWOOD	CH, ROBERT, ANNA ALLISON (WHO HAD ELIZABETH), AND JOSEPH CASTLE, GRANDSON.).
8/11/1792 11/20/1792	GLASGOW, JOHN	DERRY	WF, MARGARET. CH, JAMES, AGNES ANDERSON, MARY ANDERSON, ELIZA PARSHALL, MARY, ISABEL, SARAH, JANE.
5/10/1791 2/11/1793	MARTIN, HUGH	ARMAGH	WF, MARGARET. CH, MARGARET CHAMBERS, ALEXANDER, WILLIAM.
1/21/1793 2/28/1793	WELLS, BENJAMIN	FERMANAUGH	WF, JANE. CH, BENJAMIN, JAMES, ELIZABETH FORSYTH.
5/28/1792 3/20/1793	CAMPBELL, HERCULES	DERRY	WF, JEAN. CH, MATTHEW, MARY, MARGARET, JEAN, ROBERT, SARAH.
12/29/1792 3/25/1793	BROTHERTON, ROBERT	UNION	WF, JANE. CH, MARY (MRS. JOHN REED), JANE (MRS. THOMAS DOUGHERTY), MARGARET.

END OF MIFFLIN COUNTY WILLS

DATE	THE DECEASED	LETTERS TO	SURETIES FOR ADMINISTRATOR
1818			
5/19	DELVIN, WILLIAM	RICH. & JAS. DEVLIN	JOHN THOMPSON, BEN WALKER
8/11	HART, JOHN	ADAM BOWERS	WM. PATTERSON, JACOB BROWN
1825			
9/28	RIDDLE, WILLIAM	PETER & WM. RIDDLE	JONATHAN AYERS, JOHN HASTINGS
12/28	BREWER, HENRY	PETER BREWER	" " HENRY VAN HORN
1826			
1/31	CLAWSON, RICHARD	RICHARD CLAWSON	ALEX. LYON, JOHN THOMPSON
3/31	CRISSMAN, GEORGE	PETER CRISSMAN	HENRY LOTT, WILLIAM MCAMSH
4/7	KISSINGER, MICHAEL	ELIZ. KISSINGER	JAMES ELIOTT, JAMES TAYLOR
4/13	BEAL, PETER	FANNY BEAL	JOHN BELL, ARCHIBALD HADDON
5/31	DOUGLASS, SAMUEL, JR.	WOODROE DOUGLASS	WILLIAM DOUGLASS, TOM SHARP
6/15	LOGAN, ELIZABETH	JOHN LOGAN	JOHN LUCAS, JAMES DONNELLY
1827			
7/29	PATTERSON, THOMAS	JANE PATTERSON	ARCH. MATTHEWS, ROBERT NIXON
12/15	LEANY, HUGH	DANIEL LEANY	DAVID FERGUSON, D. JUNKINSON
12/24	HALL, WILLIAM	TOM & SAM. HALL	WILLIAM & JOHN LUCAS
12/25	DAVIS, JANE	JOHN DAVIS	JAMES HUNTER, JOHN THOMPSON
1828			
3/24	POWERS, ALEXANDER	SARAH & JOHN LUCAS	JOHN WATSON, ANDREW BARRIETT
5/8	LEWIS, JOSHUA	ISAAC LEWIS	JOHN MABON, ROBERT HAMILTON
5/28	HADDEN, BARTHOLOMEW	JAMES HADDEN	WM. HADDEN, SAMUEL TRIMBLE
5/29	STUCHELL, JACOB	WM. & JOHN STUCHELL	WM. DOUGLASS, JONATHAN JONES
8/1	THOMPSON, JONATHAN	TOM & JOS. THOMPSON	JAS. ARMSTRONG, WM. CALDWELL
8/16	MCNEIL, ROSANNA	ALEX. PATTISON	ABE LOWMAN, ANDREW UNCAPHER
8/21	ADAIR, DR. JAMES	REV. BLANY ADAIR	JONATHAN AGEY, ISAC. RICHARDS
12/23	ALLEN, THOMAS	JOHN ALLEN	DAVID PRICE, JOHN BUCHANAN
12/28	PEARCE, JOSHUA	MARTHA PEARCE	NATHL. SIMPSON, JOHN MABON
12/29	CLAWSON, ROSS	AMOS LAWRENCE	S. DAVIS, SAMUEL CLAWSON
1829			
2/7	CROSSMAN, ASA	WILLIAM CROSSMAN	WM. SEBRING, PHILIP YOUNGBLOOD
2/9	CAMPBELL, JAMES	CHRISTOPHER CAMPBELL	SAMUEL DEVLIN
2/23	GREGG, EZEKIEL	SAMUEL MARK	SIMON MARK, JOHN GREGG
3/21	LOWERY, JAMES	SAMUEL LOWRY	JOSEPH WHITE, JAMES TODD
6/24	BISHOP, JESSE	ELIZABETH BISHOP	DAVID BISHOP, E. P. EVERSON
7/29	MCCRADY, JOHN	HUGH WILEY	DAVID LINTNER, JOS. LOUGHRY
8/9	COWEN, MARGARET	DAVID JENKINSON	JAS. MCGUIRE, JOSHUA MCCRACKEN
8/7	MCKEE, ELIZABETH	JOHN JOHNSTON	AND. DICKSON, JAMES GORDON
8/19	SKELLY, PATRICK	DANIEL O'NEIL	HENRY KINTER, WILLIAM CALDWELL
8/25	CESSNA, CHARLES	SAM. H. HENDRICKSON	GEORGE REPINE, JOHN THOMPSON
9/22	DENNISTON, JOHN (ESQ.)	JAMES MCCAHAN	JOHN PATTON, WILLIAM LUCAS
10/9	JONES, WILLIAM M.	JANE C. JONES	AARON DEVINNEY, JOHN CUNNINGHAM
11/10	TINDALL, CHARLES R.	NATHANIEL TINDALL	JAMES CLADWELL, JOHN HOOVER
12/21	MCCOMB, JAMES	JOSEPH HENDERSON	DANIEL STANARD, JAMES MCCAHAN
1830			
1/1	LEWIS, DAVID	MARTHA LEWIS	JOHN & EVAN LEWIS
2/18	KERR, THOMAS	PETER JACOBY	HENRY SHOUP, ADAM ANSBAUGH
4/2	DUNN, JAMES	ELIZABETH DUNN	ROBERT SMITH, BENJAMIN ORR
4/12	SANDERSON, THOMAS	MATH. D. SANDERSON	JOHN TAYLOR, JAMES STEWART
5/5	BISHOP, DAVID K.	RICHARD B. MCCABE	W. P. STERRET, THOMAS JOHNSTON
5/21	MEALEMAN, ADAM (MEALMAN)	EDWARD CARLTON	WM. HART, SAMUEL TEMPLETON
6/29	BARTLE, LOTT	J. LUSAC, M. KNAP	FRED HETRICK, WALTER TEMPLETON
9/11	CANTWELL, JAMES	SUBAN CANTWELL	WILLIAM & THOMAS BROWN
10/4	JOHNSTON, ROBERT	JOHN JOHNSTON	JAMES GORDON, FRANCIS GOMPERS
10/18	BROWN, ANDREW	JAMES G. BROWN	WILLIAM BROWN, MACK GRIER
11/4	IRWIN, ELIPHALET	MARGARET IRWIN	JAMES & SAMUEL MARSHALL

DATE	THE DECEASED	LETTERS TO	SURETIES FOR THE ADMINISTRATOR
1831			
1/22	LEARD, ZACHARIAH	WILLIAM LEARD	JAMES M. STEWART, JOHN -------
3/29	CRAWFORD, MOSES	JOHN EWING	HENRY KINTER, ASA CROSSMAN
3/30	EMERSON, ELIZABETH	EWDARD P. EMERSON	JOHN JOHNSON, JOHN GILPIN
4/1	WAKEFIELD, JOHN	DAVID WAKEFIELD	JOHN HAROLD, ARMOUR PHILLIPS
4/23	MOORHEAD, FERGUS	JAMES MOORHEAD	JOSEPH THOMPSON, MCLANAHAN, JR.
5/17	DOUGHERTY, THOMAS	JACOB EBEY	JOHN DOUGHTERY, JOHN SHIELDS
1832			
1/7	SLOAN, SAMUEL	HENRY BUTLER	ELISHA WILKINSON, JAS. THOMPSON,
1/17	GALBRAITH, ROBERT	JOSEPH SMITH	WILLIAM & DAVID DAVIS
1/19	DAVIS, JOHN	GEORGE S. LOWMAN	TOM LOWMAN, ELLIOTT FERGUSON
4/14	CRAVEN, THOMAS	NATHANIEL CRAVEN	HUGH COLGEN, ABRAHAM LYDICK
4/23	GRUMBLING, GEORGE	JOHN GRUMBLING	JOHN & DANIEL OVERDORF
5/7	TROWBRIDGE, BENJ. H.	HENRY BEECHER	JOHN BEECHER, SIMON TRUBY
6/4	SINCLAIR, HUGH	JAMES SINCLAIR	ARCHIBALD SINCLAIR, SAM COLTER
6/15	MCGUIRE, JAMES	NEHEMIAH MCGUIRE	TOM BROWN, THOMAS LINDSAY
12/7	MARSHALL, ARCHIBALD	JAMES NOWRY	ROBERT NIXON, JOHN JOHNSON
12/8	PATTERSON, ALEXANDER	ALEX. PATTERSON	JOS. PATTERSON, ROBERT WHITBY
1833			
1/3	HOPKINS, JOHN	ALEX. MCLAM	ALEXANDER GETTY, JOHN JOHNSON
2/12	ALLISON, ROBERT	ROBT. T. ALLISON	JOHN ALLISON, ALEX. MCMILLEN
3/25	WALKER, ALEXANDER	ROBT. M. WALKER	JAMES THOMPSON
6/3	CRIBBS, DAVID (WF. CATH.)	ROBERT MCCREA	GEORGE CRIBBS, GEORGE CRIBBS, JR.
8/5	HOFF, VORIS	ELIZABETH HOFF	DAVID MAHON, SAMUEL RUSSELL
8/20	MCMULLEN, ENOS (WF. CATH.)	JOHN MCMULLEN (SON)	DANIEL BARR, JOHN SHORT
8/30	O'HARA, THOMAS	DAVID FERGUSON	JAMES MCGUIRE, JAMES TAYLOR
10/9	WILEY, ROBERT	WM. LOUGHRY	DAVID LINTNER, C. B. CAMPBELL
11/26	DAVIS, WILLIAM	ARCHIBALD DAVIS	CHRISTINA DAVIS (WIFE)
1834			
2/3	DAVIS, SIMON	PHILIP ARTHUR	WILLIAM ARTHUR, JAMES DONNELLY
2/5	HICE, HENRY	HENRY & MARY A. HICE	HENRY TAYLOR, THOMAS DICKIE
2/10	STEERE, JOS. (WF. ELINOR)	EVA STEERE	RICHARD SMITH, WILLIAM SEBRING
2/17	HOBACHER, PETER	JACOB HOBACHER	ALEXANDER REED, JOHN MCADOO
3/27	KEELY, HENRY (WF. MARY)	HENRY GROFF	THOS. JOHNSON, THOS. MCFARLAND
6/13	PATTERSON, JOHN	JOSEPH PATTERSON	JOHN ELDER, ROBERT WHITBY
8/21	WILLIAMS, JOHN	JAMES TAYLOR	WILLIAM TAYLOR, JAMES DONNELLY
11/1	STEWART, SARAH	MICHAEL STEWART	JOHN TRIMBLE, ABRAHAM STUCHELL
11/25	MCLANAHAN, JAMES	FERGUS CANNON	ROBT. MCLANAHAN, JAS. THOMPSON
12/3	MCPHERSON, MARY	JOSEPH MCPHERSON	JOHN HASTINGS, ROBERT WARDEN
12/15	FAIR, HENRY	WILLIAM LAWSON	WILLIAM FAIR, WILLIAM BARR
1835			
3/6	RUGH, CHRISTOPHER	MICHAEL RUGH	JAMES ALLISON, ROBT. HAMILTON
3/13	PURNELL, WILLIAM	JAMES KIRKPATRICK	WILLIAM COLEMAN, JAMES ELDER
4/3	FERGUSON, CHARLES	JOHN WATERSON	JOHN THOMPSON, THOS. DONNELLY
4/4	THOMPSON, JOHN	WILLIAM THOMPSON	RICHARD & SAMUEL CLAWSON
10/15	KILLEN, ANN CLARK	CHARLES KILLEN	WILLIAM LAWSON, JAMES ELLIOTT
10/22	CRIBBS, JACOB	JAMES GORDON	MARY CATHERINE & GEORGE CRIBBS
11/2	MCCRACKEN, JOSHUA	" "	JAS. ALLISON, JAMES MCLANAHAN
11/2	ALTMAN, MARGARET	JACOB ALTMAN, JR.	JACOB ALTMAN, SR., DAN STANARD
12/17	MOORHEAD, SAMUEL	JOS. MOORHEAD (BRO.)	JOHN THOMPSON, ROBERT NIXON
1836			
2/12	SHOOK, MARTIN	JAMES HILL	EDMUND BURK, THOMAS STOPHIEL
3/28	MABON, JOHN	MARGARET MABON	JAMES MABON, WILLIAM LIGHT
4/4	FLEMING, SARAH M.	PATTISON FLEMING	ARCHIBALD WEIR, GERGUS CANNON
5/2	RANKIN, MATTHEW	ADAM JOHNSTON	WILLIAM BANKS, CHARLES MCLAIN
5/2	NUGENT, ARTHUR	THOMAS NUGENT	JOHN JAMISON, MICHAEL STUMP
5/4	MCKNIGHT SUSAN	JOHN CUMMINS (BOR.)	JAMES LAPSLY, JAMES MCCOMB
6/3	DEARMIN, WILLIAM	JACOB DEARMIN	JOHN CRESSWELL, STEPHEN ADAMS

1836

Date	Name		
8/11	SCHMUCK, JACOB	JACOB SCHMUCK	WILLIAM MCCREA, WILLIAM DAVIS
9/9	JOHNSTON, TOM (S/O JOHN)	STEWART STEEL	SAMUEL STEEL, ROBERT NIXON
9/29	MOORHEAD, JOS., JR.	JOHN THOMPSON	MEEK KELLY, JAMES SUTTON
10/24	HENDERSON, REV. J. W.	THOMAS LAUGHLIN	WILLIAM HOUSTON, WILLIAM HENRY

1837

Date	Name		
1/3	CRAIG, MATTHEW	AMOS B. DAVIS	WILLIAM MCCLARREN, J. MCMASTERS
1/18	DIAS, THOMAS	RICHARD DIAS	JOHN & THOMAS DIAS
2/27	SHARETTS, REV. N. G.	FERGUS CANNON	JOSEPH & JAMES THOMPSON
2/27	GEARY, JAMES	NATHANIEL GEARY	ALEX. TEMPLETON, DAVID BLACK
2/27	DOUGHERTY, JAMES	JOHN DOUGHERTY	CHRISTOPHER LYDICK, ISAAC O'NEIL
4/29	WALKER, SARAH	FERGUS CANNON	JAMES MCKENAN, FRANCIS GOMPERS
5/4	ELDER, ROBERT	JOHN THOMPSON, JR.	JOHN THOMPSON, FERGUS CANNON
5/26	THOMPSON, JAMES, JR.	?	" " JONATHAN AYERS
6/13	MCFARLAND, THOMAS	R. B. MCCABE	STEWART DAVIS, EPHRAIM CARPENTER
6/16	FAIRMAN, JAMES	ROBT. FAIRMAN (BRO.)	JOHN & FRANCIS FAIRMAN
6/17	FINLEY, JAMES	GEORGE FINLEY	JAMES TAYLOR, ROBERT MITCHELL
7/1	RICH, PHILIP P.	ALLEN N. WORK	HENRY KINTER, WILLIAM TAYLOR
7/11	GEER, DWIGHT	AMOS B. DAVIS	JOSEPH MASTERS, JOHN BARBER
10/11	ALLISON, ANDREW, JR.	JOHN B. ALLISON	ROBERT HAMILTON, ROBERT ALLISON
10/11	" JAMES	" " "	" " " "
10/11	" WILLIAM H.	" " "	" " " "
10/21	VIRTUE, GEORGE	SCOTT MARSHALL	JOHN MAGER, JAMES KEIR
11/22	MCGARA, SAMUEL	JOHN MCGARA	MOSES MARK, CAMPBELL BOTHEL
12/27	VIRTUE, MARGERY	SCOTT MARSHALL	SAMUEL JOHNSON, SAMUEL ADAMS

1838

Date	Name		
2/16	HAZLETT, JOHN	LISLY HAZLETT	MATHIAS MILLER, JAMES HAZLETT
3/3	BRICKER, PETER	ADAM MIKESELL (S/LAW)	SUSANNA BRICKER, WIDOW
3/7	MCKELVY, JOSEPH	SAMUEL WALLACE	SARAH MCKELVY (WID.), S. MCCARTNEY
3/30	WELLS, ANN	PETER WELLS (SON)	EDWARD & JAMES WELLS (SONS)
4/23	RUMMEL, JOHN	PETER RUMMELL	ABRAHAM PEARCE, JACOB ROOF
5/21	WOLF, JOHN	SUSANA WOLF (WID)	HENRY BOUCHER, JOHN STUCHALL
5/29	ADAMS, ROBERT	GAWIN ADAMS, JR.	GAWIN ADAMS, SR., GEORGE MEYERS
6/6	KELLY, ARCHIBALD	ELIZABETH KELLY	WILLIAM CLARK, DAVID RALSTON
8/18	PATTON, JOHN	CHARLOTTE PATTON	" BANKS, JAMES MCKENNAN
8/1	DENNISTON, JOHN	JAMES MCKENNAN	JAMES & JOHN SUTTON
8/23	HAZLETT, SARAH	JAMES HAZLETT	LETTY HAZLETT, JAMES NIXON
9/26	LEECH, ARCHIBALD	WILLIAM WALKER	SAMUEL JAMISON, EDWARD CARLTON
10/22	MCCOY, JOHN	DANIEL MCPHERSON	DANEIL STANARD, WILLIAM B. CLARK
10/24	THOMPSON, JAMES	JAMES EWING	JOSEPH LOUGHRY, WILLIAM EVANS
11/5	BELL, HUGH	JOSEPH DICKSON	CHAS. B. CAMPBELL, GILLIS DOTY
11/19	CURRY, JAMES	" CURRY	JAMES CLARK, WILLIAM B. CLARK
12/6	EBY, JACOB	JAS. B. MORRISON	MAIZE MORRISON, ROBT. CRAWFORD
12/13	HOLLER, ISAAC	STEWART DAVIS	THOMAS BOYLE, RICHARD MCCABE

1839

Date	Name		
2/14	OLLIGER, NICHOLAS	JOHN OLLIGER	DANIEL OVERDORF, JOSEPH MATZ
3/11	ALLISON, ANDREW	JOHN R. ALLISON	JAMES MCKENNAN, JOS. THOMPSON
3/12	WAKEFIELD, JAMES K.	WILLIAM CLARKE	WILLIAM RANKIN, DR. JAS. STEWART
5/2	PATTISON, ALEXANDER	JOHN PATTISON	" PATTISON, WILLIAM EWING
5/11	REES, ELIZABETH	MORGAN R. BANKS	HENRY ALTMAN, JAS. MCLAUGHLIN
5/20	KELLAR, CHRISTIAN, SR.	CHRIST & GEO. KELLAR	JOHN BOWERS, THOMAS REES
6/10	KNEE, HENRY	JOHN LYTLE	ROBERT GIBSON, JAMES TAYLOR
----	MCLEAN, ALEXANDER	ANN MCLEAN (SISTER)	ADAM THOMPSON, WM. MCFARLAND
6/22	DICK, MARGARET	SIMON DICK	JOHN DICK, SAMUEL GREEN
7/1	BLACK, JAMES	WM. & DAVID BLACK	WILLIAM HOUSTON, JOHN WORK
9/3	JOHNSTON, JAMES P.	STEWART DAVIS	RICHARD MCCABE, GEORGE W. HICE
9/16	RODGERS, JAMES	JOHN C. HEMPHILL	JAMES KEIR, WM. B. CLARK
9/25	CONNER, GEORGE	ANN CONNER	" LYDICK, HETH F. CAMP
12/4	THOMPSON, ARCHIBALD	JAS. CUNNINGHAM	FERGUS CANNON, JAMES SUTTON
12/9	TINKUM, DANIEL	JOHN M. BARBER	JONATHAN AYERS, JAMES TAYLOR
12/25	LAMAR, WILLIAM	WILLIAM BARKER	WILLIAM HART, ALEXANDER WHITE

47

Date	Name		
2/4	TRAVIS, WILLIAM	TOM & JAS. TRAVIS	HEZEKIAH CRISSMAN, PETER STITLER
2/5	HERRON, WILLIAM	JAMES HERRON	PHIL. HENDRICKSON, JOHN MCNUTT
3/26	LOWRY, JOSEPH	JOSEPH LOWRY	ROBERT DOUGHIT, ALEX. GEORGE
4/21	SIMPSON, THOMAS	JAMES SIMPSON	WILLIAM & JAMES TAYLOR
4/--	ORR, JAMES	ROBERT ORR	ROBERT ORR, JR. WILLIAM ORR
6/2	FAIRBANKS, DAVID	JAMES WORK	ROBERT CRAIG, WILLIAM CARSON
6/5	O'DONALD, PATRICK	SAMUEL STEEL	GEORGE GREER, STEWART STEEL
6/25	KELLY, JOHN	WILLIAM HART	JAMES KEIR, JAMES R. DOUGHERTY
8/11	HEATER, BARBARA	HENRY KINTER	PETER KINTER, ROBERT CRAIG
8/12	SAMPLE, JOHN	JAMES SAMPLE	DAVID RALSTON, WM. B. CLARK
9/5	DOUGHERTY, NANCY	CATHERINE BUCHANAN	WILLIAM KINTER, HUGH DOUGHERTY
9/9	ADAIR, BLEANY	JOHN & JON. ADAIR	" HOUSTON, JOHN B. ALISOR
10/30	DUNCAN, SAMUEL	JOHN DUNCAN	JAMES TAYLOR, WOODROE DOUGLASS
11/25	DAVIS, ALEXANDER	JOHN DAVIS	JOS. MCMASTERS, FERGUS CANNON
12/8	MCNUTT, ALEXANDER	DAVID ANTHONY & JOSEPH HARBISON	WILLIAM ANTHONY, WILLIAM EWING
12/17	GORMAN, DAVID	JOHN GORMAN	JOSEPH STEWART, MOSES C. MARK
12/28	MCQUISTON, WILLIAM	WILLIAM LOUGHRY	PETER MULVIHILL, EDW. SHOEMAKER

Date	Name		
1/2	MORGAN, GEORGE W.	THOMAS BOYLE	JOHN PETERS, WILLIAM MCCARREN, JR.
2/19	HARKINS, JOHN	WILLIAM HARKINS	WILLIAM ROSS, DANIEL MCGUIRE
2/22	HERRON, HANNAH	JAMES HERRON	" MCNUTT, WILLIAM GLASS
2/27	OBER, CATHERINE (NEE SHAFFER)	JACOB OBER	JOHN OBER, JOHN YINGLING
3/24	CRAMER, JOHN	DANIEL CRAMER	SAMUEL GOLDEN, JOHN DICK
3/31	STINEMAN, CHRISTOPHER	JOHN MARTIN	JOS. MCMASTERS, WILLIAM LOWMAN
4/20	CLARK, MARY	WILLIAM BRACKIN	GEORGE MCCARTNEY, JOHN BRACKIN
4/28	PROUT, WILLIAM	F. CAMP	ABRAHAM WALLER, WM. THOMPSON
4/28	BEAL, BENJAMIN F.	THOMAS BOYLE	RICH. B. MCCABE, PHILIP RICE
5/22	DOUGHERTY, RACHEL (NEE ABEY)	JAMES B. MORRISON	WILLIAM TRIMBLE, WILLIAM TAYLOR
6/7	ALLIN, WILLIAM	WILLIAM GAMMILL	DAVID STEWART, WILLIAM LOWMAN
6/8	RANNELS, GEORGE	JOHN BOULER	JOHN RANNELS, REV. JAS. WAKEFIELD
7/23	SLOEY, HUGH	EDMUND BURKE	GEORGE & WILLIAM SEVERING
8/4	STEWART, ALEXANDER	THOMAS BOYLE	RICHARD B. MCCABE, ---- HOTHEM
8/13	GRAHAM, HANNAH	JONN LOGAN	ALEX. ELLIOTT, ROBERT BRANDON
9/20	SCOTT, JAMES	SAMUEL LOWERY	WILLIAM HARVEY, WILLIAM TAYLOR
9/20	MAGILL, WILLIAM H.	JOHN & JAS. MAGILL	JOHN MORRISON, HENRY NOBLE
9/11	ORR, ROBERT	JOHN G. ORR	JAMES & ROBERT ORR
10/1	DOUGHERTY, HUGH	ROBERT CRAWFORD	WM. CRAWFORD, JOS. THOMPSON
10/5	MAHAN, PATRICK	FERGUS CANNON	" TAYLOR, JAMES CLARK
10/12	AYERS, JONATHAN	EDWARD NIXON	ROBERT NIXON, JOHN SUTTON
10/29	MCFARLAND, JAMES	CHAS. B. CAMPBELL	GILLIS DOTY, JAMES PATTON
11/10	RUGH, ELIZABETH	JAMES MIKESEL	ADAM MIKESEL, WM. HENDRICKSON
11/11	ALEXANDER, JAMES	JAMES MCCOLLOM	JOHN P. LLOYD, PETER MOORHEAD
11/17	MIKESELL, PETER B.	JOHN JENKINS	PETER MIKESELL, DANIEL MIKESELL
11/19	CLAWSON, MARY	BENJAMIN CLAWSON	DANIEL STANARD, RICHARD CLAWSON
12/7	HICKS, JACOB	JOHN HICKS	JOHN WEAMER, JAMES MCKEE
12/14	O'DONALD, PATRICK	STEWART STEEL	REV. DAVID BLAIR, JOHN P. FORD
12/28	COLWELL, SAMUEL	J. G. THOMPSON	JAS. MILLER, ABDIEL COLWELL

Date	Name		
1/13	CLINGENBERGER, SAMUEL	BENJ. DORNEY	JOS. THOMPSON, JAMES MEARZE
2/10	PATCH, ALVA	WM. T. SMITH	WM. HOUSTON, WM. HENRY
3/19	AULD, WILLIAM	THOMAS AULD	THOS. FEE, JAMES PEDDICORD
3/29	SADDLER, JOHN W.	CHARLES BYRON	JOHN STEWART, JAMES BRADY
3/29	MCCONNELL, MARY ANN	JOHN R. MCCONNELL	SAM. ELDER, JAMES ELLIOTT
4/2	RAMY, CONRAD	JOHN EWING	--------- --------- ------ -----
8/11	DOTY, ZEBULAN	ROBERT DOTY	SAMUEL BLACK, MALAKIAH SUTTON
9/8	SHANKLE, HENRY, SR.	HENRY & ELIAS SHANKLE	JOHN AYERS, CHARLES RIDDLE

1842

Date	Name		
10/12	CANNON ALEXANDER	ROBERT MC CREA	WM. B. CLARK, JOSEPH TEMPLETON
11/15	HENDERSON, WILLIAM	JOS. & AND. HENDERSON	JOHN (FATHER) & SAM. HENDERSON
11/7	DICKSON, THOMAS	THOMAS GIBSON	JOHN WEIMER, FERGUS CANNON
12/28	BOSSERT, ELIZABETH	JOHN GRAFF	SAM MATTHEWS, ISABEL WATT

1843

Date	Name		
1/14	DAVIS, JOSHUA	SARAH DAVIS (WID.)	SILAS DAVIS (BROTHER)
1/21	LUKE, DAVID	GEORGE MCCARTHERY	MARY LUKE (MOTHER), WM. BRACKEN
1/13	REED, CHRISTINA	JACOB REED	FRANCIS GOMPERS, JACOB GEORGE
2/28	HAMILTON, JAMES	JOHN & ROB. HAMILTON	DAV. HAMILTON (FATH.), ROB. HOPKINS
3/3	MCKEOUN, JOHN	WM. B. BROWN	CATHERINE (WID.), CHAS. CAMPBELL
5/3	HART, ROBERT	JOHN D. HART	MOSES & JOHN HART
6/19	GREEN, SAMUEL	E. O'NEIL, JOHN YINGLING	SIMON DICK, JAMES R. BELL
6/23	HUTCHINSON, CORNELIUS	ROBT. HUTCHINSON	JAS. & ALEXANDER ELLIOTT
6/26	DAVIS, SILAS	JAMES J. DAVIS	ABE DAVIS, ANDREW BROWN
6/26	STEWART, JOHN	JAMES STEWART	WM. BRACKIN, WM. GRAHAM
6/27	EASTON, JOHN	ELIZABETH EASTON	JOHN CRAIG, JOHN EWING
6/30	HENDERSON, SAMUEL	SAMUEL LUCAS	JOHN HENDERSON, WM. LYTLE
12/4	CREPS, JACOB	SAMUEL CREPS	MARY (WID.), ANDREW BOUCHER

1844

Date	Name		
1/23	LYDICK, PATRICK	MARY LYDICK (WID.)	JOS. THOMPSON, JOHN PROTHERO
1/25	MCCURDY, SAMUEL	JOHN & SAM. MCCURDY	ABIGAIL (WID.), WM. STEWART
2/3	QUEST, SARAH	FERGUS CANNON	SAM QUEST (BRO.), JOHN MAGEE
2/6	FLEMING, JAMES	BEN CLOSSON	RICHARD B. CLAWSON
3/4	MILLEN, JAMES	ROB. HARBISON, J. MILLER	MARY ANN (WID.), DAVID RALSTON
3/8	NEAL, THOMAS	JAMES CHAMBERS	WM. NEAL, JOHN A. JAMESON
3/8	KENNEDY, HUGH	EDWARD RILEY	SOPHIA (WID.), GEORGE HICE
3/8	MCGUIRE, DANIEL	EPHRAIM A. MCGUIRE	MARGARET (WID.), JOHN PETERS
4/3	GILMORE, ALEXANDER	MARY & WM. GILMORE	THOMAS & WILLIAM LOWMAN
5/13	HUFFNAGLE, FRANKLIN	JOHN HUFFNAGLE	G. W. HUFFNAGLE, M. DONAVAN
5/18	CRISSMAN, G. W.	CORNELIUS LOWE	MARY (WID.), HEN. KINTER, J. JAMISON
5/--	LYDICK, JOSEPH	NANCY LYDICK (WID.)	JOHN & GEORGE MABON
6/25	MOFFATE, WILLIAM	JAMES DICK, JANE (WID.)	JOHN DICK, WILLIAM HICE
7/23	ELGIN DANIEL	JAMES ELGIN	" CALHOUN, " TYLOR
7/26	MURRAY, JAMES	E.F. LANT, EUNICE (WID.)	HENRY KUHN, ISAAC WATT
8/23	HAZLETT, JAMES	JOHN, SAMUEL & LESLEY HAZLETT	JAMES JACK, WILLIAM MCFARLAND
9/2	MCCOLLAM, JAMES	FRANCIS MCCOLLAM, JR.	MARTHA (WID.), JOHN PIERCE
11/16	MATHIAS, JOHN	R.B.MCCABE, ELIZABETH(WD)	GEORGE GREER, STEWART DAVIS
11/19	LEANY, DANIEL	JOS.THOMPSON, ANN (WID.)	JAMES & PETER SUTTON
12/6	HENDERSON, JOHN B.	SAM H. THOMPSON	JOS. THOMPSON, WM. L. FENTON
12/5	LEWIS, REV. DAVID	SAM MARCHALL, SR.	ELIZ. (WID) REV.ROBT. JOHNSTON
12/31	MOCK, CHRISTOPHER	JONAS MIKESELL	GEORGE MOCK, ARMOUR PHILLIPS

1845

Date	Name		
1/8	GIBSON, JAMES	JOHN MILLER	JOSEPH GIBSON, ALEXANDER ROSS
1/11	MCGUIRE, ANIEL	JOHN GRAFF	WM. HOUSTON, JOHN H. SHRYOCK
1/18	KELLY, ROBERT	JOHN KELLY, JAS. FULTON	RACHEL (WID), & SAMUEL KELLY
?	BROWN, DAVID	JAMES TAYLOR	MARTHA ("), WILLIAM TAYLOR
3/12	STINEMAN, CATHERINE	ABRAHAM WOLFE	SIMON TRUBY, NICHOLAS PEDDICORT
3/29	DOUGLASS, BARNABAS	BARNABAS DOUGLASS	EDMUND BURKE, WILLIAM HOUSTON
8/14	FULCOMER, GEORGE	ANDREW CLINE	CATHERINE (WID.), JACOB SIDES
8/15	WIGGINS, JAMES	SAM & AND. WIGGINS	MARY (WID.), & HUGH WIGGINS
8/20	THOMAS, WILLIAM	DANIEL WILLIAMS	ANN (WID.), D.W. & R.W. THOMAS
8/28	STEWART, ARCHIBALD	ARCHIBALD STEWART	JANE STEWART (WID.), JOHN BARR
9/9	STEPHENS, NANCY	THOS. W. STEPHENS	WM. (HUSB.) & WM. JR. STEPHENS
9/11	LOUGHRY, BENJAMIN	THOMAS SLOAN	NANCY (WID.), ALEX. I. MOORHEAD
9/23	THOMPSON, JAMES G.	JOHN G. THOMPSON	MATHEW WYNKOOP, ROBT. THOMPSON
9/29	DENNISTON, JOHN	WOODROE DOUGLASS	ALEX. REYNOLDS, WM. HOUSTON
10/24	MCDONALD, JOHN	SAM MCDONALD	MARTHA (WID.) & WILSON MCDONALD
11/18	WINNING, GEORGE	SUSAN WINNING	MARTIN ZIRKLE, SIDNEY MOUNTAIN
12/18	PEDDICORD, DOSSY	WM. PEDDICORD	JAS. PEDDICORD, JOSEPH YOUNG

1845			
12/19	SNYDER, THOMAS	JAMES TAYLOR	ISABELLA (WID.), JAMES GIBSON
1846			
1/12	LEWIS, TOBIAS	ELIZABETH LEWIS (WID.)	DAVID BARNETT, JOHN A. JAMESON
1/24	ELDRICKS, ADAM	JANE ELDRICKS (WID.)	SCOTT MARSHALL, WM. B. CLARK
2/23	JOHNSTON, WILLIAM	ROBT. L. JOHNSTON	JANE (WID.), SAMUEL HOWE
2/24	LYNN, THOMPSON	SMITH LYNN	MARGARET (WID.), ROB.CRAIG, J.VON
2/9	MCFARLAND, MARIAH	J. P. LAFFERTY	ALEX.MCFARLAND (BRO.),WM. MOORHEAD
3/14	MCCARTNEY, JOHN	SARAH MCCARTNEY (WID)	NATHANIEL BRYAN, JAMES TAYLOR
3/24	LYDICK, PATRICK, SR.	SAM K. LOCKARD	MARY (WID.), JAS.MCCUNN, J.THOMPSON
6/--	NORTH, ELIZABETH	JOHN & JOS. NORTH	WM. NORTH, JAMES MEARS
6/17	TURNER, JAMES E.	JOHN TURNER	ADAM M. TURNER, JOHN P. LAFFERTY
6/20	ORR, ROBERT, JR.	EDWARD CONNER	ELIZA (WID.), J.THOMPSON, J.JAMESON
6/27	CAMPBELL, MICHAEL	N. P. TURNER	ELIZABETH (MOTHER), CHAS.B.CAMPBELL
6/29	TODD, SAMUEL	JAMES TODD	MARGARET (WID.), WM. W. CALDWELL
7/6	JOHNSTON,COL.ROBT. S.	JUNE JOHNSTON (WID.)	REV.DAVID KIRKPATRICK, W. DOUGLASS
7/7	GETTY, ALEXANDER	JOHN & THOS.GETTY (SONS)	HUGH SPEDDY, ISAAC KEENER
7/18	STEPHENS, WM. T.	THOS. W. STEPHENS	ELIZABETH (WID.), W.HOUSTON,J.TALOR
8/1	COY, HENRY	DANIEL CRAMER	BARBARA (WID.), JOHN OBER, S. TRUBY
8/4	BOLER, GEORGE	JOHN BOLER	JAS. STEWART, JONATHAN A. ADAIR
8/12	HOPKINS, JANE	JAMES M. SMITH	EBENEZER HAMILL, WM. MOORHEAD
8/31	BURNS, HENRY	WILLIAM HART	NATHANIEL (FATH.), JOHN CAMPBELL
8/31	MCMILLEN, SAMUEL	ADAM M. TURNER	MARTHA (WID.), I.HENRY, WM.LAWSON
9/--	DIAS, ANDREW	THOMPSON MCREA	ANN (WID.), J.DOUGHERTY, M.SHIELDS
10/10	TAWNEY, WILLIAM	JOHN TAWNEY	JOSEPH YOUNG, CHARLES GOMPERS
10/12	BELL, THOMAS, JR.	WILLIAM MCCREA	ELEANOR (WID.), TOM BELL, G. DOTY
10/21	CANNON, FERGUS	MATH. TAYLOR	LETITIA (WID.), J. THOMPSON
11/7	STUCHEL, JACOB	FRANCIS FAIRMAN	ELLEN(WID.), WM.SHAFFER, R.SPENCE
11/13	HAFLICK, NICHOLAS	ALEX. HAMILTON	MARY ANN (WID.), WM. SHIELDS
11/27	IGON, SARAH	JACOB IGON	JAMES SCOTT, T. HANNAH
12/5	CHAPMAN, JOHN	SARAH ANN. CHAPMAN	JAMES SHIELDS, JOHN GAREE
1847			
5/1	MCELHOSE, LEVI	SAMUEL MCELHOSE	DAVID ANTHONY, JAMES MOORHEAD
5/27	JOHNSTON,ROBT.(S/O JOHN)	WOODROE DOUGLASS	DAVID KIRKPATRICK, CHAS. CAMPBELL
6/2	RUSSELL, JANE	THOS. M. ANDERSON	ROBERT MOORHEAD, SIMON TRUBY
8/18	DAVIS, JAMES I.	WM. I. DAVIS	ABE DAVIS, WM. MCCRACKEN
9/13	SMITH, GEORGE	JOHN SMITH	SAM MCCARTNEY, JOHN MONTGOMERY
9/20	FENTON, JOHN	JAMES FENTON	WM. L. FENTON, JAMES SLOAN
9/27	THOMPSON, WHITE	WM. THOMPSON	DAVID K. THOMPSON, DAVID BOUCHER
10/13	LUCAS, THOMAS SCOTT	JAMES MOORHEAD	WM. EVANS, WM. MOORHEAD
11/23	PARK, ROBERT	ALEX. GRAHAM	MICHAEL LOWMAN, JOHN GILMORE
1848			
2/9	MAHON, PATRICK	THOMAS GIBSON	I. M. WATT, THOMAS STUCHEL
2/26	DUNHAM, JOS. W.	JAMES TAYLOR	WM. TAYLOR, WM. MCCRACKEN
2/26	SMITH, ANN	ROBERT BRANDON	JACOB GAMBLE, DAVID RALSTON
8/19	FRY, CHRISTIAN	LEVI FRY	ANDREW GRAFT, BENNETT WHISSEL
9/14	SPENCER, GEORGE	JAMES Y. BRABY	DEBORAH (WID.), CHARLES GOMPERS
9/16	CANNON, WILLIAM	HUGH CANNON	JOS. & ROBT. THOMPSON
9/22	MOORHEAD, SAMUEL	MARTHA & JOS. MOORHEAD	SAM MCANULTY, JOHN SHRYOCK
10/--	MOORE, HENRY M.	ABRAHAM MOORE	REBECCA (WID.), ABE MOORE, SR.
10/4	STANARD, DAVID	JOHN SUITER	MARGARET (WID.), DAN STANARD
10/18	SHIELDS, JAMES	T. B. ALLISON	WM.,ROBT.,GEO., & JAS. SHIELDS
10/18	CULBERTSON, ISAAC	JOHN DEVINNEY	MARY (WID.), M. GRAFF, A. DAVIS
11/14	STUCHEL, JOHN	JOS. THOMPSON	MARY (WID.), WM. T. STUCHEL
1849			
1/6	DEVLIN, SAMUEL	WM. CARNAHAN	A. DEVLIN (BRO.)., G.STEEL, J.BARBER
2/13	BUTLER, ABNER	JESSE BUTLER	SOL. & CALEB BUTLER (BROS.)
2/21	THOMPSON, JAMES	JOS. & ROBT. THOMPSON	JOHN THOMPSON (BRO.), PETER SUTTON
2/27	KAUFFMAN, ABRAHAM	SAMUEL KAUFFMAN	WM. HOUSTON, BEN. HARSHBERGER
3/13	LUKE, JAMES	JOHN BOULER	WM. B. CLARK, ROBERT JOHNSTON

1847			
2/16	LUCAS, WILLIAM	JOHN LUCAS & NANCY	THOMAS LUCAS, MICHAEL LOWMAN
3/17	FAIRMAN, JAMES	JOHN FAIRMAN, JR.	FRANCIS FAIRMAN, ROBERT SPENCE
4/10	GRIFFITH, CATHERINE	JOSEPH THOMPSON	WOOD. DOUGLASS, WM. L. FENTON
4/12	WIGGINS, ROBERT L.	SMITH MOWRY	WM. LOWMAN, WM. B. CLARK
4/12	SIDES, JANE	JACOB SIDES (BRO.?)	JAMES & ALEXANDER ELLIOTT
1849			
3/26	HENRY, ELIZABETH ANN	ROBERT HARBISON	THOMAS WALKER, ROBERT P. MCCREA
	(MOTHER, LUCINDA CLAWSON, SISTER, MARGARET HENRY)		
4/7	TRIMBLE, GEORGE	SAMUEL TRIMBLE, JR.	TOM TRIMBLE (SON), WM. HAMILTON
4/10	RISINGER, JOHN	DANIEL RISINGER	MICHAEL HESS, ALEXANDER DICK
4/20	PERRY, SAMUEL	ROBERT HARBISON	ELIZ. PERRY (MOTH.), C. B. CAMPBELL
4/23	LEIBENGOOD, JACOB	CHRISTOPHER LEIBENGOOD	MARGARET (WID.), JOHN ELDER, SAMUEL MARSHALL
5/1	CAMERON, FINDLEY	JOHN BRACKEN	MARTHA (WID.), T. DAVIS, W. BRACKEN
5/3	CAMP, HETH F.	EBENEZER B. CAMP	JOHN & WM. ARMSTRONG
5/3	OVERDORF, JOHN JR.	FRED. HARLINGER	SUSAN (WID.), JOHN GRUMBLING
6/16	HOSACK, SAMUEL R.	WILLIAM MCCREA	RACHEL (WID.), J. HOOD, C. CAMPBELL
8/9	ST. CLAIR, SAMUEL	CATH. & JOHN ST. CLAIR	HUGH ST. CLAIR, WM. CAMPBELL
8/30	PATTERSON, ALEX.	JAS. STEWART, WM. LYDY	MARTHA (WID.), B. O'NEAL,
9/25	HOOD, ROBERT	JAMES HOOD	SARAH (WID.), S. TRIMBLE, S. HENDERSON
9/25	BOYLE, THOMAS	HENRY GRAFF, JR.	MARIA (WID.) C. CAMPBELL, J. PETERS
10/15	SILVERS, GEORGE	CHARLES GOMPERS	FRANCIS & WM. GOMPERS
11/9	MCKEE, JOSEPH	ELSEY MCKEE	WILLIAM MOORHEAD, ROBT. MITCHELL
11/13	MCCONAHEY, JAMES	JAMES SIMPSON	MARY (DAU.) S. DICKSON, W. TAYLOR

END OF INDIANA COUNTY, PENNSYLVANIA, LETTERS OF ADMINISTRATION.

WILLS OF INDIANA COUNTY, PENNSYLVANIA.
(1817-1849)

INDIANA COUNTY WAS FORMED FROM WESTMORELAND AND PART OF LYCOMING COUNTIES. LYCOMING WAS FORMED FROM NORTHUMBERLAND COUNTY, THE LARGEST IN PENNSYLVANIA. INDIAN COUNTY WAS FORMED IN 1803, AND INDIANA, PA., IS THE COUNTY SEAT. THIS LIST IS NOT COMPLETE FROM THE FORMATION OF THE COUNTY.

WILL DATE PROBATED	THE DECEASED	TOWN OR TOWNSHIP	HEIRS
10/1/1817 12/27/1817	WEIR, HUGH	CLINTON CO., OHIO	W. REBECCA. CH. SARAH, ELIZA, CATHERINE, JOHN, SAMUEL, JESSE C., WILLIAM C., DINAH. BROTHER, GEORGE.
2/27/1818 ——/1818	LYTLE, ANNA	ARMSTRONG	NEPHEWS, ROBERT S/O TOM WIGONS, ROBERT CLIFFERT SISTERS, MARGARET WALKER, CATHERINE LYTLE.
3/5/1810 ——-/1818	THOMPSON, WILLIAM	CONEMAUGH	WF. AGNES. CH. JOHN, WILLIAM, POLLY, AGNES, ROBERT.
3/24/1818 ——-/1818	WIGGINS, WILLIAM	WASHINGTON	WF. ELIZABETH. CH. SAMUEL, ROBERT, JOHN, ANDREW, MARGARET.
9/3/1817 5/16/1818	MCGEE, PATRICK	BLACKLICK	WF. ESTHER. CH. JAMES, ROBERT, JOHN.
3/6/1825 8/4/1825	BRACKIN, WILLIAM	?	WF. MARGARET. HAD CHILDREN, NOT NAMED.
1/26/1825 9/27/1825	LEARD, JUDITH (NEE ELLIOTT)	CONEMAUGH	CH. MARY (MRS. JAS. HART), WILLIAM, ELEANOR MCCOMB, JOHN, JUDITH, STEWART (WHO HAD A DAUGHTER, MARY ANN), ZACHARIAH. MOTHER, JUDITH ELLIOTT.
8/15/1825 10/4/1825	LOUGHRY, WILLIAM	?	CH. REBECCA SUTTON, JAMES, JOSEPH, WILLIAM, JOHN, POLLY, SALLY, BENJAMIN.
12/15/1825 1/23/1826	RIDDLE, POLLY (WID. OF WM.)	MAHONING	CH. WILLIA, PETER, CATHERINE, MARGARET.
4/18/1822 5/3/1826	RANKIN, WILLIAM	ARMSTRONG	WF. JANE. CH. HANNAH MCKINLEY, ISABEL MILLER, MARGARET MCMICHAEL, JANE MCMICHAEL, MARY MILLER, MATTHEW, WILLIAM.
4/14/1825 7/23/1826	MONTGOMERY, DORCAS	BLACKLICK	HEIRS; ELIZABETH (MRS. JAS. ELDER), JANE (MRS. ROBT. ELDER), REBECCA (MRS. THOMAS ELDER, WHO HAD DAUGHTER, DORCAS), ELIZABETH MCCUTCHEON, ALEX. MCCUTCHEON, ISABEL (MRS. ALEX. THOMPSON), CATHERINE ALLEN (COLORED GIRL).
4/10/1826 7/29/1826	GETTY, ANDREW	CONEMAUGH	WF. CATHERINE. CH. JOHN, MARGARET SHEARER, ALEXANDER, ELIZABETH SCOTT, JAMES.
12/27/1823 3/1/1827	DOUTHET, NATHANIEL	ARMSTRONG	CH. ROBERT, MARY HART (WHO HAD NATHANIEL) JOHN JOSEPH, ELIZABETH. BROTHER, JAMES.
1/22/1827 4/13/1827	MCPHERSON, THOMAS	?	WF. MARY. CH. DAVID, ELIZA MCGAUGHNEY, JANE TRAVIS, JOHN, PEGGY, JOSEPH, THOMAS.
5/25/1827 6/22/1827	CUMMINS, JOHN	?	WF. ELEANOR. CH. DAVID, SAMUEL, MARGARET, ELEANOR, SUSAN, JANE, STEWART, WILLIAM, JOHN.
6/21/1825 8/1/1827	REES, HUGH	GREEN	WF. ELIZABETH. CH. ANN, JEREMIAH, MARY, CATHERINE, THOMAS, HANNAH.
3/21/1827 9/8/1827	WILSON, JOHN	?	CH. MARY ALLISON, ELIZABETH, ANN LOUGHRY (WHO HAD SON, ALEXANDER).
7/18/1827 10/8/1827	ELDER, ANN	CONEMAUGH	NEPHEW, JOSHUA EWING. NIECE, MARY ANN LEARD. AUNT, MARY ANN SMITH. SISTER, MARGARET EWING. MOTHER, MARY ELDER.
10/13/1827 11/26/1827	PEARCE, JOSHUA	?	WF. MARTHA. CH. EDWARD, ANN ADAMS, WILLIAM, ZILPHA, LYDIA, SALLY, JOB, ISAAC. G'SON,, WILLIAM P. BOYD.

3/26/1826 12/26/1827	LEANY, HUGH	WHEATFIELD	WF. MARGARET. CH. MILTON
10/2/1827 3/5/1828	HARROLD, JOHN (A COUSIN OF THE HERROLDS OF SNYDER CO., PENNSYLVANIA)	BLACKLICK	WF. BARBARA. CH. JACOB (DEAD, LEAVING CHRIST- INA, JACOB, & OTHERS), CHRISTOPHER, SUSAN (MRS. JOS. PISOR), JOHN, DANIEL, SALLY (MRS. ROBT. ARMSTRONG), JOSEPH, HENRY, BETSY (MRS. JACOB DOWELL), MARTHA (MRS. HENRY BAKER), BARBARA (MRS. CHRISTOPHER HARROLD, JR.).
1/11/1828 3/13/1828	WHITBY, GEORGE	?	WF. RACHEAL. BROTHER, ROBERT.
3/14/1828 4/4/1828	LAFFERTY, ROBERT	CONEMAUGH	WF. PRISCILLA. CH. JOHN, JONATHAN, SAMUEL, JAMES, WILLIAM, MARY RICHEY, SARAH MARTIN.
9/5/1825 4/7/1828	MARLIN, JOSHUA, SR.	?	CH. JOSHUA, SARAH (MRS. ALEX. WALKER), NANCY (MRS. WM. DOUGLASS), LETITIA (MRS. GEO. BALL- ENTINE), ROBERT, WILLIAM B.
7/25/1825 4/22/1828	TURNER, GEORGE	?	WF. NOT NAMED. CH. EDWARD, SAMUEL, SEVERAL DAUGHTERS, NOT NAMED.
9/6/1826 5/5/1828	THOMPSON, JAMES	CENTER	WF. POLLY. CH. JOH, REBECCA, JAMES, WILLIAM, BETSY DICAS, NANCY MOORHEAD, POLLY KELLY, ROBERT (DECEASED)
8/2/1828 9/24/1828	CLARKE, GEORGE	?	WF. MARY. CH. HAD SOME, NOT NAMED. SISTER, RUTH.
7/21/1828 10/15/1828	TAYLOR, ALEXANDER	INDIANA	WF. SARAH. CH. ROBERT C., MATTHEW, MOLLY, WILLIAM. BROTHER, JOHN.
10/23/1823 12/10/1828	HARROLD, CHRISTOPHER (BROTHER OF JOHN, MENTIONED ABOVE)	BLACKLICK ?	CH. WILLIAM, JOHN, CHRISTOPHER, JR., LUCINDA, MARY, CATHERINE, ELIZABETH, SARAH, NANCY, MARTHA, GDAU., SARAH BORLAND.
10/10/1822 12/15/1828	WALKER, THOMAS	CONEMAUGH	WF. MARGARET KERR, D/O THOMAS. CH. HUGH, REBECCA, ELIZABETH, MARGARET CLARK, THOMAS KERR.
12/18/1828 1/22/1829	CAMPBELL, GEN. CHAS. (FOUNDER OF CAMP- BELLS MILLS, PA.)	BLACKLICK	CH. MICHAEL, REBECCA (MRS. SAM. DENNISTON), SARAH (MRS. FULLERTON WOODS), MARY (DEAD, 1ST WIFE OF JOHN DENNISTON), JAMES, THOMAS, PHANNEL D., ELIZA (MRS. ALEX. SPEERS), CHARLES, BARBARA (DEAD, MRS. JAMES MCCLAIN).
4/13/1825 4/6/1829	MCKISSON, DANIEL	CENTER	WF. MARGARET. CH. ROBERT, WILLIAM, JOHN, SALLY, JAMES, ELIZABETH,
1/6/1829 5/2/1829	SUTTON, PETER, SR.	INDIANA	CH. GAWIN, THOMAS, PHEBE (MRS. WM. HARROLD), MALEKIAH, PETER (DEAD, LEFT WIDOW, MARTHA), POLLY NIJON. GSON., JAMES SUTTON,
4/15/1829 5/29/1829	BRICKER, JOHN	BLACKLICK	WF. SUSAN. CH. DAVID, ADAM, JACOB, JOHN, & PERHAPS OTHERS.
2/9/1813 5/30/1829	MCKEE, WILLIAM	CENTER	WF. ELIZABETH. CH. NONE MENTIONED.
6/6/1829 6/27/1829	THOMPSON, HUGH	WASHINGTON	WF. MARTHA. CH. ROBERT, WILLIAM, JOHN, MARY, JANE, JOSEPH, JAMES, B/L HUGH CANNON.
11/16/1828 7/2/1829	MORRISON, ROBT. W.	?	WF. MARGARET. CH. JAMES L., JOHN MARY F., ROBERT, ANDREW, REBECCA, JANE.
4/12/1824 7/28/1829	REES, JOHN	GREEN	CH. THOMAS, ELIZABETH, CATHERINE, ANN, WILL- IAM, MARGARET. SON/LAW, DAVID MOSES, HAD DAU., LEAH. NEPHEW, JOHN THOMAS.
6/23/1829 8/28/1829	MCFARLAND, JOHN	CONEMAUGH	CH. ANN, ELIZABETH, WILLIAM, ROGERT, CHRIST- INE, JEAN, JOHN, NANCY, MARGARET, JAMES, CATHERINE, ALEXANDER.
10/12/1825 8/29/1829	SMITH, THOMAS	CONEMAUGH	CH. JAMES, WHO HAD A SON, THOMAS.
8/19/1823 9/28/1829	HAMILTON, ROBERT	MAHONING	WF. JANE. CH. ROBERT, HUGH, JAMES, MARTHA WORK, MARY HAMILTON.
7/14/1829 9/29/1829	BLAKENEY, FERGUS W.	?	WF. MARY. CH. MARGARET, WM., JANE (MRS. JAMES CRAVEN), SAMUEL, ANN (MRS. DAVID WHITE).

53

Date	Name	Place	Details
9/9/1828 10/1/1829	McCUNE, MARY (W/O ARCHIBALD)	BLACKLICK	BRO. ANDREW (WHO HAD ELIZABETH JENNINGS, MARGARET FERGUSON, AARON, CHAROLTTE KERNS, RACHEL WAINRIGHT, ANDREW, REBECCA, PHEBE, ELISHA). BRO WILLIAM (HAD SON, JOHN).
5/27/1829	REPINE, CATHERINE (W/O CHRISTOPHER?)	?	CH. SOPHIA JEWEL, MARGARET HOOVER, ELIZABETH, JOSEPH, JOHN (WHO HAD CATHERINE & CHRISTOPHER), GEORGE (WHO HAD CATHERINE & CHRISTOPHER). B/L GEORGE MEYER.
10/8/1829 12/23/1829	BROWN, JEREMIAH	MAHONING	WF. ELIZABETH. CH. DAVID, WILLIAM, JOSEPH, SAMUEL, NANCY WORK, AND 3 OTHER DAUS.
7/2/1825 1/1/1830	BOGLE, JAMES	?	WF. SALLIE, HEIRS, SALLY McCRACKEN, DANIEL MORRISON.
1/12/1830 1/19/1830	SAMPLE, JANE	CENTER	CH. ROBERT, MARGARET HAMILTON, MATTIE DUNHAM, POLLY, BETSY, REBECCA.
3/8/1830 3/12/1830	CUNNINGHAM, DAVID	CONEMAUGH	WF. JANE. HAD CHILDREN, NOT NAMED.
3/3/1830 3/19/1830	FEE, ANDREW	WHEATFIELD	CH. JANNET, JOSIAH, JEAN DALTON, THOMAS, AGNES, JAMES, ELIZABETH (MRS. TOM MARTIN), GCH. JAMES & JEAN LOUTHER.
12/23/1829 4/9/1830	RICHARDS, MARTHA	CENTER	CH. JAMES (WHO HAD, MARY, MARTHA, ELIZABETH, JAMES, ROBERT, LUCINDA), JOHN, WILLIAM, ALEXANDER, ROBERT, ELIZABETH SMITH, MARY CRAIG (WHO HAD MARTHA & AMANDA), MARTHA HUGHES.
4/10/1830 5/4/1830	WRAY, DANIEL	CONEMAUGH	CH. WILLIAM H., ROBERT, ELIZABETH, MARGARET.
3/26/1830 5/17/1830	GETTY, JOHN	"	HAD WIFE AND CHILDREN, DID NOT NAME THEM. ROBERT MAY HAVE BEEN A SON.
4/17/1829 7/28/1830	DUNN, JAMES	?	WF. ELIZABETH. HEIR, SAMUEL DEVLIN.
7/6/1830 7/30/1830	MONTGOMERY, JAMES	CENTER	WF. ANNA. CH. JAMES, JOHN, ROBERT, MARGARET.
10/21/1823 8/5/1830	McCOMB, ALLEN	?	WF. HANNAH. CH. CHARLES, WILLIAM, JEAN WILSON, ALLEN, HANNAH, DAVID.
9/9/1830 9/21/1830	FISHER, JOHN	BLAIRSVILLE	WF. SARAH. NO CHILDREN MENTIONED.
7/6/1830 11/13/1830	McBRIDE, JOHN, SR.	PERRY TWP., JEFFERSON CO.	CH. REBECCA (MRS. JOHN STONEKEN), JOHN (HAD SON, JOHN), BENJAMIN, NANCY BOWERSOCK, JANE McGEE, JAMES, MARY, ELIZABETH.
11/2/1827 10/16/1830	MILLER, ROBERT	CONEMAUGH	CH. SAMUEL, DAVID, MARY WILSON, JAMES, HANNAH, ROBERT.
2/12/1830 12/16/1830	McCREADY, MARGARET	BLACKLICK	SON, JOSEPH SCOTT (WHO HAD SON, JOHN), DAU. MARGARET. HUGH & SARAH CASADY WILEY.
8/10/1830 12/18/1830	COLEMAN, JOHN	GREEN	CH. MARGARET (MRS. HENRY C. McDOWELL), GSONS., JOHN & WILLIAM COLEMAN.
2/18/1831 3/25/1831	DAVIS, SIMON (D. 2/21/1831)	"	WF., NOT NAMES, CH. SARAH (MRS. THOMAS BROTHERLINE), WILLIAM H.
4/29/1828 3/26/1831	STEWART, ARCHIBALD	CENTER	WF. ELEANOR. CH. ARCHIBALD, JOHN, SAMUEL, JANE, MAY, ELEANOR, MARGARET. GSON., JAMES STEWART SIMPSON.
3/9/1831 4/--/1831	MOONEY, HESTER	EBENSBURG	SISTERS, RACHEL SEELY, SARAH FISHER, ELIZABETH BROWN, MARY McANULLY, -----------.
3/29/1831 4/9/1831	DAVIS, CATHERINE (W/O SIMON)	CENTER	CH. ANN (MRS. PHILIP ARTHUR).
3/31/1831 4/19/1831	RICHEY, GEORGE	WASHINGTON	CH. JAMES, ELIZABETH.
12/7/1829 4/29/1831	GRIFFITH, JESSE	CENTER	WF. ELIZABETH. CH. JOSEPH, JESSE, EVE, REBECCA, ELIZABETH, MARGARET.
---------- 5/7/1831	FRY, PETER	?	WF. CATHERINE. CH. PETER, MARY, JOHN, MICHAEL, ELIZABETH, JACOB, DAN, SAM, GEORGE, RACHEL, SUSAN.

——— 5/17/1831	SAMPLE, REBECCA	CENTER	BROTHERS, JOHN, ROBERT, SISTER, JANE.
9/9/1828 6/1/1831	LEWIS, JOHN	CONEMAUGH	WF. NANCY. CH. JAMES, EVANS, DAVID, REUBEN, CATHERINE MCFARLIN, REBECCA ROBINSON, PEGGY MCFARLIN.
11/16/1818 8/27/1831	CUMMINS, JANNET	CENTER	CH. ELIZABETH, (MRS. JEREMIAH BROWN), MARY MORROW, WILLIAM
8/18/1831 9/19/1831	CLARK, WILLIAM	WHEATFIELD	CH. THOMAS, MARTHA BUTLER, WILLIAM, GEORGE (WHO HAD MARTHA, ELIZABETH, SARAH, MATILDA, EMILY), RUTH, MARY WAKEFIELD.
11/12/1831 1/28/1832	MCDONALD, JOHN	YOUNG	CH. JAMES (WHO HAD JAMES & WILLIAM), AND PERHAPS OTHERS.
9/15/1828 2/2/1832	REES, ELIZABETH	GREEN	CH. REES, THOMAS, ANN, JEMIMA, MARY, CATHERINE, HANNAH.
——— ——-1832	AYERS, JONATHAN	MAHONING	WF. SUSAN. CH. SYLVESTER, AND POSSIBLY OTHERS.
6/1/1831 4/28/1832	MCLAUGHLIN, DANIEL	WHEATFIELD	WF. EVE. CH. GEORGE, ELIZABETH, JAMES, ANN, MARY, JOHN, KITTY GEORGE. BROTHER, MICHAEL.
11/21/1829 5/15/1832	WORK, ROBERT (STONECUTTER)	CONEMAUGH	NEPHEW, JOHN WORK, DECEASED, WHO LEFT A NUMBER OF CHILDREN NOT NAMED IN WILL.
9/28/1831 5/19/1832	SUTTON, ROBERT	WHEATFIELD	WF. JANE. CH. HENRY, ROBERT, WILLIAM, MARIA, LOUISA, CHRISTINA (MRS. GEO. HILL), CAROLINE (MRS. JAMES WHITE). ALSO ROBERT, HENRY, WILLIAM & DANIEL ANDERSON.
11/30/1831 5/25/1832	CLARKE, RUTH (D/O WILLIAM)	"	BROS. GEORGE, WILLIAM, SISTERS, MARY WAKEFIELD, ANN KILLIN, MARTHA BUTLER. OTHERS, SARAH DUNKEN, ANN CAMERON, MARY HERRELL, DANIEL KILLIN (PROBABLY BROTHER-IN-LAW).
4/13/1830 6/8/1832	WILLIAMS, CATHERINE	CENTER	CH. BENONI, REBECCA (MRS. MICHAEL RISINGER). MRS. JAMES STEWART. GDAU. CATH. TRIMBLE.
12/22/1831 6/26/1832	LUKE, JAMES, SR.	WHEATFIELD	WF. MARY. NO CHILDREN MENTIONED.
4/26/1832 7/13/1832	DUFFIELD, DR. SAM	BLAIRSVILLE	BROTHERS, GEORGE, JOHN D. SISTER, ELIZA ANN. OTHERS, MARY (MRS. NATHAN MCDOWELL), MARTHA MCFARLAND (WHO HAD SON SAMUEL DUFFIELD MCFARLAND.
12/29/1831 9/26/1832	MCLAUGHLIN, JOHN	WASHINGTON	BROS. WILLIAM, JAMES, SR.
7/4/1831 10/1/1832	STEWART, ELEANOR (W/O ARCHIBALD)	CENTER	CH. JANE, POLLY, ELEANOR, MARGARET. GSON. JAMES STEWART SIMPSON.
8/28/1832 10/5/1832	MITCHELL, JAMES	?	WF. UNNAMED. CH. WILLIAM, JAMES.
6/4/1832 10/23/1832	EARHART, ANTHONY	CONEMAUGH	WF. ELIZABETH. CH. JOHN, DAVID, MICHAEL, ANTHONY, JACOB, HENRY, POLLY, SALLY.
10/6/1832 12/14/1832	CAMPBELL, MICHAEL	BLACKLICK	WF. ELIZABETH. CH. SARAH, JANE, MARY, ALICE, THOMAS, JOHN, GEORGE, CHARLES.
11/10/1832 2/9/1833	SUTTON, THOMAS	INDIANA, PA.	WF. REBECCA. CH. MARGARET, WILLIAM, PETER, ROBERT, JAMES, JOHN, REBECCA, PHEBE. BROTHER-IN-LAW, JAMES LOUGHRY.
1/20/1833 4/5/1833	JOHNSTON, JOHN (LAWYER)	"	BROS. ROBERT (WHO MARRIED LAVINA AND HAD 3 SONS), ADAM, JAMES, WILLIAN. NIECE, MARY RANKIN.
4/16/1832 4/16/1833	GRAHAM, JOSEPH	WHEATFIELD	WF. HANNAH. CH. ANN, RUTH, JAMES, ISABEL LOGAN, MARY HISE, HANNAH HISE.
5/2/1833 6/25/1833	SIMPSON, NATHANIEL	MAHONING	WF. CATHERINE. CH. JOHN, DAVID, WILLIAM, JAMES, NATHANIEL, SOLOMON, ELIZABETH. BROTHER, JOHN.
1/3/1833 8/26/1833	MILLEN, JAMES	YOUNG	CH. WILLIAM, JAMES, BARBARA UNCAPHER, ANN GRAHAM, POLLY HARBISON.
12/30/1830 10/4/1833	GRAHAM, JOHN	WHEATFIELD	WF. REBECCA. SEVERAL YOUNG CHILDREN, NO NAMES GIVE.

55

-------- 10/11/1833	HUSTON, THOMAS	GREEN	WF. MARGARET. CH. JOHN, HUGH, MARY, ROBERT (DEAD, WIFE JANE.)
-------- 10/11/1833	ALLISON, JOHN	?	CH. JAMES, ROBERT, JOHN, JANE (MRS. WM. H. DICKIE) HANNAH (MRS. RICHARD PEDDICORD).
3/8/1826 11/26/1833	BURNS, THOMAS	CENTER	WF. SARAH. CH. WILLIAM, THOMAS, JANE, CATHERINE AND PERHAPS OTHERS.
11/8/1833 11/27/1833	ROBINSON, ROBT., S.	CONEMAUGH	WF. ELIZABETH. CH. ROBERT, JOHN, JAMES, THOMAS, WILLIAM, DAVID, ELIZABETH. BROTHER, JOHN.
11/23/1833 11/30/1833	HICE, GEORGE	WHEATFIELD	CH. ROBERT, HENRY, ELIZABETH (MRS. HENRY TAYLOR), SAMUEL, WILLIAM, MARGARET (MRS. PETER MILLIRON), MARY.
3/4/1831 1/17/1834	MULLEN, MICHAEL	CENTER	CH. SARAH (WIDOW OF TOM BURNS), WILLIAM, THOMAS, CATHERINE, JANE BURNS.
12/30/1833 1/30/1834	RANKIN, JAMES	BLAIRSVILLE	HEIRS, SUSAN MAHAN, REBECCA & JOHN MCCLURE, STEWART DAVIS AND SON, ROBERT, JOHN CUNNINGHAM, ELIZABETH WEIR.
3/1/1834 3/8/1834	RUTHERFORD, JOHN	?	WF. MARGARET. CH. HAD SOME, NO NAMES GIVEN.
3/16/1831 3/19/1834	SWEASY, JOHN	?	WF. POLLY. CH. JANE, JOHN, REBECCA.
2/1/1834 4/12/1834	MCGARA, CLEMENCE	WASHINGTON	WF. SARAH. CH. SAMUEL, JOHN, MARTHA WILSON (WHO HAD JOHN & SAMUEL), GCH. SAMUEL W. & PEGGY BELL.
4/12/1834 5/6/1834	HAMILTON, JANE	?	BRO. MORRIS MCMANNIS, SIS. ELIZABETH MCMANNIS. OTHERS, ELEANOR BAKER, JANE OWENS, REBECCA SLONINGER, HUGH HAMILTON.
6/20/1833 6/--/1834	NESBIT, NATHANIAL, SR.	?	WF. ELIZABETH. CH. NATHANIEL, JACOB, MRS. DANIEL STONEBERGER, AND OTHER DAUGHTERS.
5/17/1834 9/27/1834	MOYER, MARTIN, SR.	GREEN	WF. JANE. CH. MARTIN, SIMON, JACOB, MATTHIAS, JOHN, BARBARA, MARY. GDAU. ELIZ. MCDONNELL.
-------- 10/6/1834	MCCLANAHAN, JAMES	?	CH. JAMES, ROBERT, THOMAS, JANE RANKIN.
3/19/1830 11/13/1834	FEALS, ALEXANDER	BLACKLICK	CH. JOHN, THOMAS, ALEXANDER, HANNAH REPINE, SARAH CRISSMAN, RICHARD, DAVID, SUSAN.
2/10/1834 11/22/1834	CREMER, JOHN, SR.	WHEATFIELD	WF. MARY. CH. DANIEL, JACOB, JOHN. ALSO, JACOB HEINER, A RELATIVE.
4/9/1834 12/19/1834	MCPHERSON, HUGH	?	WF. NANCY. NO CHILDREN MENTIONED.
4/15/1834 1/21/1835	WILSON, ALEXANDER	WHEATFIELD	CH. JAMES, POLLY, GEORGE, RICHARD, WILLIAM, SARAH MCCORMICK,
11/28/1834 2/3/1835	RUGH, MICHAEL	BLACKLICK	CH. JACOB, HENRY, DANIEL, SIBILLA, SAUL, PAUL, JESSE, ELIZABETH, SARAH, PAMELIA. 2ND WIFE, KISSIAH (WHO HAD MARY ANN & SUSAN SPIRES, BY A FORMER MARRIAGE).
1/30/1835 2/13/1835	SMITH, JAMES	BLACKLICK	WF. THERESA WAINWRIGHT, D/O SAMUEL. CH. GEORGE, WILLIAM, ALARETTA, ELIZABETH, SARAH. B/L, ISAAC WAINWRIGHT.
12/29/1834 3/4/1835	DICK, JOHN	WHEATFIELD	WF. BARBARA. BROS. WILLIAM, JAMES, THOMAS. SISTER, MARY (MRS. JAMES WHERRY, WHO HAD A SON, JAMES). HALF-SISTERS, MARGARET & JANE, OF IRELAND.
12/26/1786 4/13/1790	GILPIN, JOSEPH, SR.	CECIL CO., MARYLAND	WF. ELIZABETH. CH. HANNAH, ELIZABETH, MARY, RACHEL, JOHN, JOSEPH, SISTER, SARAH ALLISON. BROTHER, SAMUEL, S/O JOHN.
4/10/1822	PARTRIDGE, JOSEPH, G.	BALTIMORE, MARYLAND	FATHER, JAMES. OTHERS, MARY, JOHN, HENRY, AND JAMES PARTRIDGE.
6/7/1832 7/21/1832	GILPIN, JOSEPH, JR.	CECIL CO., MARYLAND	BROTHERS & SISTERS, MARY, HENRY H., JOHN, WILLIAM H.

NOTE: THE THREE WILLS ABOVE WERE PROBATED IN MARYLAND, BUT COPIES WERE RECORDED IN INDIANA COUNTY, PA., TO PROVE RELATIONSHIP OF SOMEONE LIVING THERE.

1/--/1834 -------- 1835	JORDEN, ROBERT	MAHONING	WF. CATHERINE. CH. ALEXANDER, MARGARET MATSON, JAMES, SAMUEL, JOSEPH, HANNAH BELL, MARTHA MCHENRY, JANE MCPHERSON, NANCY CHRISTMAN, MARY MOGLE, BY 2ND WIFE, CATHERINE; MARGARET, JOHN, WILLIAM.
4/20/1826 3/24/1835	BRONSTON, JAMES (BROWNSTON)	?	WF. NANCY. CH. GEORGE.
6/25/1832 5/9/1835	PHILLIPS, ARMOUR	CENTER	WF. MARTHA. CH. ARMOUR, JONATHAN, ROBERT, JANE, FANNY, MARTHA.
3/18/1835 5/25/1835	LYTLE, ALEXANDER	CONEMAUGH	WF. ELIZABETH. CH. WILLIAM, JOHN, JAMES, SARAH, ELIZABETH, RACHEL MCGABEY.
5/28/1835 6/8/1835	LLOYD, ANTHONY	PLEASANT TOWNSHIP MARION CO., OHIO.	CH. WILLIAM, MARY, THOMAS, DAVID.
1/9/1833 6/23/1835	GIBSON, NANCY	YOUNG	CH. JANE, JEAN, ELIZABETH BLACKLEY.
11/17/1834 6/25/1835	CRAIG, ROBERT	MAHONING	WF. AGNES. HAD CHILDREN, GAVE NO NAMES.
4/16/1829 7/14/1835	GETTY, JAMES	WASHINGTON	CH. JAMES, JOHN, ISABEL WILSON, MARGARET SHIELDS.
1/19/1835 8/14/1835	MCLAIN, JAMES	CENTER	CH. MARGARET HOWARD, JAMES, CHARLES, THOMAS, LOIZA, MARY.
6/8/1835 8/19/1835	THOMPSON, SAMUEL	MAHONING	WF. MARY. CH. JAMES, MARGERET JOHNSON, SUSAN, MOSES, SAMUEL, LEVINA, CATHERINE, NANCY, MARY, DAVID, BENJAMIN.
11/4/1834 9/4/1835	PILSON, JOHN	CENTER	WF. NANCY. CH. JOHN, SAMUEL, SUSAN, GRIFFITHS, POLLY, NANCY.
8/24/1829 9/28/1835	GAILEY, JAMES	CONEMAUGH	WF. LETTIS. CH. ANDREW (WHO HAD JAMES), NEIL, SAMUEL, JAMES, CORNELIUS, THOMAS, ANN.
2/2/1836 2/22/1836	MCLAUGHLIN, JAS., SR.	WASHINGTON	CH. JAMES, WILLIAM, ANN MARLIN, S/L, JOSEPH LAWSON.
7/2/1835 5/4/1836	KINTER, JOHN, SR.	"	WF. ISABEL. CH. ISAAC, WILLIAM, PETER, MARY BORLAND (WIDOW), CATHERINE (MRS. JAS. COLTER), JOHN, HENRY, ARCHIBALD, FINDLEY.
4/26/1833 5/12/1836	REED, THOMAS	CONEMAUGH	WF. RACHEL. CH. MARTHA MCGAUGHEY, ELIZABETH MCCREA. GCH. ROBERT MCCREA, TOM R. MCGAUGHEY, S/O TOM. TOM R. MCGAUGHEY, S/O WILLIAM.
11/20/1835 5/28/1836	GRAHAM, JOHN	BRUSHVALLEY	WF. ANNA. CH. JANE (MRS. WM. DUNCAN), MARGARET (MRS. JOHN LOMAN), SARAH (MRS. SAM DUNCAN), WILLIAM, ANN (MRS. JOHN DUNCAN), JOHN (DEAD).
5/19/1836 5/31/1836	HAROLD, JOHN	BLAIRSVILLE	SISTERS, NANCY, MARTHA, LUCINDA. NIECES, ELIZABETH ANN & MARGARET HENRY.
5/20/1836 6/12/1836	MCENTIRE, HUGH	BLACKLICK	WF. MARY. CH. JOHN, DANIEL, JAMES, ANDREW, ELIZABETH, MARY, ELINOR, SIDNEY, HUGH.
4/30/1836 8/12/1836	HICE, SAMUEL	WHEATFIELD	WF. MARGARET. HEIR, SAMUEL MILLIRON, S/O PAUL,
10/18/1836 11/12/1836	SHULTS, HENRY	BRUSHVALLEY	WF. ELIZABETH. CH. JAMES, MICHAEL, JACOB, MARY, SAMUEL, JOHN, CATHERINE, HENRY, SARAH, WILLIAM.
1/14/1837 1/--/1837	MCCAFFERY, JAMES	GREEN	WF. CATHERINE. CH. BERNARD, THOMAS, PATRICK, NANCY O'NEIL, CATHERINE O'NEIL, ELLEN LAPSLY.
5/10/1834 3/7/1837	NESBIT, JOHN	CONEMAUGH	WF. CATHERINE. CH. NATHANIEL, SAMUEL, JOHN, JAMES, ELIZABETH HOUSE, FRANCES KEATON, ANNA, CATHERINE.
2/6/1837 3/11/1837	STRONG, JAMES	BRUSHVALLEY	WF. CATHERINE. CH. MICHAEL, JACOB, JOHN, ELIZABETH SHULTZ, CATHERINE MICHAEL, MARGARET MILLER, SUSANNA BENNETT, MARY LAYPOLE.
2/14/1837 3/16/1837	HENDERSON, BRICE	"	WF. ANN. CH. MARGARET, NANCY, SAMUEL, JESSE, BRICE, JOHN. SOME CHILDREN UNDER 21.

1/30/1837 3/20/1837	GRAHAM, ALLEN	WHEATFIELD	WF. JANE. CH. JAMES, JOHN, WILLIAM, GEORGE,
3/11/1837 3/23/1837	MURPHEY, JOHN	BRUSHVALLEY	WF. MARY. CH. WILLIAM, JAMES, GEORGE, SISTER, MARY.
5/5/1834 4/24/1837	STEWART, MARGARET	?	CH. JOHN (WHO HAD WM., FLORANA, ELIZA, ROBERT, LENA, ALEXANDER, MARIA, ARCHIBALD, MARTHA), MARTHA PATTISON (HAD CHILDREN), MARY ARCHIBALD (WHO HAD A SON ARCHIBALD ARCHIBALD).
2/4/1837 3/26/1837	ELLIOTT, JOH, SR.	MAHONING	SON, THOMAS. GDAUS. RACHEL & JANE ELLIOTT.
8/17/1837 8/28/1837	WILEY, JOHN	BLACKLICK	WF. LIVING, NO NAME. CH. JAMES, SAMUEL (WHO HAD MARGARET), JANE MCCRACKEN (DEAD), ROBERT (DEAD, LEFT WIDOW, JANE, AND MARGARET GRANT, SUSAN FORESHAW, JOHN, HUGH).
5/28/1835 9/15/1837	ARMSTRONG, JAMES	ARMSTRONG	WF. ELIZABETH. CH. THOMAS, JAMES, ROBERT, ANN, ELIZA WALKER, NANCY LOWERY, POLLY GEORGE, JANE MCCRACKIN, MARGARET, ISABEL, LYDIA.
1/24/1838 2/26/1838	ARMSTRONG, ELIZABETH	"	CH. JAMES, LYDIA, ANN, MARGARET, THOMAS, ELIZA WALKER, ROBERT, DAVID.
12/16/1834 4/1/1835	COOPER, BEN. B.	BORN IN GLOUCESTER CO., N. J.	CH. RALPH, SARAH ANN, WILLIAM, COUSINS, BEN & REBECCA COOPER. (OWNED LARGE TRACTS OF LAND IN PENNSYLVANIA AND NEW JERSEY).
2/12/1838 3/9/1838	MCCONAHEY, JOHN	WASHINGTON	WF. RACHEL. CH. WILLIAM, JOSEPH, DAVID K., RACHEL WILLIAMS, ELIZABETH WEIR, SARAH, MARGARET WILLIAMS, HANNAH SMITTEN, GCH., MARGARET BARKLEY, RACHEL WHITE.
3/8/1838 3/26/1838	LYDICK, ISAAC	MAHONING	WF. ELIZA. CH. GEORGE T., JOSEPH M., & OTHERS. BROTHER, PATRICK.
3/20/1838 3/27/1838	MCNUTT, SAMUEL	ARMSTRONG	BROS. JOSEPH, ROBERT, ALEXANDER. NIECES, MARGARET & ISABEL RUTHERFORD. MARGARET, ELIZABETH & SARAH MCNUTT. NEPHEWS, WILLIAM REA, WILLIAM ROSS.
4/12/1834 3/27/1838	MCKESSICK, JAMES	YOUNG	CH. JAMES, MARGARET (MRS. WM. COCHRAN), ROBERT (WHO HAD DAUGHTER, LETTY).
1/4/1838 4/--/1838	UNCAPHER, PHILIP	GREEN	LEFT WIFE AND SMALL CHILDREN, BUT DID NOT NAME THEM.
4/25/1838 5/7/1838	MABON, WILLIAM	WHEATFIELD	WF. ESTHER. CH. HAD SEVERAL, DID NOT NAME THEM.
5/14/1838 5/25/1838	EWING, ROBERT	CONEMAUGH	WF. MARTHA. CH. JAMES, ROBERT, JANE, MARTHA, WILLIAM, ELINOR ROBINSON.
1/17/1838 5/28/1838	MOONSHOWER, JOHN	CENTER	WF. CATHERINE. CH. SAMUEL, JOSEPH, HANNAH, DANIEL, DAVID, ELIZABETH, JOHN, CATHERINE, NICHOLAS, MARY.
5/14/1838 5/31/1838	GRAHAM, JANE (WID OF ALLEN)	WHEATFIELD	CH. JOHN, JAMES, WILLIAM, GEORGE.
11/26/1833 8/7/1838	SCOTT, THOMAS	BLACKLICK	CH. JOHN, ELIZABETH, MARY, JAMES, MARGARET CLAWSON, AGNES, SARAH.
8/1/1838 8/16/1838	ARMSTRONG, WM.	YOUNG	WF. MARY. CH. BENJAMIN, ALEXANDER, WILLIAM, ROBERT, LEANY ANN, MARGARET JEAN.
3/21/1838 8/7/1838	ORR, BENJAMIN	BLACKLICK	WF. MARY. CH. SAMUEL, WILLIAM ELIZA (MRS. JOHN SCOTT). GCH. BEN & MARY ANDERSON.
8/15/1838 9/22/1838	MCKEE, JAMES	WASHINGTON	WF. ANN. CH. ROBERT, CLAUDIUS, NANCY, MARY.
8/28/1838 9/24/1838	GRIER, MARK	BLAIRSVILLE	HAD WIFE AND CHILDREN, BUT DID NOT NAME THEM IN WILL.
2/10/1818 9/26/1838	MCDOWELL, JANE	"	CH. MARY, CATHERINE WILLIAMS (WHO HAD LOUISA JANE), JAMES, NATHAN. AUNT, ELIZ. MCCALMONT.
2/25/1835 10/10/1838	LAWRENCE, AMOS	BLACKLICK	WF. ELIZABETH. CH. ANNA (MRS. WM. LAWRENCE), WARREN. OTHERS, AMOS, SAMUEL, CHESTER DAVIS, GSONS. AMOS AND WARREN LAWRENCE.

3/10/1838	DICK, JAMES	WHEATFIELD	WF. NOT NAMED. CH. JEAN, ALEXANDER, ROBERT,
9/27/1838			JOHN, WILLIAM, JAMES, THOMAS. BRO. JOHN.
5/5/1838	THOMAS, ISRAEL	ARMSTRONG	WF. MARGARET. CH. WILLIAM, NANCY ANTHONY,
1/21/1839			MARY CARR, RUTH MOOR, ELIZABETH WALKER, MARG-
			ARET GIPSON, JOHN.
2/23/1839	LOUGHRY, SUSANNA	BLAIRSVILLE	HEIRS, HER BROTHERS AND SISTERS, ONLY WILLIAM
3/25/1839			& JOSEPH WERE NAMED.
1/26/1839	KIER, DAVID	CONEMAUGH	WF. ELIZABETH. CH. JAMES, ANDREW, AND PROBABLY
4/4/1839			OTHERS. STEPSON, THOMAS KIER.
8/14/1838	WEAMER, ANDREW	MAHONING	WF. ELIZABETH. CH. ADAM, SUSAN RUSSELL, NANCY
4/24/1839			MARSHALL, SARAH, HANNAH, MARY, DANIEL, GEORGE,
			ABRAHAM, JOHN.
12/30/1837	MCCONAUGHY, JEAN	WHEATFIELD	CH. ESTHER, MATTHEW, JANE, GEORGE, SAMUEL,
4/26/1839			ROBERT, JOHN, JAMES. MARY RUSSELL'S CHILDREN,
			JEAN ELDER'S CHILDREN.
--------	ARMSTRONG, ALEX.	ARMSTRONG	CH. NANCY, LENA.
5/21/1839			
5/21/1831	HAMILTON, WILLIAM	CENTER	WF. JANE. CH. THOMAS, JAMES, ROBERT, HUGH,
7/20/1839			JOHN, REBECCA, PEGGY, NANCY.
5/23/1838	LOTZ, JACOB	WASHINGTON	WF. CATHERINE. CH. SUSAN, SARAH, SOPHIA, JOHN,
7/20/1839			GEORGE, SAMUEL. BROTHER, JOHN.
8/16/1838	MARLIN, JOSHUA	SALTSBURG	WF. ELIZA. CH. NONE MENTIONED.
8/13/1839			
2/5/1836	ADAMS, NANCY	CENTER	CH. ROBERT, POLLY (ARCHIBALD ADAMS), JANE (MRS.
9/2/1839	(BORN CA. 1750)		WM. HADD), NANCY (MRS. GEO. MCCARTNEY), PEN-
			ELOPE, ISABEL, JAMES, GAWIN. GCH. PENELOPE
			ADAMS, GAWIN MCCARTNEY.
9/16/1839	MEAKIN, JOHN	BRUSHVALLEY	WF. EVE. CH. WILLIAM, MARY BENNETT, JOHN, PETER
10/11/1839			ELIZABETH RICHEY, ADAM, ABRAHAM.
9/9/1839	LUCAS, WILLIAM	WASHINGTON	WF. MARY. CH. WILLIAM, MATILDA, MARGARET,
11/11/1839			THOMAS, MARY, ISAAC, EDWIN.
6/30/1839	LEARD, WILLIAM	YOUNG	CH. MARGARET (MRS. ROBT. THOMPSON), ZACHARIAH
12/3/1839			(DEAD, LEAVING ELINOR & MARY ANN) GCH. MARG-
			ARET BLACKLEY, JR., WM. L. FOSTER, WM. L.
			STEWART.
10/17/1839	MCCABE, CAPT. ROBT.	----------	BRO. RICHARD B. MCCABE. NEPH. JOHN MCCABE,
12/23/1830	(5TH U. S. INFTY.)		S/O JOHN.
3/15/1839	MCFARLAND, WM.	BLACKLICK	2ND WF. MARY. CH. WILLIA, MARY LYONS, JANE
1/30/1840			RAMSAY, ELIZABETH BELL, JOHN (DEAD). SONS-IN-
			LAW, ALEX. LYONS, JOHN RAMSAY.
5/16/1840	ADAMS, GAWIN	INDIANA	WF. SUSAN. CH. PENELOPE (MRS. CHAS. C. MCLAIN-
5/20/1840			WHO HAD SON GAWIN ADAMS MCLAIN).
5/30/1840	ARNSTRONG, NANCY	ARMSTRONG	SISTER, LENA.
8/13/1840			
7/13/1840	SPENCE, JAMES	WASHINGTON	CH. ROBERT, SARAH, SAMUEL, ELIZABETH.
8/22/1840			
6/15/1840	ASKIN, JOSEPH	GREEN	CH. THOMAS, WILLIAM, NANCY, ELIZA, LAVINA.
10/3/1840			GDAU. LAVINA DUNWOODY.
9/14/1840	REED, REV. JOHN	INDIANA	WF. ISABELLA. CH. MARGARET, LINN, SARAH REED,
10/8/1840			WILLIAM, JOHN, MARY.
8/15/1840	LOW, JAMES	GREEN	DAU. BETHSHEBA (MRS. ELIAS MOOSE).
10/1/1840			
7/13/1840	STEPHENS, ABRAHAM	GREEN	WF. HANNAH. NO CHILDREN MENTIONED.
10/12/1840			
11/20/1839	OAKS, JOHN	BLACKLICK	CH. JOHN (DEAD, LEAVING JOHN, JANE, EDWARD),
10/20/1840			SUSIAVIN PALMER.
7/22/1840	MONTGOMERY, JOHN	?	HEIRS, RACHEL, D/O JAS. MONTGOMERY. JANE &
11/16/1840			MARTHA EWING, DAUGHTERS OF ROBERT. PUBLIC
			SCHOOL, AND SABBATH SCHOOL LIBRARY.

8/17/1835 12/8/1840	MCDONALD, JOSEPH	WHEATFIELD	CH. HUGH, JOSEPH, THEOPOLIUS, CATHERINE.
2/24/1841 3/23/1841	HARRISON, JAMES	WASHINGTON	WF. REBECCA. NO CHILDREN MENTIONED.
10/13/1836 4/5/1841	GARDNER, JOHN	?	SISTER, MARGARET. FATHER, JAMES.
11/23/1839 4/19/1841	RANKIN, REBECCA	CENTER	CH. JAMES, JUINEY M., MARIA RHEA.
5/17/1839 4/21/1841	KATON, SAMUEL, SR.	WASHINGTON	CH. MARY, MARTHA COLEMAN, ELIZABETH KELLY. MARGARET ELDRIX.
4/27/1841 5/3/1841	ADAIR, SUSANA (W/O BLEANYO	CENTER	SISTER, MARY HILL, BROTHER, SAMUEL HILL. HUSBANDS CH. MARIA BOYLE, NANCY, HUGH ADAIR.
5/16/1840 5/18/1841	JONES, WILLIAM	MAHONING	WF. HANNAH. CH. JOHN, MARY.
2/23/1829 6/29/1841	EWING, ALEXANDER	?	HEIR, ALEXANDER EWING, S/O JOHN EWING.
4/19/1841 7/5/1841	BRAUGHLER, ADAM	MONTGOMERY	CH. SOLOMON, TOBIAS.
6/2/1841 7/7/1841	JOHNSTON, JOHN	"	WF. SARAH. CH. MARGARET, WILLIAM M., JOHN, ELIZABETH (MRS. SAM. WORK), JANE (MRS. JAMES KIRKPATRICK), THOMAS.
8/10/1841 9/11/1841	REPINE, JOSEPH	BLACKLICK	WF. NOT NAMED. CH. RACHEL, CATHERINE, JOSEPH, WIFE'S DAUGHTER, ELIZA ANN (MRS. JAS. WALLACE)
7/24/1841 9/--/1841	EARHART, ELIZABETH	CONEMAUGH	BROTHER-IN-LAW, GEORGE GILBERT.
5/13/1840 10/8/1841	DAVIS, JOSHUA, SR.	MAHONING	WF. HANNAH, WHO HAD DAUGHTER, SARAH. CH. JOSHUA, SILAS, SAMUEL.
4/21/1841 10/21/1841	WILEY, MARGARET	BLACKLICK	CH. MARY, MARTHA, ELIZABETH, JAMES, WHO HAD A DAUGHTER, MARGARET.
1/2/1838 4/28/1841	SIDES, ANN	WHEATFIELD	CH. CATHERINE BRANTLINGER, ANN, ELIZABETH, JOHN, JOSEPH, JACOB, LYDIA, JANE, ADAM (DEAD, LEAVING JANE, ADAM, JOHN),
10/12/1841 11/17/1841	CUMPTON, RUBEN	BLACKLICK	WF. MARY ANN. CH. MARY ANN, ANDREW.
6/24/1841 11/25/1841	ADAMS, ROBERT	"	WF. MARGARET. CH. MARY ORR, SARAH ANN ADAMS, THOMAS A., MARGARET FAIR, ELEANOR GOURLEY.
------- 11/29/1841	HUSTON, JAMES	CENTER	WF. MARY. CH. JAMES, WILLIAM, NANCY, EMILY, OTHERS, MARY REED, D/O SAMUEL REED.
9/25/1841 12/13/1841	STEEL, SAMUEL	BLAIRSVILLE	WF. NANCY. CH. WILLIAM, ANDREW, DAVID.
8/18/1838 12/24/1841	TOMB, DAVID	WHEATFIELD	WF. ELIZABETH. CH. HUGH, JOHN, MARY KILLEN, RICHARD D., DAVID.
2/6/1841 12/30/1841	ANDERSON, THOMAS	GREEN	WF. ELIZABETH. CH. JONATHAN, ROBERT, JAMES, THOMAS, ANDREW, ELIZABETH, RACHEL WHITEHEAD, MARY HORTON, SARAH S.
3/29/1821 1/14/1842	GRAY, JOHN	CONEMAUGH	WF. MARGARET. CH. JAMES, MARY MCCURDY, HANNAH, NANCY, JANE.
12/30/1841 1/14/1842	HICE, HENRY	WHEATFIELD	WF. MARY. CH. JOHN, ELIZABETH (MRS. HENRY R. HICE), SARAH, MILDRED, MARY ANN.
12/8/1841 1/29/1842	EWING, JOHN, SR.	YOUNG	CH. JOHN, ALEXANDER, JAMES, SARAH MCCURDY, REBECCA HARBISON, ROBERT.
------- 2/14/1842	ROOF, JACOB, SR.	MAHONING	WF. CATHERINE. CH. DANIEL, MARY ANN, CHARLOTTE, JACOB, FREDERICK, WASHINGTON, WILLIAM.
1/21/1842 2/18/1842	MCFEATHERS, JOHN	?	WF. NOT NAMED. HAD CHILDREN, DID NOT NAME THEM.
7/26/1842 8/12/1842	SAMPLE, JOHN	ARMSTRONG	NEPHEWS & NIECES, JOS. W. DUNHAM, WM. L. HAMIL- TON, ROBERT HAMILTON, JANE (MRS. PATRICK LYDICK, D/O JAS. HAMILTON), ELIZABETH (MRS. WM. F. TEMPLETON), MATILDA (MRS. JON. TRIMBLE).

-------- 8/13/1842	PALMER, CHARLES	BLACKLICK	WF. JANE, CH. SAMUEL, ELIZABETH, JANE, SUSAN, JESSE. (ELIZABETH LIVINGSTON)
8/22/1842 9/27/1842	LYTLE, JAMES	CONEMAUGH	BROTHERS, WILLIAM, JOHN. SISTERS, ELIZABETH, MARIA MCFARLAND.
8/11/1842 12/30/1842	SHERIDAN, MARY (WID./O JAMES)	CENTER	GRANDSON, JOHN CAMPBELL.
9/6/1842 1/24/1843	CARRY, JOHN (KEARY)	MONTGOMERY	WF. MARY MADALIN. GSON. JACOB MAGINLEY
1/6/1843 2/6/1843	JOHNSTON, REBEKAH	BLAIRSVILLE	DECEASED HUSBAND'S DAUGHTER, SARAH. HER CHILDREN, ROSANNA & JOHN WILEY.
6/--/1838 2/6/1843	KENNING, CHARLES	INDIANA	SONS, TWO UNNAMED, JOSEPH (WHO HAD JOHN ISAAC AND FOUR DAUGHTERS).
2/21/1843 4/25/1843	BROOKS, SAMUEL	MAHONING	WF. ELEANOR. CH. HAD SOME, NOT NAMED.
4/25/1829 5/12/1843	CRAIGE, WILLIAM	?	WF. MARY, NEE GAMBLE. CH. JOHN, ANN JOHNSTON, MARGARET CAMPBELL, HUGH.
7/23/1841 5/18/1843	KELLEY, MEEK (LAWYER)	?	CH. SARAH, PHINY, EUPHEMA, ANN, JANE, LOUISA, JAMES, FERGUS. BROTHER, ABNER.
5/25/1843 6/8/1843	MCCREA, JOHN	ARMAGH	WF. MARTHA. CH. JOHN MCCLURE MCCREA.
-------- 6/23/1843	WILSON, RICHARD	BRUSHVALLEY	CH. RICHARD, JAMES, JOHN, WILLIAM, GEORGE, MARY (MRS. ALLEN ROSE).
6/15/1842 7/21/1843	BOALS, THOMAS	"	WF. JANE. CH. MRS. WILLIAM WILSON (NEE JANE SIDES), WHO HAD THOMAS B., JANE,
5/20/1843 8/5/1843	KENNING, REBECCA (W/O CHARLES)	INDIANA	CH. LETITIA FULTON, REBECCA FULTON, JOSEPH KENNING (WHO HAD DAU., REBECCA), SON-IN-LAW, WILLIAM HENRY (WHO HAD SON, JOHN)
7/24/1843 8/8/1843	CUNNINGHAM, ROBT.	YOUNG	SISTER-IN-LAW, REBECCA HOPKINS.
3/31/1842 8/19/1843	DODSON, RICHARD	MAHONING	WF. MARY. CH. ELEANOR RIDDLE, THOMAS, WILLIAM, ELIZABETH ADAMS, MARY ANN MCGAHAGAN, ELIZA PENNINGTON, TRAVIS, RICHARD.
11/5/1841 11/7/1843	PATTISON, JOHN	ARMSTRONG	CH. OF ALEXANDER PATTISON (DECEASED), NAMELY, JOHN JOSEPH & EIRLIN PATTISON.
7/8/1843 11/18/1843	JOHNSTON, JAMES	CENTER	CH. ADAM, WILLIA, JAMES, ELIZABETH RANKIN, ANNE HAMILTON, MARY DIXON, SARAH LEWIS.
11/8/1842 11/28/1843	MCFARLAND, MARY	BLACKLICK	CH. RUTH LATIMORE (WHO HAD CATHERINE, POLLY, ROBERT). GDAU. MARY HOLDEN. OTHERS, JANE & MARY, DAUGHTERS OF TOBIAS BRICKER.
11/28/1843 12/8/1843	WALKER, BENJ, SR.	ARMSTRONG	CH. ROBERT, JANE (WHO HAD BEN & MARGARET), MARY ARMSTRONG (WHO HAD BEN), MARGARET JOHN-STON, JAMES, BENJAMIN, ALEXANDER.
12/9/1843 12/15/1843	CAMPBELL, CORNELIUS	"	WF. REBECCA. CH. ESTHER, JAMES, DAVID.
12/7/1843 12/22/1843	FERGUSON, SAMUEL	CENTER	WF. SUSANNA. CH. JOHN, WILLIAM, DAVIS, MARY, BELINDA, ELIZABETH, SUSANNA, JAMES (MINOR),
1/29/1840 12/26/1843	NORTH, JOHN	MAHONING	WF. ELIZABETH. CH. JOHN, ELIZABETH MEANS, JOSEPH, DEBORAH PONGE, PHEBE, DANIEL, THOMAS, WILLIAM.
----1843 1/31/1844	SCHNEIDER, JOSEPH	BLAIRSVILLE	WRITTEN IN GERMAN.
1/--/1841 2/14/1844	MCCLELLAND, JAMES	MAHONING	WF. ISABELLA. BROS. WILLIAM, JOHN (WHO HAD JOSEPH, WILLIAM, MARY, ALICE). SIS. JANE CARSON
1/20/1844 2/26/1844	MCCREERY, SAMUEL	CONEMAUGH	WF. MARGARET JANE. CH. ROBERT, ANDREW, SAMUEL.
2/23/1844 3/2/1844	DUNWOODY, ROBERT	GREEN	WF. NANCY. CH. LAVINA, ANN, MARY, LIZA JANE, ROBERT, THOMAS, WILLIAM.
12/18/1843 3/4/1844	LONG, THOMAS	MONTGOMERY	WF. CATHERINE (HAD SON ABRAHAM). SISTERS, RACHEL, JANE (SON PHILIP), MARY, ISABELLA, MARTHA.

Date	Name	Township	Details
1/15/1844 3/11/1844	HEFFELFINGER, PETER	ARMSTRONG	CH. POLLY THOMAS, BARBARA LAPSLY, DAVID, WILLIAM, JAMES.
3/1/1844 3/11/1844	CRAWFORD, WM. SR.	INDIANA	WF. MARY. CH. ROBERT, WILLIAM.
8/31/1838 3/11/1844	ALTMAN, LOUISA	BLACKLICK	CH. JACOB, HENRY, SUSAN HARROLD, CATHERINE EARHART, BETSY EARHART, LUCINDA, POLLY STEFFY.
1/12/1844 3/26/1844	DICKEY, WILLIAM	SATTSBURG	WF. SARAH. FRIENDS, JOHN M. ROBISON, N. B. LOUGHRY.
3/11/1842 4/10/1844	MCNUTT, ROBERT	ARMSTRONG	CH. MARTHA ARMSTRONG, JANE MCCURDY, SARAH, MARGARET HARBISON, ELIZABETH ANTHONY. BROTHER, JOSEPH. OTHERS, ROBT. M. ARMSTRONG.
3/8/1843 4/15/1844	LUCAS, THOMAS	WASHINGTON	WF. SUSAN. CH. SAMUEL H., MARGARET LOUGHRY, SUSANA SHIELDS, ELIZA JANE, JAMES, WILLIAM.
3/18/1842 5/10/1844	LYONS, SAMUEL, SR.	CONEMAUGH	WF. HANNAH. CH. EZEKIEL, SAMUEL, ALEX, WILL-IAM, MARTHA DOUGHERTY, ANNA KIER, SARAH GRAHAM, ELIZA KIER.
2/13/1844 5/14/1844	DICK, JOHN	GREEN	WF. MARGARET. HAD CHILDREN, DID NOT NAME THEM.
7/14/1843 6/20/1844	SHERIDAN, JOHN	(CENTER CO.)	WF. CATHERINE. CH. MANASAH, WILLIAM, GREGORY, JAMES, POLLY MELOY.
7/1/1841 7/2/1844	LAFFERTY, MARY A.	CONEMAUGH	BROS. & SISTERS, ELIZABETH STEPHENS, JOHN, ROBERT, MARTHA. MOTHER LIVING.
1/30/1844 7/16/1844	MARSHALL, JAMES	MAHONING	WF. MARGARET. SEVERAL CHILDREN, NOT NAMED.
7/3/1844 7/17/1844	CRISMAN, FRED.	BLACKLICK	CH. ELIJAH, SUSANA HARTSOCK, DOLLY, DAVID, RACHEL STEER, REBECCA BURKET, ENOCH, JOHN, SAMUEL. S/L, GEORGE STEER.
4/10/1844 7/19/1844	THOMPSON, JOHN	WASHINGTON	CH. JAMES, MILLER, JOHN, MARTHA, MARGARET.
4/28/1844 8/26/1844	DAVIS, WILLIAM	BLACKLICK	CH. JOHN, ARCHIBALD, LYMAN, DAVID, JANE, RACHEL.
8/2/1844 11/2/1844	HENDERSON, ALEX.	YOUNG	WF. HANNAH. CH. MARGARET, ROBERT. GCH. HANNAH JOHN, ROBERT, MATILDA, WILLIAM, AND ELIZABETH ROBERTSON.
11/9/1839 11/9/1844	HENRY, ROBERT	?	WF. MARTHA. CH. JOHN, NANCY, MARTHA, MARY, RACHEL.
6/15/1833 12/5/1844	TEMPLETON, JAS.	ARMSTRONG	CH. JOHN, ANNE.
11/5/1839 12/14/1844	MOORHEAD, JOSEPH (BORN 1768)	CENTER	CH. JOSEPH (DEAD), JOHN, SUSAN, WILLIAM. S/L, JOSEPH THOMPSON.
3/13/1844 12/24/1844	CLYDE, JOHN	MAHONING	CH. NANCY, JOHN, SOLOMON, WILLIAM, ISABEL MARSHALL, SARAH KIRKPATRICK, ROBERT, THOMAS, ELIZABETH PILSON.
6/28/1844 12/28/1844	SHOCKY, SUSANNA	?	SON, DANIEL SHOOP. DAUGHTER, PHEBE REFFNER.
6/9/1844 1/3/1845	PORTER, PATRICK	MAHONING	WF. ELEANOR. GSON. DAVID R. PORTER.
10/26/1844 1/4/1845	LEASURE, JOHN, SR.	"	CH. CATHERINE COLKETT, JANE HALL, REBECCA WORK, JOHN, SARAH MABON, SOLOMON, MARY THOMP-SON, ABRAHAM, ELIZABETH BRADY.
12/31/1844 1/11/1845	SWAN, THOMAS	WASHINGTON	CH. JAMES, MARY MCGARA, JANE, WILLIAM, GEORGE.
1/27/1845 1/30/1845	GEORGE, JOHN C.	INDIANA	BROS. SAM. P., JAMES, ALEXANDER, WASHINGTON. OTHERS. MRS. MARGARET RALSTON.
1/20/1845 2/4/1845	JACK, HENRY	BLAIRSVILLE	WF. ELIZABETH (WHO HAD, ELIZABETH). CH. JANE, ELIZA, LETITIA.
2/17/1844 2/7/1845	KEENER, JACOB	ARMSTRONG	WF. SUSANNA. CH. HAD SOME, NOT NAMED. GSON., SOLOMON B. KEENER.
2/8/1845 2/19/1845	MCINTYRE, MARY	BLACKLICK	CH. JAMES, ANDREW, HUGH, SIDNEY CRISMAN, ELIZABETH LAWRENCE, JOHN.

2/26/1845 3/1/1845	GRIFFITH, EVAN	GREEN	WF. SARAH. CH. ISAAC, SAMUEL, WILLIAM, ALEEDNIG, JOHN.
12/31/1844 3/17/1845	CLINEBERGER, PHILIP	?	MOTHER, ELIZABETH. BROS. JOSEPH, JACOB.
12/20/1844 3/24/1845	MARDIS, GEORGE	BRUSHVALLEY	WF. EVE. OTHERS, PERHAPS GCH. MARY ANN & DAVID MARDIS, WILLIAM REED, THOS. STOPHEL.
9/23/1845 10/22/1845	RICHEY, JOHN	?	MOTHER, SARAH. SISTERS, SARAH & RACHEL.
4/8/1845 10/11/1845	NICKLE, WILLIAM	GREEN	WF. MARY. CH. ARCHIBALD, JAMES.
11/5/1845 11/21/1845	LOUGHRY, WM.	STRONGSTOWN	WF. SARAH. SISTER, REBECCA MCQUISTON.
1/3/1845 12/18/1845	WILLSON, ROBT.	CONEMAUGH	CH. JOHN, ELIZABETH GRAHAM, AGNES LEECH, DANIEL, JOSEPH, JAMES, ROBERT.
9/2/1844 12/6/1845	CALHOUN, DAVID	CENTER	WF. MOLLY. CH. JOHN (OF OHIO), MARIA, MARG- ARET (MRS. JOHN MCCOMB), MARTHA (MRS. JAMES ELGIN), JANE (MRS. THOS. RANKIN), REBECCA (MRS. WILLIAM RANKIN).
5/1/1844 1/7/1845	GEER, ROGER (REV. SOLDIER)	BLAIRSVILLE	SON, JAMES. APPLIED FOR ARREARS PAY FOR SERVICE IN THE REVOLUTION.
12/10/1845 1/20/1846	MAHAN, JOHN	WASHINGTON	CH. MARTHA, REBECCA STUCHELL, PATRICK (HAD MARGARET), JANE STUCHELL.
5/3/1844 1/20/1846	WHARRY, JAMES	?	WF. MARY. CH. SAMUEL, JOHN, JAMES, WILLIAM, MARY (MRS. ALEX. VAN HORN), NANCY (MRS. CHAS. BARR), MARGARET.
1/1/1846 2/2/1846	HOOVER, GEORGE	MAHONING	WF. LIVING BUT NOT NAMED. CH. ADAM C., GEORGE W.
5/17/1845 2/3/1846	MCNUTT, JOSEPH	ARMSTRONG	CH. JANE MCCURDY, ISABEL RUTHERFORD, ELLEN ARMSTRONG, MARGARET HARBISON, ELIZABETH ANTHONY, SARAH SHARP.
8/6/1844 2/17/1846	TRIMBLE, WILLIAM	WHITE	WF. JANE. CH. JANE HAMILL, GEORGE, SUSAN ADAMS, MARGARET HOOD. BRO. SAMUEL, SONS-IN- LAW, ROBERT HAMILL, JAMES HOOD.
2/9/1846 2/19/1846	REPINE, JOHN	BLACKLICK	WF. RUTH. CH. BOWDEN, DANIEL, THOMAS, MARIA (MRS. MATHEW CANEDY), MARGARET, MARY WILEY.
2/17/1846 3/3/1846	LYDICK, SAM. JR.	RAYNE	WF. SARAH. CH. LUCINDA, ELLEN (BOTH UNDER 15). BROTHER, PATRICK.
1/2/1846 3/5/1846	FERGUSON, JAMES	BLACKLICK	WF. MARGARET. CH. ELLIOTT, ELIZABETH PETTICORD, AARON, WILLIAM, JAMES, ANDREW, JOHN, DAVID, MARGARET, ELI, JOSEPH.
10/28/1845 3/23/1846	MCCONNELL, JAMES	?	WF. MARGORY. CH. JOHN.
5/15/1846 6/13/1846	ROSS, JOHN	CENTER	WF. ELLEN. CH. ELIZA, MARGARET, JOHN D., JAMES, ALEX, ISABELL(MRS. ROBT. MCKEE), JOSEPH, ELLEN SIMPSON, SAMUEL.
10/3/1845 6/13/1846	MARSHALL, SAMUEL	CONEMAUGH	WF. MARY. CH. JOSEPH, JOHN, MARY, ELIZABETH, JANE, REBECCA, WALTER, WM., SAM, ARCHIBALD.
4/18/1846 5/11/1846	ISENBARGER, GABRIEL	GREEN	WF. NOT NAMED. CH. PETER, JOHN, HENRY.
6/12/1846 6/24/1846	KINTER, A. F.	W. MAHONING	WF. CATHERINE. CH. CHRISTIANA, I. R., HENRY A. JOHN A.
6/8/1846 6/25/1846	WILSON, JOHN	CENTER	WF. MARTHA. CH. WILLIAM, MARY CUMMINS, AND PERHAPS OTHERS.
11/5/1845 7/21/1846	LOGAN, JOHN	WHEATFIELD	WF. ISABELLA. CH. SAMUEL, HANNAH HICE, MAR- GARET, ANN.
4/3/1843 4/12/1847	DILL, MATTHEW	BRUSHVALLEY	WF. MARY. CH. JOHN, GEORGE, JAMES, MARGARET DAVIS.
3/29/1847 4/13/1847	CARREL, PATRICK	GREEN	WF. ROSE ANN. CH. JAMES, MARY ANN.
1/22/1846 5/14/1847	WEAMER, FRED	MAHONING	WF. MARGARET. CH. CASPER, DAN, ABE, GEORGE, FRED, ADAM, CATH. SMITH, ELIZ. POLLIUS.

4/27/1847 5/17/1847	SMILEY, DAVID	MAHONING	WF. MARY. CH. JOHN, OTHERS NOT NAMED.
7/--/1829 4/27/1847	LEWIS, SARAH	WASHINGTON	CH. ELIZABETH (MRS. WM. DOUGHERTY), ANN (MRS. EVAN LEWIS), DAVID, JOSHUA, JOHN, BROTHER, ABE HICKS OF HUNTINGDON CO., PA.
5/28/1847 7/13/1847	MCCLAREN, WM. JR.	INDIANA	WF. PHEBE. CH. NONE MENTIONED.
3/1/1847 8/17/1847	MCLAUGHLIN, WM.	RAYNE	WF. ELIZABETH. CH. MADISON, JAMES, ISABEL, JANE, HARRIET ANN.
7/17/1829 8/21/1847	TURNER, JOSEPH	BLACKLICK	WF. MARGARET. CH. ELEANOR, JAMES, WM., NATHANIEL. S/L, DAVID LUTMAN.
1/26/1847 8/25/1847	ROUSH, HENRY, SR.	W. MAHONING	WF. ANN. HENRY, JOHN, ANDREW, GEORGE, SAMUEL, ELLEN, ANN, CATHERINE (HAD HEN. & CATH. STEER)
11/2/1846 9/1/1847	WALKER, ROBT. M.	ARMSTRONG	WF. JANE. CH. SAMUEL, JAMES, MARTHA, JOHN, BENJAMIN, SUSANNA, ROBERT F.
7/13/1844 9/28/1847	WILSON, JANE	CONEMAUGH	DAU. JANE MARSHALL. OTHERS, SAMUEL & WM. C. MARSHALL.
3/--/1837 10/15/1847	MCCURDY, JAS. SR.	WHEATFIELD	CH. ARCHIBALD, ISAAC, ISABELLA, SARAH, JAMES, POLLY, HANNAH, JOHN, JANE, MARTIN, GEORGE (DEAD), WF. SARAH.
1/10/1848 2/2/1848	ANGUISH, DANIEL	GREEN	WF. BARBARA. OTHERS, DANIEL ANGUISH, S/O JOHN, ABRAHAM BRECHBILL.
1/2/1848 2/17/1848	AYERS, SYLVANUS	MAHONING	WF. ELEANOR. CH. JONATHAN, JAMES (MINORS).
2/18/1848 2/25/1848	TRIMBLE, JOHN	E. MAHONING	WF. ANN. CH. MARY HUTCHISON, GEORGE. GSON. JOHN M. TRIMBLE. BRO SAMUEL TRIMBLE.
12/16/1845 3/28/1848	ROBISON, ELIZABETH	ARMSTRONG	CH. JAMES, SAMUEL, JOSEPH, SARAH.
3/15/1845 4/4/1848	GRIER, ADORA	BLACKLICH	BRO. GEORGE GRIER & WIFE, MARTHA. BROTHER, MARK GRIER (DEAD).
-------- 4/10/1848	HOCKINGBERRY, THOS.	S. MAHONING	SON, ALEXANDER.
3/2/1848 4/12/1848	ALLISON, JOHN G.	GREEN	WF. MARGARET. CH. THOMAS, JACOB, AGNES, MARGARET, REBECCA. CATHERINE BARR, JOHN, MARY (MRS. THOMAS ALLISON.)
11/18/1847 4/26/1848	RENDRIXON, AMARIAH	CENTER	WF. ELIZABETH. CH. PHILIP, ESTHER DRENNING, SARAH GRIFFITH, POLLY MIKESELL, NANCY WHETSTONE, ANNA WIDDICK, MARTHA, WID OF WM. HENDRIXON.
5/8/1848 --------	TAYLOR, MARY	SALTSBURG	CH. ANDREW, HARRISON, JAMES, THOMAS, ELIZABETH, JANE.
1/--/1842 8/14/1848	DAVIS, STEWART	BLAIRSVILLE	WF. ELIZABETH. CH. ROBERT S., ROCHE STREETER, AMOS B., CHESTER C., SAMUEL H., ENICE.
4/24/1848 9/7/1848	EARHART, DAVID (D. 6/3/1848)	(SCOTT CO., IOWA.)	WF. KATHERINE. CH. SAMUEL, PHILIP, DAVID, WM., HENRY, DANIEL, JOSEPH, ROBERT, JOHN. LUCY RICE, MARY.
2/20/1848 9/20/1848	BROWN, WILLIAM	BLACKLICK	WF. ELIZABETH. CH. ANDREW, JOHN, WILLIAM, GEORGE, ELIZABETH, REBECCA.
9/25/1848 9/29/1848	BELL, WALTER	WHITE	WF. ELIZABETH. CH. JOHN, JAMES, JACKSON, GEORGE W., MOSES C., JANE, WALTER, MARY MONTGOMERY.
8/17/1844 10/7/1848	FETTERMAN, MICH.	BRUSHVALLEY	WF. CATHERINE. CH. DAVID, EMANUEL, ELIZABETH CRAMER, JOHN, MICHAEL, ANDREW, SOPHIA DICK, DANIEL, JACOB, CATHERINE OLIVILIER, MARY GEORGE.
8/26/1848 11/1/1848	BURKE, EDMUND	STRONGSTOWN	DAU. ELLEM M. OTHERS, ELIZA ROBINSON, THOS. CRISWELL, JAS. CRISWELL, JAMES SWEENY.
11/11/1848 12/7/1848	STUMP, MICHAEL	S. MAHONING	WF. PRUDENCE. CH. ANDREW P., AND OTHERS, NOT NAMED.
8/21/1847 12/12/1848	MCAFFEE, PATRICK	BLAIRSVILLE	WF. ANN. CH. JOHN, JAMES, ANN, MARGARET, SARAH, ELIZABETH, DANIEL, MARY MULLEN.

64

6/17/1847 1/26/1849	HARTSOCK, JOHN	BLACKLICK	WF. SUSANNA. CH. CHRISTINA, RACHEL, HANNAH, SAMUEL, JONATHAN, FREDERICK, JOSEPH, REBECCA, ELIZABETH.
4/15/1848 2/12/1849	ROSS, ELENOR	CENTER	CH. ISABELLA, ELIZA, JANE, MARGARET, JOSEPH, ALEXANDER, SAMUEL, GSONS. JOHN ROSS, JOHN MCGEE.
11/28/1848 1/23/1849	COLEMAN, JOHN T.	WF. MAHONING	WF. SUSAN. BROS. HENRY, ELIJAH.
1/4/1847 2/3/1849	HENRY, JOHN	ARMSTRONG	SISTER, NANCY (MRS. JOHN MCCAHEN, LONDONDERRY, IRELAND), BRO. ROBERT, AND HIS WIDOW, MARGARET. MARY (MRS. MATHEW HARBISON.)
12/13/1848 3/22/1849	CRAIG, JOHN	RAYNE	CH. ANN. OTHERS, ALFRED S. & ANN ELIZABETH SHIELDS.
2/9/1849 3/27/1849	SUTTER, JACOB	N. MAHONING	WF. ELIZABETH. CH. NONE MENTIONED.
2/14/1849 3/27/1849	LUCAS, JOHN	ARMSTRONG	CH. ALEX, NANCY TEMPLETON, MARY ANN, MARTHA MEARS, ELIZA, SARAH, ADALINE.
9/25/1835 4/5/1849	BELL, THOMAS	BLACKLICK	WF. MARY. CH. NONE MENTIONED.
10/29/1847 6/14/1849	PHILLIPS, JANE	?	FRIEND, CURENCE (MRS. FREDERICK LYDICK).
6/4/1842 3/12/1847	BUCHANAN, JOHN, SR.	?	CH. JAMES, JOHN, CHARLES, MRS. ROBERT GETTY. GDAU. JANE CRAIG.
6/13/1845 3/22/1847	WEIRS, JOSEPH	BLACKLICK	BRO. ABRAHAM (WHO HAD SONS, JOSEPH & WILLIAM).
8/16/1845 4/12/1847	WIGGINS, ANDREW	ARMSTRONG	WF. REBECCA. CH. SAMUEL, OTHERS MENTIONED. NOT NAMES.
1/26/1842 8/13/1849	MOORE, ABE. SR.	WASHINGTON	WF. FRANCES. CH. JAMES, MARGARET (MRS. JOHN BROWN), FANNY (MRS. SAM. HALL), ABRAHAM, HENRY.
6/11/1849 8/21/1849	GUTTS, JOHN	N MAHONING	WF. MARY. CH. SEVERAL, NOT NAMED.
11/30/1848 10/11/1849	LOSE, MARGARET	BLAIRSVILLE	HUSBAND, GEORGE. CH. NONE MENTIONED.
———— 11/5/1849	BROWN, THOMAS	BLACKLICK	WF. ELENOR. CH. THOMAS, HENRIETTA, ELEANOR, ANDREW, MICHAEL, PETER.

END OF INDIANA COUNTY WILLS.

DATE	GRANTOR	GRANTEE	TOWNSHIP	DESCRIPTION
5/29/1798	ROG. & RACHEL ROBINSON	THOMAS HINDMAN	CONEMAUGH	ON KISKY RIVER
4/28/1804	JOHN & SARAH HINDMAN	" "	"	" " RIVER
4/1/1805	WM. & MARY KEIR	GEORGE SCOTT	"	PAT. TO ANN TODD
3/4/1806	TOM MCCARTNEY, SHERIFF	GEO. EMFILED (MILLER)	WHEATFIELD	ON YELLOW CREEK
1/24/1805	TOM & DORCAS DUNCAN	JOHN LONG	CONEMAUGH	ON BLACKLICK "
11/1/1805	DR. BENJ. SAY (PHILA.)	MICH. KENNY HEIRS	?	ON YELLOW CREEK
------ 1806	SIMON HOVEY	CHARLES CAMPBELL	?	ADJ. MOORHEAD
3/23/1807	ROD. GORDON, SR.;	WM. GORDON (SON)	WASHINGTON	LIVESTOCK, ETC.
9/6/1806	THOMAS LITTLE	SAMUEL TALMADGE	?	" "
"	" " "	THOMAS N. SLOAN	?	" "
2/14/1801	WILLIAM NEIL	MARY NEIL	ARMSTRONG	ON ALTMAN RUN
4/24/1806	THOMAS & MARGARET MCGAUGHEY	WILLIAM HALL	"	" STONY "
------ 1806	THOMAS BRACKEN	THOMAS CLARKE	WHEATFIELD	" BLACKLICK CREEK
11/12/1806	JAS. & MARY ORR	JOHN BEATTY (IRELAND)	ARMSTRONG	?
9/7/1805	GEO. & ELIZ. CLYMER	INDIANA COUNTY	?	NEAR CENTER OF CO.
3/23/1807	JAS. & JANE BLACK	THOS. N. SLOAN	?	ON CONEMAUGH RIVER
4/6/1795	SAM KIRKPATRICK	HEN. KIRKPATRICK	?	" ALTMANS RUN
7/9/1794	ROBERT LOWERS	DAVID DUNCAN	?	ADJ. MOSES STEWART
1/29/1807	DAVID DUNCAN EST.	HUGH WEIR	?	?
6/3/1807	ALEX. MOORHEAD	JOHN ARMITAGE	CENTER	179 ACRES.
"	" " "	WM. & JOHN CUMMINS	"	ADJ. CHAS. MCGUIRE
8/1/1806	ISAAC DECKER	THOMAS KERR	WHEATFIELD	ARMAGH TOWNSITE
---- 1790	JAS. WILKINS, SR.	JAS. WILKENS, JR.	ARMSTRONG	ON TWOLICK CREEK
7/10/1807	ROBERT FRAZER	WILLIAM FRAZER,	?	ALL HIS CHILDREN,
		MARY MCDONALD,		TO WHOM HE DEEDE
		ELIZABETH FRAZER,		ALL PERSONAL &
		JINEY GORDON		REAL PROPERTY
5/9/1806	WM. COCHRAN	DAVID GILLILAND	CONEMAUGH	(NANCY, WIFE OF WM.)
4/13/1806	INDIANA COUNTY	WM. FALLOON	INDIANA	TOWN LOT NO 85
7/20/1807	JACOB CRIBBS	JOHN CUMMINS	CENTER	?
6/20/1807	ALEX. & JEAN TAYLOR	THOMAS BURNS	"	277 ACRES
7/20/1807	ALEX. KERNAHAN	JAMES MCDONALD & SAMUEL PARKER	?	LIVESTOCK, ETC.
------ 1807	CONRAD HEATER	ROBERT UNDERWOOD	WASHINGTON (D.C.)	POWER OF ATTORNEY
------ 1807	BENJ. WALKER	ROBT. WALKER (SON)	?	LIVESTOCK, ETC.

END OF EARLY INDIANA COUNTY DEEDS.

INDEX

BOWERSOX, PAUL	13	CALHOUN, DAVID	63	COLE, WILLIAM, SR.	38
BOYD, ARCHIBALD	7	CAMERON, CHARLES	42	COLEMAN, JOHN	54
BOYER, GEORGE	16	DUNCAN	8, 44	JOHN T.	65
SAMUEL	40	FINDLEY	51	COLLINGS, WILLIAM	25
BOYLE, THOMAS	51	CAMP, HENRY	17	COLLINS, JOHN	44
BRACKEN, THOMAS	66	HETH	51	COLWELL, SAMUEL	48
WILLIAM	52	CAMPBELL, ALEXANDER	18	COOK, JAMES	43
BRADY, CAPT. JOHN	2	ANDREW	4	JOHN	14
JOHN	10, 15	GEN. CHARLES	53	COL., WILLIAM	30
BRAIZLER, ROBERT	6	CORNELIUS	61	COOL, CAPT. SIMON	3
BRAUCHER, ADAM	60	JAMES	7, 45	COOLY, JONATHAN	5
BREEZE, NEHEMIAH	1	JOHN	1, 3	COOPER, BENJAMIN B.	58
BRENNER, FRANCIS PETER	32	HERCULES	44	CONNER, GEORGE	47
JOHN	6	MICHAEL	50, 55	JOSEPH	38
LUDWIG	4	WILLIAM	2	CONRAD, ADAM	27
BREON, GEORGE	10	CANNON, ALEXANDER	49	JACOB	37
BREWER, HENRY	45	FERGUS	50	CORL, JOHN	19
BRICKER, JOHN	53	WILLIAM	50	CORNELIUS, JOHN	14
PETER	47	CANTWELL, JAMES	45	WILLIAM	43
BRIDGENS, THOMAS	1	CARIF, MILES	6	CORTING, GEORGE	6
BRIGGS, JOHN, SR.	37	CARLING, GEORGE	7	COTNER, TOBIAS	4
BRIGHT, GEORGE	11	CARRELL, PATRICK	63	COURSIN, JAMES	25
BRINSER, PHILIP	17	CARRY, JOHN	61	COVENHOVEN, ALBRIGHT	1
BRITTAIN, ZEBOETH	22	CARSCADDON, JAMES	34	COWEN, MARGARET	45
BROMLEY, JOHN	6	CARSON, ADAM	21	COX, SAMUEL	2
BRONSTON, ROBERT	57	CARTER, MARY	32	COY, HENRY	50
BROOK, SAMUEL	10, 61	RICHARD	8	CRAIG, HENRY	65
BROSIUS, SEBASTIAN	22	CASE, PETER	37	MATTHEW	47
BROTHERTON, ROBERT	44	CATHERMAN, DAVID	13, 32, 43	ROBERT	13, 57
BROUSE, ADAM	10	CATIN, IGNATIUS	10	CRAIGE, WILLIAM	61
BROWN, ALEXANDER	44	CAUSERT, JAMES	17	CRAMER, JOHN	48
ANDREW	45	CESSNA, CHARLES	45	CRAVEN, THOMAS	46
CHRISTIAN	39	CHAMBERLAIN, COL. WM.	41	CRAWFORD, HENRY	1
DANIEL	1	CHAPMAN, JOHN	11, 50	MOSES	46
DAVID	49	CHENEY, JAMES	12	WILLIAM	2
ELIAS	4	JOHN	28	WILLIAM, SR.	62
JAMES	9	CHARRY, JAMES	31	CREECE, JOHN	29
JANE	16	CHILD, JOHN	35	CREIGHTON, EDWARD	33
JEREMIAH	54	CHRIST, ADAM	33	CREMER, JOHN, SR.	56
JOHN	40	CHRISTMAN, MICHAEL	13	CREPS, JACOB	49
MATTHEW	20	CHRISTMAN, GEORGE	38, 53	CRIBBS, DAVID	46
THOMAS	65	JAMES	2	JACOB	46, 66
WILLIAM	5, 64	JOHN	18, 34, 35	CRISSMAN, GEORGE	45
BRUNNER, JACOB	30	MARY	48	G. W.	49
ULRICH	16	ROBERT	26	FREDERICK	62
BUCHANAN, ARTHUR	44	SAMUEL	18	CROCKETT, THOMAS	3
JOHN, SR.	65	RUTH	55	CROOKS, SAMUEL	3
BUNDY, WILLIAM	17	WILLIAM	16, 18, 29, 25	CROTZER (KRATZER), JOHN	9
BUOY, EDWARD	13	CLAWSON, JOSIAH	11	CROWNOVER, JAMES	1
BURGET, GEORGE	33	MARY	48	CROSSMAN, ASA	45
BURK, HENRY	21	RICHARD	45	CULBERTSON, ISAAC	50
BURKE, EDMUND	64	ROSS	45	CULP, TILMAN	13
BURLEW, ALEXANDER	17	CLELAND, WILLIAM	5, 21	CUMMINGS, JOHN	15
BURNS, HENRY	50	CLEMENS, PETER	10	CUMMINS, JOHN	52
THOMAS	56	CLENDENIN, WM. SR.	18	JANET	55
BUTLER, ABNER	50	CLINEBERGER, PHILIP	63	CUMPTON, REUBEN	60
RICHARD	6	SAMUEL	48	CUNNINGHAM, DAVID	54
ROBERT	18	CLYDE, JOHN	62	ROBERT	61
		CLYMER, GEORGE	66	CURRY, JAMES	47
CALDWELL, EDWARD	14	COCH (KOCH), ADAM	11	JOHN	6
JOHN	33	COCHRAN, JAMES	23, 27	ROBERT	2
CALHOON, CAPT. GEORGE	20	WILLIAM	66	CUTTER, ROBERT	34

DALE, SAMUEL	30	
DARROUGH, JOHN	42	
DASSON, DANIEL	2	
DAUGHERTY, WILLIAM	1	
DAVIDSON, JAMES	6	
DAVIS, ALEXANDER	48	
CATHERINE	54	
JAMES I,	50	
JANE	45	
JOHN	46	
JOSHUA	60, 49	
MARGARET	5	
SILAS	49	
SIMON	46, 54	
STEPHEN	5	
STEWART	64	
WILLIAM	34, 46, 62	
DEAL, HENRY	18	
JOHN	18	
PHILIP	9	
DEAN, DAVID	2	
DEARMIN, WILLIAM	46	
DECKER, ISAAC	66	
DEELMAN, PETER	7	
DEEM, ADAM	2	
DEHAAS, COL. PHILIP	32	
DELL, LEONARD	6	
DELONGCHAMP, CHAS. J.	7	
DELVIN, WILLIAM	45	
DENNISTON, JOHN	45, 47, 49	
DERR, FREDERICK	9	
LUDWIG	4	
DEVER, JOHN	15	
DEVLIN, SAMUEL	50	
DEVORE, DAVID	6	
DEVORS, JOHN	12	
DEWART, WILLIAM, JR.	35	
DEWITT, ABRAHAM	3	
ISAAC	11	
PAUL	1, 10	
DIAS, ANDREW	50	
THOMAS	47	
DICK, JAMES	59	
JOHN	56	
MARGARET	47	
MARY	44	
DICKSON, JOHN	35	
THOMAS	49	
DICKEY, WILLIAM	62	
DIEM, THOMAS	3	
DIETRICH, JOHN	34	
DILDINE, HENRY	34	
DILL, MATTHEW	63	
DIMM, JACOB	36	
DIMSY, CORNELIUS	4	
DINIUS, JOHN	17	
DISSLER, DAVID	13, 15, 31	
DRAKE, JOHN	1	
DREESE, JACOB	23	
JOHN, SR.	15	
DREISBACH, JACOB	30	
MARTIN, SR.	11	

DRESHER, SAMUEL	16	
DRUM, CATHERINE	10	
MAJ. CHARLES	16	
DRUCKENMILLER, FREDERICK	22	
PETER	22, 42	
DODDERER, PHILIP	7	
DODSON, RICHARD	61	
DOEBLER, JOSEPH	24	
DONALDSON, ALEXANDER	4	
JOHN	19, 33	
WILLIAM	33	
DONAT, PETER	15	
DONMEYER, JOHN	13	
DORNSIFE, JOHN	7	
DOTY, ZEBULON	48	
DOUGAN, WILLIAM	2	
DOUGHERTY, HUGH	48	
JAMES	47	
JOHN	11	
ELINOR	26	
GEORGE	34	
NANCY	48	
RACHEL	48	
THOMAS	46	
DOUGLASS, BARNABAS	49	
SAMUEL	45	
WILLIAM	16	
DOUTHET, NATHANIEL	52	
DUCK (DOCK), NINEVAH	22	
DUFFIELD, DR. SAMUEL	55	
DUNCAN, DAVID	66	
SAMUEL	48	
TIMOTHY	66	
DUNHAM, JOSEPH W.	50	
DUNKLEBERGER, PHILIP	3	
DUNKLE, JACOB	43	
WILLIAM	40	
DUNLAP, JOHN	20	
DUNN, JAMES	45, 54	
DUNNING, CATHERINE	14	
SAMUEL	14, 34	
DUNWOODY, ROBERT	61	
DUNSCOMB, JAMES	6	
DURHAM, JAMES	37	
DUSING, NICHOLAS	23	
EAGLER, WILLIAM	42	
EARHART, ANTHONY	55	
DAVID	64	
ELIZABETH	60	
EASTWOOD, CHARLES	6	
EASTERLY, GEORGE	28	
EASTON, JOHN	49	
EBY, JACOB	47	
ECKENROTE, ADAM	18	
CHRISTIAN	38	
ECKHART, JACOB	35	
EGBERT, NICHOLAS	38	
ELDER, ANN	52	
ROBERT	47	
ELDRICKS, ADAM	50	
ELGIN, DANIEL	49	
EICHENMOYER, ANDREW	16	

EICHINGER, HENRY	17	
ELLIOTT, JOHN	15, 58	
EMERICH, MICHAEL	31	
EMERSON, ELIZABETH	46	
EMERY, DAVID	4, 9	
EMMET, JOHN	31, 35	
ENOCH, ABRAHAM	7	
EPLER, JOHN	13	
EPLEY, CHRISTIAN	14	
JOHN	16	
MARTIN	10	
ERNE, ELIZABETH	33	
ERTLE, VALENTINE, SR.	7	
ERWIN, SAMUEL	37	
ESBENSHIP, JACOB	3	
ESCHBACH, JOHN	18	
WILLIAM	34	
ESPER, SIMON	1	
ESPY, GEORGE	12	
JAMES	25	
ETZWEILER, GEORGE	2	
EVANS, CALEB	29	
EVAN R.	17	
JOSEPH	36	
NATHANIEL	11	
ROGER	1	
EVERETT, OBED	15	
EVES, JOHN	28	
EWIG, ADAM, SR.	28	
PHILIP	1	
EWING, ALEXANDER	60	
JASPER	27	
JOHN, SR.	60	
ROBERT	58	
FAIR, HENRY	46	
FAIRBANKS, DAVID	48	
FAIRMAN, JAMES	47, 51	
FAIRWEATHER, EDMOND	16, 18	
FALLS, JAMES	18	
FAULKNER, JOHN	21	
FEALS, ALEXANDER	56	
FEE, ANDREW	54	
FELKER, JOHN	12	
JOHN HENRY	36	
FENTON, JOHN	50	
FERGUSON, CHARLES	46	
JAMES	23, 63	
SAMUEL	61	
FERSTER, PETER	9	
FERTICH (FERTIG), ADAM	42	
FETTER, ELIZABETH	43	
JACOB	42	
FETTERMAN, MICHAEL	64	
FINLEY, JAMES	47, 49	
JOHN	1	
FISHER, JOHN	6, 24, 50	
MARY	11	
WILLIAM	7	
FITMAN, PHILIP	37	
FITZSIMMONS, JOHN	10	
FLEMING, JAMES	22	

FLEMING, JOHN 20
SARAH M. 46
FLICK, PETER 35
FLICKINGER, PETER 14
FLIN, LAWRENCE 24
FOCHT, JONAS 22
FOLLMER, FREDERICK 36
JACOB 30
MICHAEL 6, 23
FOLTZ, FRANCIS 12
FOLWEILER, HENRY 11
FORCE, JACOB 13
FORESMAN, SARAH 14
FORSTER, JAMES 22
JOHN 21
MARGARET 22
SARAH 23
THOMAS 11
FOULK, OWEN 14
FOUST, ABRAHAM 8
JACOB, SR. 7
FOWLER, DAVID 32
FOX, ANDREW 7
JOHN 4, 11
FRANKLIN, DANIEL 14
FRANTZ, LEWIS 12
MICHAEL 11
FRAZER, ROBERT 66
FREALY, PHILIP 14
FREDERICK, GEORGE 11, 42
FREDERICKI, CHARLES 34
FREELAND, GARRET 4
FREEMAN, NATHANIEL 9
FREES, PETER, SR. 12, 13
FREY, ANDREW 16
JACOB 12
FRICK, JOHN 36
PHILIP 35
FRICKEY, CHRISTIAN 24
FRIENDLY, JOHN 42
FROAS, HENRY 16
FULCOMER, GEORGE 49
FULLER, FREDERICK 36
FULLERTON, WILLIAM 31
FURROW, STOPHEL 2
FURY, PATRICK 10

GABLE, DANIEL 5
FREDERICK 7
GAILEY, JAMES 57
GALBRAITH, ROBERT 46
GALLAHER, ELIZABETH 36
GARDNER, JOHN 60
GARMAN, JOHN 21
GARRET, ELISHA 3
GARY, WILLIAM 12
GASKINS, THOMAS 38
GASTEN, JOHN 18
ROBERT 23
GAUGLER, GEORGE 19
NICHOLAS 13
GAUGH, CHARLES 21
CATHERINE 27
GEARHART, ISAAC 17
JACOB 32, 38, 40
PHILIP 31
GEARY, JAMES 47
GEER, DWIGHT 47
ROGER 63
GEIGER, VALENTINE 20
GEIST, CONRAD 11
JOHN 18
GEORGE, JOHN C. 62
WILLIAM 2
GETTIG, CHRISTOPHER 22, 25
" JR 28
FREDERICK 11
GETTY, ALEXANDER 50
ANDREW 52
JOHN 54
JAMES 57
GETZ, PETER 9
GIBBONS, EDWARD 6
GIBSON, DAVID 8
GEORGE 8
JAMES 49
NANCY 57
THOMAS 3
GILBERT, PAUL 31
GILLESPIE, WILLIAM 3
GILMORE, ALEXANDER 49
GILPIN, JOSEPH JR. & SR. 56
GINGLES, JAMES 10
GINGLES, JOHN 33
WILLIAM 12
GIRTON, WILLIAM 38
GLASGOW, JOHN 44
WILLIAM 12
GLASS, EVE 43
JOHN 36
JOHN GEORGE 29
GLENN, JOHN 10
GOBIN, CHARLES 8
HUGH 6
GODDARD, JOHN 9
GODHART, JOHN 25
GOODLANDER, CHRISTIAN 13
GOODMAN, HENRY 6
GORDON, ROBERT 66
GORMAN, CHARLES 3
DAVID 48
GOSSLER, ANDREW 15
GRAHAM, ALLEN 58
HANNAH 48
JANE 58
JOHN 55, 57
JOSEPH 55
GRANT, ALEXANDER 1
GEORGE 5
GRAY, JOHN 60
NEIL 4
ROBERT 18
GRAY, WILLIAM 40
GRAYBILL, JOHN 31
GREEN, JOSEPH 32
CAPT. JOSEPH 32
MARGARET 4
SAMUEL 49
GREENLEE, WILLIAM 5
GREGG, EZEKIEL 45
ROBERT 1
WILLIAM 5
GRIER, ADORA 64
MARK 58
GRIFFITH, CATHERINE 51
EVAN 63
JESSE 54
GRONER, HENRY 7
GRONINGER, LEONARD 22
GROSSCUP, SAMUEL 10
GROVE, GEORGE MICHAEL 4
MICHAEL 8
GRUBB, JACOB 40
GRUBER, JOHN GEORGE 23
GRUMBACH, GEORGE H. 43
GRUMBLING, GEORGE 46

HAAS, HENRY 12
LAWRENCE 11
HADDEN, BERTHOLOMEW 45
HAGER, JOHN 8
HAGGERTY, JOHN 43
HAFLICH, NICHOLAS 50
HAFFLICH, JACOB 40
JOHN 19
HAHN, MICHAEL, SR. 27
HAIN, GEORGE, SR. 4, 26
WILLIAM 5
HAINES, JAMES 2
JOHN 39
JOSIAH 24
HALL, JOHN 4
PETER 4
WILLIAM 45
HAMILTON, ALEXANDER 2
JAMES 5, 16, 49
JANE 56
ROBERT 53
THOMAS 33
WILLIAM 58
HAMMER, THOMAS 13
HAMMOND, DAVID 27
GEORGE 17
HAMPTON, JOSEPH 29
HANEY, CHRISTOPHER, SR. 22
HARE, JOSEPH 13
HARLAN, THOMAS 38
HANNA, WILLIAM 9
HARRIS, LAIRD 13
ROBERT 15
SAMUEL 23
WILLIAM 33
HARRISON, GEORGE 13

HARRISON, JAMES	30, 60	
JOHN	21	
HARROLD, CHRISTOPHER	53	
JOHN	53, 57	
HART, JOHN, ROBERT	49, 45	
HARTER, JOHN	27	
HARTMAN, THOMAS	38	
HARTSOCK, JOHN	65	
HASLET, JANE	39	
ROBERT	8	
HASSINGER, JACOB	29	
JOHN	9, 35	
HAUN, SAMUEL	6	
HAVERLING, JACOB	25	
HAWK, GEORGE	5	
HAYNES, BARTHOLOMEW	21	
HAZLET, JAMES	49	
JOHN	47	
SARAH	47	
HARKINS, JOHN	48	
HEATER, BARBARA	48	
CONRAD	66	
HECKERT, ANN E.	27	
JOHN	9	
HEDDEN, WILLIAM, SR.	12	
HEFFER, ANDREW	5	
ELIZABETH	15	
HEFFELFINGER, PETER	62	
HEHN, CONRAD	43	
HEIDENRICH, JOHN	9	
HEILMAN, JACOB	14	
HELMAN, HERMAN	8	
HENNING, HIRONOMUS	8	
JOHN	9	
HENDERSON, ALEXANDER	62	
BRICE	57	
JAMES	3	
REV. J. W.	47	
JOHN	49	
SAMUEL & WILL.	49	
HENDERSHOT, MICHAEL	35	
HENDRICKS, JACOB	39	
JOHN	40	
SAMUEL	16	
HENDRICKSON, PETER	13	
HENDRIXON, AMARIAH	64	
HENNEBACH, DANIEL	14	
HEPBURN, SAMUEL	10	
HENRY, ELIZABETH A.	51	
JOHN	65	
ROBERT	62	
HERROLD, JOHN GEORGE	29	
HERRON, HANNAH	48	
WILLIAM	48	
HETTRICK, NICHOLAS	32	
HEWITT, EDWARD	10	
HILLEBRAND, LEVI	37	
HICE, HENRY	46, 60	
GEORGE	56	
SAMUEL	57	
HICKS, JACOB	48	
HINDMAN, JOHN	66	
HIORN, WILLIAM	4	
HOAR, BENJAMIN	28	
HOBACHER, PETER	46	
HOCKENBERRY, THOMAS	64	
HODGENS, SAMUEL	6	
HOFF, VORIS	46	
HOFFMAN, GEORGE	41	
PETER	17	
HOGE, GEORGE	17	
REV. JOHN	32	
JOSEPH	14	
HOGG, JAMES	4	
HOLLENBACH, JACOB	18	
HOLLER, ISAAC	47	
HOLSTEIN, GEORGE	36	
HOLTZAPPLE, HENRY	28	
HOPKINS, JANE	50	
JOHN	46	
ROBERT	3	
HOOD, JOHN	9, 25	
ROBERT	51	
HOOK, STEPHEN	15, 24	
HOOVER, GEORGE	63	
JOHN	14	
HORSEFALL, WILLIAM	3	
HOSACK, SAMUEL R.	51	
HOSTERMAN, COL. PETER	12	
HOUCK, JACOB	3	
HOUSEL, MARTIN	31	
PETER	8	
HOVEY, SIMON	66	
HOW, SAMUEL	8	
HOWER, BARBARA	31	
JOHN FREDERICK	28	
HUDSON, JOSEPH	25	
HUFFMAN, PETER	34	
PHILIP	4	
HUFFNAGLE, FRANK	49	
HUGHES, ELLIS	17, 27	
GARRETT	8	
GEORGE	8	
JAMES, JR.	3	
JAMES, SR.	4	
JOHN	37	
MARY	9	
THOMAS	14	
HULL, PHINEAS	13	
HURLEY, MARGARET	7	
HUMMEL, GEORGE ADAM	33	
JOHN	10, 12	
HUMPHREY, JOHN	11	
HUNT, WILSON	11	
HUNTER, ALEXANDER	16	
JAMES	18	
COL. SAMUEL	20	
WILLIAM	11	
HUNT, CHARLES	44	
AGNES	28	
HURSH, PHILIP	11	
HUSTON, JAMES	60	
HUSTON, THOMAS	56	
HUTCHINSON, CORNELIUS	49	
JOSEPH	30	
MARY	35	
MARGARET	37	
THOMAS	10	
IDDINGS, WILLIAM	12	
IGON, SARAH	50	
IKELER, WILLIAM	14	
INGLEDOE, THOMAS	6	
IRWIN, ALEXANDER	4	
ELIPHALET	45	
FRANCIS	31	
JACOB	15	
JOHN	22, 25	
RICHARD	1, 39, 41	
ROBERT	18	
WILLIAM	24	
ISENBARGER, GABRIEL	63	
JACK, HENRY	62	
JACKSON, JEREMIAH	9, 10, 11	
JACOBY, MARY	18	
JAMES, ISAAC	7	
JENKINS, JAMES	4, 11	
PHEBE	29	
JOB, JOHN	3	
JOHN, GRIFFITH	36	
ISAAC	30	
JOHNSON, JOHN	3, 5, 6	
RICHARD	1	
ROBERT	10, 45	
THOMAS	47	
WILLIAM	2	
JOHNSTON, JAMES	47, 61	
JOHN	55, 60	
REBECCA	61	
COL. ROBERT	50	
ROBERT	50	
JONES, ELIZABETH	32	
LEVI	1	
WILLIAM	45, 60	
JODON, PETER	14	
JORDAN, GEORGE	9	
PETER	13	
JORDEN, ROBERT	57	
JORDON, WILLIAM	8	
KADERMAN, PHILIP	26	
KAIN, JOHN	56	
KALABASH, ANTHONY	6	
KANNELL, MARK	11	
KARSNER, PETER	18	
KATON, SAMUEL, SR.	60	
KAUFMAN, ABRAHAM	50	
KEALY, ABEL	4	
KEELY, HENRY	46	
KEEN, GEORGE	42	
KEENER, JACOB	62	
KEIGER, GEORGE	5	

KEIR, WILLIAM	66
KEISTER, GEORGE	24
KELLER, CHRISTIAN, SR.	47
HENRY	24
KELLY, ARCHIBALD	47
EDWARD	18
JOHN	48
MEEK	61
ROBERT	49
SARAH	1
KEMPLE, JOHN ADAM	27
KEMPLIN, CAPT. THOMAS	2
KENNEDY, HUGH	49
JAMES	4
KENNING, CHARLES	61
REBECCA	61
KERLIN, THOMAS	33
KERN, GEORGE	7
MICHAEL, SR.	11
KERNAHAN, ALEXANDER	66
KERR, ABRAHAM	20
ROBERT	1
THOMAS	45
KERSHNER, GEORGE	12
JACOB	1
KERSTETTER, LEONARD	5
MARTIN	26 ,40
MAGDALENE	31
SEBASTIAN	21
KEPHART, JOHN PHILIP	43
KESSLER, GEORGE	18
PETER	13, 18
KESTER, PAUL	36
PETER	38
KETSEL, MARGARET	5
KETTERLY, PETER	4
KIEHL, JOHN	25
PETER	14
KIER, DAVID	59
KILLEN, ANN C.	46
KING, JAMES	18
KINKEAD, JOHN	7
KINTER, A. F.	63
JOHN, SR.	57
KIRK, MOSES	22
KIRKPATRICK, SAMUEL	66
KISNER, JOHN	31
KISSINGER, MICHAEL	45
KITCHEN, JACOB	10
KLINE, ABRAHAM	42
LUDWIG	8
KNEE, HENRY	47
KNEELAND, THOMAS	6
KNEIB, JACOB	15
KNEPP, CALEB	1
KNEPP (SCHNEPP), HENRY	39
KOBEL (KABEL), ISAAC	8
KOCHER, JOHN	13
KRAMER, GEORGE	37
GEORGE ADAM	8
KRANKS, JAMES	7
KRATZER, FREDERICK	29

KRAUSE, CHRISTIAN	13
KREBS, HENRY	16
KREBS, JOHN HENRY	26
KREIDLER, DANIEL	16
KREITZER, FREDERICK	43
KRITZ, SIMON	37
KUNTZ, PETER	16
LAFFERTY, MARY	62
ROBERT	53
LAMAR, WILLIAM	47
LAMB, MICHAEL	3
LAMPHLEY, SARAH	18
LANGS, GEORGE	16
LANTZ, HENRY, SR.	10
JOHN	10
LASH, STEPHEN	2
LATELY, JOHN	6
LATHY, WILLIAM K.	34
LATSHA, ABRAHAM	5
JOHN	10, 35
LAUDENSLAGER, VALENTINE	13
LAUGHLIN, ADAM	39
WILLIAM	2
LAUVER, BALTZER	11
LAVERTY, ISAAC	9
LAVISTON, JOHN	3
LAWRENCE, AMOS	58
LAWSON, MATHIAS	11
LEACOCK, WILLIAM	4
LEANY, DANIEL	49
HUGH	45 53
LEARD, JUDITH	52
WILLIAM	59
ZACHARIAH	46
LEARY, DENNIS	5
LEASURE, JOHN, SR.	62
LEBO (LEBEAU), PAUL	14
LECHNER, JACOB	40
LEE, EDWARD	2
JESSE	8
MAJ. JOHN	2
STEPHEN	4
LEECH, ARCHIBALD	47
DANIEL	7
LEEPORT, JOHN	16
LEFFLER, GOTTLIEB	8,11
LEHMAN, TOBIAS	12,13
LEIBENGOOD, JACOB	51
LEISENRING, ANDREW	25
LEMON, JOHN	15
LENKER, MICHAEL	8
LEPLEY, JACOB	40
MICHAEL	1
LETTERMAN, PETER, JR.	25
LEVINSTON, DAVID	5
LEWIS, DAVID	45, 49
JOHN	55
JOSHUA	45
LEMUEL	4
SARAH	64
TOBIAS	50

LIEFF, FRED	2
LIKENS, JOSEPH	38
LILLY, LEONARD	15
LINDEMUTH, MICHAEL	18
LINDSEY, JOHN	2
LINN, JOHN	15
LITTLE, THOMAS	26, 66
LIVINGOOD, GEORGE	2
JACOB	7
LODGE, JONATHAN	3
LOGAN, ELIZABETH	45
JOHN	63
LONG, JACOB	42
JOSEPH	10, 26
PETER	29
SIDNEY	15
THOMAS	61
LONGBAUCH, HENRY	17
LOSE, MARGARET	65
LOUGHRY, BENJAMIN	49
SUSAN	59
WILLIAM	52, 63
LOW, JAMES	59
LOWDEN, MAJ. JOHN	25
LOWERS, ROBERT	66
LOWERY, JAMES	45
LOWRY, JOSEPH	48
LOY, ADAM	4
LUCAS, JOHN	65
THOMAS	50,62
WILLIAM	59
LUKE, DAVID	49
JAMES	50,55
WILLIAM	51
LUNGER, JACOB	24
MARTIN	18
LUTZ, JACOB	59
JOHN	25
ULRICH	22
LYCANS, JOSEPH	3
LYDICK, ISAAC	58
JOSEPH	49
PATRICK	49, 50
SAMUEL, JR.	63
LYMAN, JOHN	14
LYNN, THOMPSON	50
LYON, JOHN	28
SAMUEL , SR.	62
LYTLE, ALEXANDER	57
ANN	52
ELEANOR	39
JAMES	61
MCAFFEE, PATRICK	64
MCBATH, ANN	14
MCBRIDE, HUGH	15
JAMES	18
JOHN, SR.	54
MCCAM, JONATHAN	8
MCCANDLISH, WILLIAM	3,4, 20
MCCLANAHAN, DAVID	5
JAMES	5,20, 56

Name	Page	Name	Page	Name	Page
McCAFFERY, JAMES	57	McGENNETT, CHARLES	3	MANN, SAMUEL	32
McCALLA, ALEXANDER	9	McGIBBON, JOHN	6	MANTZ, NICHOLAS	16
JOHN	17, 35	McGINLEY, HUGH	4, 21	MARCH, JACOB	11
McCARTNEY, JOHN	50	McGRADY, ALEXANDER	23	MARDIS, GEORGE	63
McCLINTOCK, SAMUEL	37	McGUIRE, ANIEL	49	MARKLEY, ELIZABETH	7
McCLURE, JAMES	22	DANIEL	49	PETER	5
McCLASKY, FELIX	7	JAMES	46	SIMON	5
McCOMB, ALLEN	54	McINTYRE, MARY	62	DR. SOLOMON	18
JAMES	45	McKEE, ELIZABETH	45	MARLIN, JOSHUA	53, 59
McCONAHEY, JAMES	51	JAMES	58	MARR, JOSEPH	8
JOHN	58	JOSEPH	51	MARSHALL, ARCHIBALD	46
McCORD, WILLIAM	16, 27	SAMUEL	21	JAMES	62
McCORLEY, ROBERT	23	WILLIAM	53	JOHN	17
McCRACKEN, HENRY	2	McKELVY, JOSEPH	47	JOSEPH	4
JOSHUA	46	McKENNY, DAVID	3	SAMUEL	63
McCRADY, JOHN	45	MORDECAI	2	MARTIN, GEORGE	31
MARGARET	54	McKEOUN, JOHN	49	HUGH	44
McCORMICK, ALEXANDER	3	McKESSICK, JAMES	58	JAMES	24, 14, 18
WILLIAM	13	McKIM, WILLIAM	14	JOHN	2, 43
McCOY, JOHN	47	McKINLEY, JOHN	5	JOHN LUDWIG	11
McCURDY, SAMUEL	49	McKISSON, DANIEL	53	ROBERT, JR.	31
THOMAS	11	McKNIGHT, JAMES	2	MARTZ, JACOB	29
WILLIAM	23	SUSAN	46	PETER, SR.	18
McCURLEY, JAMES	34	WILLIAM	27	MASSER, JOHN	38
McCLUNG, JOHN	21	McKUSH, JOHN	6	MATHER, SAMUEL	11
McCULLEY, ALEXANDER	9	McLAM, JAMES	57	MATHIAS, JOHN	49
ELIZABETH	21	McLANAHAN, JAMES	46	MAURER, PETER	32
McCONNELL, JAMES	63	McLAUGHLIN, DANIEL	55	MAWHORTER, HENRY	41
MARY A.	48	JAMES	13, 57	MAXWELL, WILLIAM	14
McCABE, CAPT. ROBERT	59	JOHN	55	MAZE, ELIZABETH	28
McCARTNEY, THOMAS	66	HUGH	42	MEADS, ASHAEL	2
McCLELLAND, JAMES	61	WILLIAM	64	MEAKIN, JOHN	59
McCLAREN, WILLIAM	64	McLEAN, ALEXANDER	47	MEARS, SAMUEL	38
McCOLLAM, JAMES	49	McMAHAN, JOHN	34	THOMAS	31
McCONAUGHTY, JEAN	59	McMAUREN, JAMES	13	MECONKEY, JOHN	17
McCREA, JOHN	61	McMONIGAL, ALEXANDER	12, 30	MEECK (MICK), ANDREW	30
McCREARY, SAMUEL	61	McMULLEN, ENOS	46	MEISER, HENRY	27
McCURDY, JAMES	64	SAMUEL	50	JOHN	24
McCUNE, MARY	54	McNEIL, ROSANA	45	MICHAEL	3
McDONALD, JOHN	35, 49, 55	McNUTT, ALEXANDER	48	MELICK, PETER, SR.	22
JOSEPH	60	JOSEPH	63	MELISH, PETER	5
McDOWELL, JANE	58	ROBERT	62	MENGES, JOHN ADAM	39
McELHOSE, LEVI	50	SAMUEL	58	MERTZ, NICHOLAS	10
McENTIRE, DONALD	1	McPHERSON, HUGH	56	PHILIP	29
HUGH	57	MARY	46	METZGER, DANIEL	14
McFADDEN, HUGH	4	THOMAS	52	MEYER, ABSALOM	12
JOHN	23	McQUIRE, THOMAS	20	CAPT. CHARLES	16
McFALL, JAMES	7, 9	McQUISTON, WILLIAM	48	CHRISTINA	12, 31
McFARLAND, JAMES	48	McWHORTER, JOHN	8	CHRISTOPHER	8
JOHN	53	McWILLIAMS, HUGH	1	DAVID	11
MARIA	50	ROBERT	1	ELIZABETH	42
MARY	61	MABON, JOHN	46	HENRY	14
THOMAS	47	WILLIAM	58	JACOB	14
WILLIAM	59	MACHAMER, PHILIP	10	MANEVAL	12
McFAIN, JOHN	15	MACLAY, HON. SAMUEL	36	MICHAELS, GEORGE	12
McFARLANE, JAMES	6	MACKEY, JOHN	28	MIDDLESWORTH, JOHN	42
McFEATHERS, JOHN	60	MACKLEHENNY, THOMAS	17	MIKESEL, PETER	48
McGARA, CLEM	56	MADDEN, NEAL	15	MILES, JAMES	9
SAMUEL	47	MAGER, GEORGE	9	JOHN	20
McGAUGHEY, THOMAS	66	MAGILL, WILLIAM	48	MILLEN, JAMES	49, 55
McGEE, JOHN	13	MAHAN, PATRICK	48, 50	MILLER, ALEXANDER	6
PATRICK	52	JOHN	63	CHRISTIAN	8

74

RABUCK, VALENTINE — 10
RADDICK, JOHN — 21
RAKER, MARTIN — 10
RAMY, CONRAD — 48
RANK, ADAM — 35
RANKIN, JAMES — 56
    MATTHEW — 46
    REBECCA — 60
    WILLIAM — 46
RANNELS, GEORGE — 48
RAY, GEORGE — 28
READER, JOSEPH — 3
READING, DAVID — 39
REARICK, JOHN — 5
    MARY — 16
REED, CAPT. CASPER — 29
    CHRISTINA — 49
    REV. JOHN — 59
    THOMAS — 57
REEDY, CONRAD — 35
REES, ELIZABETH — 47, 55
    HUGH — 52
    JOHN — 53
REESE, DANIEL — 30
REICHENBACH, JOHN, JR. — 35
REICHLEY, CONRAD — 12
REICHSTONE, PATER — 14
REILEY, FREDERICK — 21
RENFREW, JACOB — 39
RENTZ, ANDREW — 10
REPINE, CATHERINE — 54
    JOHN — 63
    JOSEPH — 60
REUBENDALL, JACOB — 12
REYNOLDS, BENJAMIN — 42
REZNOR, JOHN, SR. — 28
    DAVID — 37
RHOANDS, CAPT. FRANCIS W. — 36
    JACOB — 12
    JOHN — 5, 6
    PETER — 18
RICH, PHILIP — 47
RICHARDS, JAMES — 12
    MARTHA — 54
    ROBERT — 34
RICHART, WILLIAM — 35
RICHEY, GEORGE — 54
    JOHN — 63
RICHTER, CHRISTIAN — 8
RIDDLE, GEORGE — 25
    POLLY — 52
    WILLIAM — 45
RIEHLE, JOHN — 12
RIHLE, FRED — 12
RINE, GEORGE — 14
    HENRY — 39
RISHEL, HENRY — 17
RISINGER, JOHN — 51
ROBB, JOHN — 23
    WILLIAM — 43
ROBBINS, WILLIAM — 20
    ZACHARIAH — 15

ROBERTS, DAVID — 29
    HIRAM — 17
ROBERTSON, WILLIAM — 38
ROBESON, THOMAS — 1
ROBINSON, JAMES — 12
    RICHARD — 12
    ROBERT — 34, 56
ROBISON, ELIZABETH — 64
    PETER — 4
    ROBERT — 66
ROCKEY, JOHN — 8
    WILLIAM — 40
RODGERS, JAMES — 47
RODMAN, WILLIAM — 8
RODY (RUDY), PETER — 7
ROENKER, JOSEPH — 14
ROOF, JACOB — 60
ROSE, ADAM — 40
ROSEBURY, JOSEPH — 26
ROSMAN, JOHN — 14
ROSS, ADAM — 16
    ELINOR — 65
    GUSTAVUS — 3
    JOHN — 63
ROUSH, JOHN — 6
    HENRY — 64
ROUSHER, JOHN NICHOLAS — 3, 25
ROTTAN, JOSEPH — 20
ROW, GEORGE — 2
    JACOB — 8
    LEWIS — 14
ROYER, JOHN — 15
RUCKMAN, THOMAS — 12
RUGH, CHRISTOPHER — 46
    ELIZABETH — 48
    MICHAEL — 56
RUMMEL, JOHN — 47
RUNYAN, BONHAM — 13
RUSH, JOHN — 24
RUSHER, JACOB — 15
RUSSELL, ANDREW — 35
    JANE — 50
    ROBERT — 34
RUTHERFORD, JOHN — 56
RYAN, WILLIAM — 12
(VOWEL 2ND LETTERS)
SADDLER, JOHN — 48
SALTSMAN, ARTHUR — 1
    GEORGE — 2
SAMPLE, JANE — 54
    JOHN — 48, 60
    REBECCA — 55
SANDERSON, EZEKIEL — 33
    THOMAS — 45
SANDOS, JOHN — 7, 8
SASSAMAN, HENRY — 7
SAX, JACOB — 17
SAY, DR. BENJAMIN — 66
SECHLER, JACOB — 37
    JOSEPH — 12
SECHRIST, CHRISTIAN — 8
SEEBOLD, CHRISTOPHER — 38

SEELEY, ISAAC — 5
    ROBERT — 18
SELIN, MAJ. ANTHONY — 5
SEILER, VALENTINE — 9
SERVER, PETER — 7
SEVERSON, ERNEST — 19
SIDES, ANN — 60
    JANE — 51
SIERER, JOHN — 18
SIGLER, GEORGE — 44
SILVER, AMOS — 6
    GEORGE — 51
SIMPSON, JOHN — 30
    NATHANIEL — 55
    RACHEL — 16
    THOMAS — 48
SINDLEY, WILLIAM — 14
SINCLAIR, HUGH — 46
    NEAL — 12
SOCKMAN, ANDREW — 6
SOLOMON, JOHN — 2
SULLIVAN, THOMAS — 6
SUMMERS, JOB — 15
SUTTER, JACOB — 65
SUTTON, PETER — 53
    ROBERT — 55
    THOMAS — 55
(CONSONANT 2ND LETTERS)
SCHOCH, JOHN — 9
    MATTHIAS — 17
SCHMELCHER, JACOB — 42
SCHNEIDER, JOHN — 12
    JOSEPH — 61
SCHOUFLER, CHRISTIAN — 13, 14
SCHMUCK, JACOB — 47
SCHULTZ, JACOB — 11
SCHWARTZ, PHILIP — 13
SCOTT, ABRAHAM — 9
    JAMES — 48
    THOMAS — 58
SCUDDER, JOHN — 4
SHAFFER, ANDREW — 40
    CHRISTOPHER — 23
    GEORGE — 8
    HENRY — 40
    JOHN — 15, 17, 21
SHAFFLET, FRANCIS — 6
SHAMBACH, GEORGE — 42
SHANKLE, HENRY — 48
SHANNON, DAVID — 16
    ROBERT — 23
SHAPEL, DANIEL — 12
SHARRETS, REV. N. G. — 47
SHATZBERGER, CHRISTOPHER — 42
SHAW, WILLIAM — 36
SHAWVER, PHILIP — 10
SHEFFER, CONRAD — 2
    FRANCES — 6
SHELLENBERGER, JACOB — 37
    MARTIN — 33
SHERIDAN, JOHN — 62
    MARY — 61

SHERMAN, SIMON 8
SHETTERLY, DAVID 10
SHIELDS, EDWARD 1
    JAMES 50
SHIPMAN, JOHN 4
SHIRK, JOHN 23
SHIVELY, MARTIN 17
SHOCKEY, SUSAN 62
SHOEMAKER, PETER 5
SHOOK, MARTIN 46
SHOLLY, LUCAS 14
SHOWER, ADAM, SR. 31
SHRADER, HENRY 42
SHRINER, MICHAEL 13
SHULER, VALENTINE 17
SHULL, DAVID 8
SHUMAN, RUDOLPH 37
SHULTS, HENRY 57
SHULTZ, PETER 42
SKELLY, PATRICK 45
SLACK, JOHN 23
SLOAN, SAMUEL 46
SLEAR, CHARLES, SR. 15
SLOEY, HUGH 48
SMILEY, DAVID 64
SMITH, ADAM 3
    ANN 50
    ANNA MARY 24
    BALTHASER 25
    DAVID 28
    ELIZABETH 38
    EZEKIEL 7
    GEORGE 24, 50
    GIDEON 42
    JAMES 56
    JOHN 2,13,16,23,35,38
    MATTHEW 7
    MELCHOIR 43
    MICHAEL 31
    NICHOLAS 7
    PETER 16, 25, 37
    THOMAS 53
SNOOK, PETER 43
    WILLIAM 43
SNYDER, ABRAHAM 23
    DANIEL 42
    JACOB 30
    JOHN 4, 8, 31
    THOMAS 50
    WILLIAM 17
SPADE, SEBASTIAN 28
SPENCE, JAMES 59
SPENCER, GEORGE 50
SPRINGER, CONRAD 36
SPYKER, HENRY 41
STACKHOUSE, ELINOR 31
    JOSEPH 14
    THOMAS 25
STADDON, THOMAS 25 •
STAHL, JACOB 32
    JOHN 34

STAHL, PHILIP 26
STANARD, GEORGE 50
STARK, ZEPHNIAH 44
STEANS, CATHERINE 37
STEEDMAN, CHARLES 16
    JAMES 27
STEEL, DAVID 43
    JOHN 36
    SAMUEL 60
    WILLIAM 13
STEERE, JOSEPH 46
STEESE, BARBARA 16
STEFFEN, JOHN 36
STEPHENS, ABRAHAM 59
    JOHN 3, 6
    NANCY 49
    WILLIAM 50
STEINBRUCH, ABRAHAM 27
STERN, JACOB 39
STEWART, ALEXANDER 18, 48
    ARCHIBALD 49, 54
    ELINOR 55
    MARGARET 58
    SARAH 40
STIDLER, JOHN, SR. 17
STILWELL, DANIEL 26
STINE, MICHAEL 9
STINEMAN, CHRISTOPHER 48
    CATHERINE 49
STITES, JOSEPH 30
STOCK, PETER 9
    MELCHOIR, SR. 26
STONE, ABRAHAM 1
STRAEHLE, CASPER 9
STRAPHON, JOSEPH 8
STREUB, ANDREW 32
STRAWYER, LUDWIG 7
STRAYER, MATHIAS 22
STRONG, JAMES 57
STRUBLE, ADAM 39
STOTT, ALEXANDER 32
STUCHELL, JACOB 45, 50
    JOHN 50
STUMP, MICHAEL 64
STUTZ, MARGARET 17
SWAN, THOMAS 62
SWARTZ, PETER 11
SWEASEY, JOHN 56
SWENGLE, MICHAEL 7
SWINEHART, ANDREW 12
    GEORGE 16
SWINEFORD, ALBRIGHT 35
    GEO. MICHAEL 37
    JOHN 12, 17, 43
SWISHER, LOW 5
    PHILIP 3
TAGGART, DAVID 17
    THOMAS 4
TATE, EDWARD 7
TAWNEY, WILLIAM 50

TAYLOR, ALEXANDER 53, 66
    FREDERICK 11
    JAMES 9
    JOHN 8
    MARY 64
    THOMAS 13
    WILLIAM 17
TEEPLE, GEORGE 5
TEMPLETON, JAMES 62
    ROBERT 26
THOM, JAMES 2
THOMAS, DAVID 12, 14
    ISRAEL 59
    JOB 9
    JOHN 15
    WILLIAM 49
THOMPSON, ARCHIBALD 47
    HUGH 53
    JAMES 47, 49, 50, 53
    JOHN 28, 46, 62
    JONATHAN 45
    JOSEPH 28
    MATTHEW 3
    MICHAEL 58
    SAMUEL 57
    WHITE 50
    WILLIAM 33, 52
THORNBAUGH, JOHN 8
THORNTON, JAMES 19
    JOHN 43
    MICHAEL 16
THROPTOE, ANDREW 5
TIETSWORTH, JOHN 10, 11
TINDALL, CHARLES 45
TINKUM, DANIEL 47
TODD, SAMUEL 50
TOMB, DAVID 60
    JOHN 5
TONNER, JOHN 7
TORBET, JOHN 5
TORNEY, JOHN 6
TOMLINSON, ANN 16
    HENRY 26
    JAMES 16, 27
    THOMAS 12
TRAVIS, WILLIAM 48
TREASTER, GEORGE 2
    MARTIN 2
TREMBLY, JOHN 37
TREON, JACOB 42
TRIMBLE, GEORGE 51
    JOHN 64
    WILLIAM 63
TRINKLE, MATHIAS 3
TROWBRIDGE, BENJAMIN 46
TROUTMAN, PETER 34
TROXEL, JOHN 42
TRUCKENMILLER, JOHN 9
TRUTT, ANDREW 40
TURNER, ANDREW 1
    GEORGE 53

ERRATA

PAGE 5, IETSEL IS KETSEL
 37, JACOB SHELLENBERGER
 26, DREBS IS KREBS
 26, DERSTETTER IS KER-
     STETTER

* * * * * * * * * * * * *

ADDITION

ON PAGE 44 IT SHOULD BE
STATED THAT MIFFLIN COUNTY
WAS FORMED FROM CUMBERLAND
AND NORTHUMBERLAND COUNTIES.

www.ingramcontent.com/pod-product-compliance
Lightning Source LLC
Chambersburg PA
CBHW020516030426
42337CB00011B/417